The Private Life
of General Omar N. Bradley

The Private Life of General Omar N. Bradley

Jeffrey D. Lavoie

Foreword by Alan Axelrod

McFarland & Company, Inc., Publishers
Jefferson, North Carolina

LIBRARY OF CONGRESS CATALOGUING-IN-PUBLICATION DATA

Names: Lavoie, Jeffrey D., 1981– author.
Title: The private life of General Omar N. Bradley / Jeffrey D. Lavoie ; foreword by Alan Axelrod.
Description: Jefferson, North Carolina : McFarland & Company, Inc., Publishers, 2015. | Includes bibliographical references and index.
Identifiers: LCCN 2015040422 | ISBN 9780786498390 (softcover : acid free paper) | ISBN 9781476620152 (ebook)
Subjects: LCSH: Bradley, Omar Nelson, 1893–1981. | Generals—United States—Biography. | United States. Army—Biography. | World War, 1939–1945—Campaigns.
Classification: LCC E745.B7 L38 2015 | DDC 355.0092—dc23
LC record available at http://lccn.loc.gov/2015040422

BRITISH LIBRARY CATALOGUING DATA ARE AVAILABLE

© 2015 Jeffrey D. Lavoie. All rights reserved

No part of this book may be reproduced or transmitted in any form or by any means, electronic or mechanical, including photocopying or recording, or by any information storage and retrieval system, without permission in writing from the publisher.

Cover image: Gen. Bradley at his desk with portraits of his daughter and wife close at hand (Joseph Fansler Petit Collection, West Point Academy)

Printed in the United States of America

McFarland & Company, Inc., Publishers
  Box 611, Jefferson, North Carolina 28640
  www.mcfarlandpub.com

To Laurie, Emma, and Wesley Lavoie.
May Omar Bradley's life story remind you
that you can accomplish anything
you set your mind to do!

Table of Contents

Foreword by Alan Axelrod 1
Preface 5
Introduction 11

I. Prewar

1. The Early Life of an American Patriot 17
2. Welcome to West Point 25
3. Groom-ing an Officer 28
4. Close but No Cigar 34
5. Here, There, and Back Again 38
6. Hello, Hawaii 42
7. Back to School 47
8. WAR-ning 55
9. There's No Place Like the 82nd Division 61

II. War

10. We Missed the Bombs Down in Africa 66
11. Sicily or Bust 71
12. Operation Overlord 75
13. Today Is D-Day 80
14. Cherbourg and Alcohol in the Army 89
15. Bulging Out 94
16. Partying with the Russians 108

III. Postwar

17. Omar the Entertainer	119
18. In Love with Kitty	129
19. From Mary to Kitty	137
20. The Final Years	147
21. Reflections	154

Appendices:
I. General Omar Nelson Bradley: Leader or Lucky?	163
II. The Screen Credits of Kitty Buhler Bradley: Connecting Washington, D.C., to Hollywood	187
Chapter Notes	199
Bibliography	209
Index	213

Foreword
by Alan Axelrod

In 1970, 20th Century–Fox released one of the most compelling war movies ever made, which was also among the greatest of filmed biographies. Directed by Franklin J. Schaffner, *Patton* starred George C. Scott in the performance of a lifetime. He created a bigger-than-life screen presence for a commander who was famously—or infamously—bigger than life. In the key supporting role of Omar Bradley was Karl Malden, who also delivered a brilliant performance—brilliant precisely because it was *not* bigger than life, but rather of dimensions that fit a military leader who perfectly fit the needs and the values of an American army.

Patton is a great film because it presents the commander of the Third U.S. Army in all his disturbing ambiguity. Germany's Field Marshal Gerd von Rundstedt, whom Patton defeated at the Battle of the Bulge, pronounced him America's "best" general, whereas the late Andy Rooney, of *60 Minutes* television fame but a young war correspondent in World War II, "detested Patton" and declared that it "was because we had so few soldiers like him that we won the war." Oddly enough, it may have been Hollywood gossip columnist Liz Smith who put it best when she described Scott's Patton for her *Cosmopolitan* magazine readers as a "hero-villain in all his glorious and vainglorious humanity."

Detested, hero-villain, glorious, vainglorious. None of these words was ever or would ever be applied to Omar Nelson Bradley. It was not that he was a perfect general. Far from it. It was that he was so thoroughly suited to be an *American* general.

Americans—Patton's troops, his superiors, his colleagues, political leaders, and, most of all, the American public—never quite knew what to think and feel about Patton: a warrior as capable of slapping his own ailing and battle-weary soldiers as he was of killing the enemy.

But they always knew what to think and feel about Bradley. Why? Because they knew and felt him to be one of them.

Among the charges the Declaration of Independence lodged against King George III was his forcing a large standing army upon the colonists. Americans have never fully trusted the military establishment and have never supported the creation of an autocratic military class. They certainly admire warriors like Patton, but ultimately they cannot tolerate them—not in a nation founded on democratic principles. In Bradley, Americans believed they had found the all-but-impossible ideal: a democratic warrior, a GI general, a commander of the people, by the people, and for the people.

Just as there is a generous ration of popular mythology behind the historical image of Patton, so myth and media portrayal (beginning with the evocative sketches provided by World War II correspondent Ernie Pyle) have shaped the Bradley image. Jeffrey D. Lavoie's biography makes a fresh, insightful, and authoritative effort to separate image from reality. The reality, he reveals, is both more complex and more intriguing than the image. Yet his study also finds much truth in that image. Whereas the Patton façade—he faithfully practiced what he called his "war face" in front of a mirror—hid as much as it revealed, in Omar Bradley what you saw was, to a remarkable degree, what you got.

And this presents any Bradley biographer with a critical problem. Hidden motives, inner conflicts, men who wear a "war face" and who qualify as "hero-villains" are naturally dramatic. The virtues of quiet courage, rational humanity, common sense, and essential competence are far more difficult to portray compellingly. No wonder the fiery Scott played Patton and the blue-collar Malden, Bradley. Yet it is also no wonder that Francis Ford Coppola and Edmund H. North, who together wrote the *Patton* script, drew heavily on Bradley's own memoir, *A Soldier's Story*, and that the studio hired Bradley himself as a screen-credited "Senior Military Advisor." Not only was Bradley present as the Patton story unfolded, he was the kind of Everyman leader, the normative insider, the trusted interpreter who could help his fellow Americans make sense of that often alien-seeming warrior.

The greatest irony in a film that subordinates the character of Bradley to that of Patton is that, in reality, Bradley rapidly eclipsed Patton, quickly rising to the top Allied field command in Europe, presiding over the Normandy D-Day landings as well as what Eisenhower so aptly called the "Crusade in Europe" that followed them. Patton was an unparalleled tactical commander, but it was to Bradley that George C. Marshall and Dwight D. Eisenhower entrusted the topmost strategic field command. They knew it was the kind of command that Patton neither wanted nor could have handled successfully. Although Bradley made his share of errors, he proved himself in this strategic role to be what James T. Flexner memorably called George Washington: the indispensable man.

In this biography, Jeffrey D. Lavoie focuses not on military history—Bradley's part in such history has been explored and debated in many previous books—but on the private life lived by this indispensable man. The portrait that emerges is the uniquely American story of a hard-working and intensely decent individual who combined the qualities of leader and mentor on his journey toward mastery of the military art.

There are surprises along the way, as in Lavoie's exploration of Bradley's longtime affair with the journalist, screenwriter, and (unpublished) Bradley biographer Kitty Buhler, thirty years his junior. In this, some readers may detect a foreshadowing of General David Petraeus, who resigned as CIA director after the revelation of his affair with his biographer, Paula Broadwell. Bradley, however, was far more discreet, his wife, Mary Bradley, far more tolerant, and the outcome far happier. After Mary's death, Kitty became Bradley's second wife.

Indeed, Lavoie takes us where previous biographers have tread but lightly—into Omar Bradley's life and career after World War II, not only as a civilian (with an appetite for celebrity social life many readers will find entirely unexpected) but, first, as the postwar head of the Veterans Administration. If Bradley's relationship with Kitty Buhler invites comparison with the Petraeus affair, his brilliant leadership of the VA—including his reform of veterans' health care from a passive policy of warehousing the disabled wounded to the active practice of rehabilitating them and his vigorous promotion of the educational benefits under the GI Bill of Rights—makes a stark contrast with today's climate of disgraceful mismanagement, corruption, and scandal in veterans' affairs.

Nor does Lavoie give short shrift to Bradley's role as the nation's very first chairman of the Joint Chiefs of Staff, in which he worked against heavy institutional resistance to actually create the unified

American military mandated by the epoch-making National Security Act of 1947.

Beyond Bradley's leadership of the VA, the Joint Chiefs, and the much-reduced U.S. military during the ordeal of the Korean War, this book portrays Bradley's long Indian Summer of creative productivity after his retirement from active military service, with important positions in business, achievements as both a memoirist and an autobiographer, and an unexpected but richly deserved celebrity among celebrities. The joy and grace with which this general of the Army gradually withdrew from public life created an enduring legacy and template of the ideal soldier in service to democracy.

Alan Axelrod is the author of three books on George S. Patton, Jr.: *Patton's Drive: The Making of America's Greatest General* (2009), *Patton: A Biography* (2006), and *Patton on Leadership* (1999) as well as a brief biography of Omar Bradley (*Bradley: A Biography*, 2006).

Preface

"There are no more good deals left on eBay" a friend muttered to me after he had received in the mail a cheap "could be authentic" World War II dagger that had looked legitimate in its picture but in real life appeared more like a cheap Chinese knock-off. The age-old adage rings true—"you get what you pay for." At least that's what I thought before I began my research into the fascinating life of Omar N. Bradley.

It all began as I was searching on eBay for various unpublished manuscripts (as I regularly do when I am procrastinating from my writing) when I came across a curious typed book by some Hollywood writer named Kitty Buhler; the title of this book was called *Horses Make Strange Bedfellows*. I proceeded to conduct a Google search and made a library query only to find out that no such book by this title had ever been formally published. This seemed to be an original work, yet I was a little confused, as this auction had been going on for many weeks and there were still no bidders. Based on its description, this work focused on the life of Omar N. Bradley as told from his second wife's perspective. Omar Bradley: Now there was a name I recognized.

I have always considered myself a bit of a World War II enthusiast, and Omar was a major figure in this vicious war, leading the U.S. troops on the D-Day Normandy invasion and in the Battle of the Bulge. Yet if this really were an unpublished biography of famous five-star general Omar N. Bradley, then why was there no one bidding on it and why was it offered at such a low purchase price? Not only that, but it had been on sale for several weeks, and no one cared to bid or even make an offer. It seemed suspicious, but still I decided I would take the gamble and make an offer for this manuscript. I clicked the mouse and felt the surge of adrenaline that goes along with winning an online auction. I made the payment, and all I had left to do was to sit back and wait for the United States Postal Service to bring this potential treasure to my doorstep. After all, the mystery surrounding auction sites such as eBay is that you very often don't know what you're buying until it arrives in the mail. That was certainly the case in this instance.

When the package did arrive, I was a little disappointed. Though the paper was aged and typesetting appeared typical for the time period in which it was supposed to have been created, nevertheless it was not a complete biography as the description had claimed. Rather, it seemed to be an outline of an autobiography. This proposal had been written circa 1981 by Kitty about her years spent with Omar Bradley, and it also contained key events of her own life. Surprisingly, Kitty's life has never warranted much attention by any researcher either from a World War II or pop-culture perspective. Yet I still felt like I had overspent on purchasing a book proposal with no real depth to it, and I proceeded to contact the seller to initiate a return … until I began to explore its pages more fully.

As I read the pages of this curious, yellowing-with-age proposal (which came complete with a hand-signed letter on "Mrs. Omar N. Bradley" official stationery, squelching any further objections to its authenticity), I realized that it recorded intimate details of the general's life that had never before been published. Not only that, but certain secrets were divulged in its pages that had been intentionally hidden from the public view. These details are for the first time in history put forth in this work, and they begin to clarify why Kitty was so protective of her husband's life story.

The truth is that very few details are known of Bradley's later life. There is a reason only a handful of biographies have been written on him as opposed to other World War II leaders such as General Dwight Eisenhower or General George Patton, whose lives have been fully documented by various researchers—both have more than thirty full-length works devoted to them. No such detailed biographies of Omar Bradley exist. Of the only two genuine full-length biographies on Bradley, both end in 1951, thirty years before his death. This is largely due to the fact that there are very few sources about him after this time period. This prompts the question: "Why?" This is the very question that this work will begin to answer.

Omar Bradley's life remains one of the most incredible examples of the famous "American Dream," confirming that with perseverance and hard work (mixed with a little bit of luck), anyone can climb up the ladder of success in America. Yet with this dramatic and glamorous rise to power came many impulsive decisions that would ultimately hurt the lives of his family and subordinates.

Great care has been used in communicating this delicate information in an appropriate manner, contextualizing it in the life of a true American hero. As one of Kitty's associates noted about their relationship when she and Bradley were finally married: "That had to be the best kept secret since the atom bomb." It could be argued that this secret was actually better kept than the atomic bomb, which was revealed to the world in 1945. This secret has been kept until 2015. Yet time gets the better of everyone, including five-star generals, and it is finally time for the public to know the true story of the private life of General Omar N. Bradley.

Kitty the Controller: A Word on Critical Investigation

This book is not an in-depth scholarly analysis in the sense that it will not pick apart every decision Bradley made and either justify or condemn it. Rather, this is a narrative of Bradley's fascinating life and his journey from the woods of Missouri to his status as a celebrated World War II hero. As noted previously, the main obstacle in writing a biography on the general is a severe lack of sources on his later life. As such, most of this research centers on the writings of both Bradley himself and his second wife, Kitty.

It must be noted that several researchers have disputed the picture of Omar that the Bradleys have painted in their writings. Instead, certain researchers have critically suggested that Bradley was more a calculated opportunist than his writings portray to the public. As one recent researcher, Martin Blumenson, claimed, "Underneath the mask was a cold and ruthless mind."[1]

While there are researchers on both extreme sides of this issue (i.e., pro–Bradley and anti–Bradley, some of which borders on conspiracy theory), any definitive answers are not as obvious, given the severe lack of sources available from this later stage. As such, Kitty's writings are relied upon heavily throughout this book because that is the only detailed perspective available from this time in history. It is my belief, based on further investigation, that Kitty did a satisfactory job documenting her husband's life, yet it must be remembered that she was writing from the perspective of a doting wife (even though she still aired his dirty laundry in her unpublished autobiography).

Kitty, George and Omar

It seems that if the average American has heard of Omar Bradley, it is likely from the 1970 movie *Patton*, in which his character is played by Karl Malden. It has recently been argued that the image of Bradley portrayed in this movie was one that he and Kitty worked hard to create. This perception seemingly began with S. L. A. Marshall, the military historian, who claimed: "The Bradley name gets heavy billing on a picture of [a] comrade that, while not caricature, is the likeness of a victorious glory-seeking buffoon.... Napoleon once said that the art of the general is not strategy but knowing how to mold human nature.... Maybe that is all producer Frank McCarthy and Gen. Bradley, his chief advisor, are trying to say." Marshall's opinions of Bradley are dissected in an addendum to this work, and his actual views on the general are clearly revealed for the first time in print.

A similar critique was implied by Carlo D'Este in his biography *Patton: A Genius for War*: "It was ironical that Bradley received a considerable sum of money, including a percentage of the gross receipts, for his professional consultation on a film about a comrade-in-arms he despised and never understood.... What inevitably emerges in the film is the portrayal of a brash, swashbuckling, controversial warrior. Yet, as one critic noted, if the film glorified anyone, it was Omar Bradley, not Patton."[2]

D'Este, the very capable and articulate military researcher, fails to cite any source to back up his opinion that Bradley "despised" Patton even though he claims this in several of his other works. In fact, Bradley recorded just the opposite in both of his major writings, calling Patton a "magnificent soldier" and "a superb field general and leader—perhaps our very best."[3] Yet, if Bradley considered himself a fair and effective leader, then why wouldn't he portray himself this way in this film, regardless of who the main character is? Perhaps the blame should be directed at the screenwriters who hired and relied upon one general to tell the life story of another. It remains unfortunate that the screenwriters could not access Patton's own diary and personal papers and instead had to rely solely upon Bradley's testimony and a biography written by Ladislas Farago. Thus, while Patton fans have legitimate cause for concern with the writing process for the movie *Patton*, it seems their frustration has been directed wrongly in criticizing Omar Bradley. Furthermore, it seems unfair to claim that Bradley was attempting to manipulate his public image, as no one really knows the exact level of influence he had on this movie, and the American presumption of innocence maintains "innocent until proven guilty."

The Latin expression *prima facie* is a commonly used legal term that means *at first sight* or *at first encounter*. In law, a *prima facie* case is a cause of action or defense that is sufficiently established by a party's evidence to justify a verdict in his or her favor, provided such evidence is not rebutted by the other party. It is my belief that Omar Bradley's reputation (as put forth in Kitty Bradley's writings) must be taken at face value until (or unless) there is evidence directly refuting these writings. If no party introduces new evidence, the case must stand or fall simply on this *prima facie* evidence.

The mystery of Bradley's competency can be solved at this later stage only by piecing together the accounts of the men who served under him, such as George Waple III, Walter Bedell "Beetle" Smith, and Chet Hansen, whose own diary reflects his day-to-day contact and personal reflections of Bradley as a leader. Even the news reporter Ernie Pyle spent time with Bradley and wrote about this experience favorably *while the war was going on* (though it must be remembered that these reports were intended to boost the morale of the American public). These accounts are all incorporated into the following narrative account of Bradley's life, and together they assemble a picture of both a responsible and likeable leader, though not without human shortcomings.

It has also been suggested to me, throughout my research and conversations with various World War II researchers, that Kitty was very protective of the general's life story. She seemingly destroyed his papers and allowed only certain pieces of information to leak out into the media. Rumors have even been circulated that implicate Kitty as a co-conspirator, working for her husband to rewrite World War II history and censor it in great detail. If this were true, there would be grounds to see a larger conspiracy theory of World War II. However, the main reason why Kitty was so protective of Bradley's life seemingly has a much more logical and practical solution suggested in this book: embarrassment. In my opinion, this secrecy was due to Kitty's desire to keep the general's reputation untarnished (to say nothing of his first wife's feelings). This may not be as dramatic as certain researchers would like it to be, as it requires no government conspiracies or cover-ups, yet in my opinion it seems most likely.[4]

It must also be remembered that Kitty was actually the one who revealed Bradley's darkest secrets to the world, and even though she clearly loved him, she was the one who in fact gave out the intimate details of his private affairs, down to identifiable descriptions and the code names employed. Therefore, the question remains: Why would she include this information if she was (as some have claimed) trying to build an alternate history and paint her husband as the famous "GI's general"? Rather, it seems much more plausible that instead of hiding a covert government conspiracy, Kitty was merely protecting Bradley's family and loved ones. This seems to be validated through the limited testimony of those who served under him, most of whom seemed to share a similar perspective that he was both a "solid and safe" general.[5]

In the interest of full disclosure, I should explain that when I originally began my research I was convinced that Bradley was a womanizing war hero who just got "lucky" in his placements and assignments. However, through my studies, I have come to respect him and have realized that he is the real, genuine American hero that history has determined him to be. While Bradley certainly had his own issues, which are clearly outlined in this book, he nevertheless remains one of the greatest military leaders in history—calculative, balanced, and solid.

There also are some soldiers and subordinate officers who didn't care for Bradley's style of leadership, yet they seemed to be of the minority opinion. Thus, it seems probable that while Bradley was a great leader, there were times when he made mistakes (such as Operation Cobra) and hesitated in battle (Battle of the Bulge). Still, these differing points of view must be acknowledged, and for anyone desiring a more thorough defense of this position, an addendum has been included with a more academic analysis of Bradley's leadership abilities and a defense of his reputation (including a detailed analysis of S. L. A. Marshall's infamous quote). It seems that if there is an Omar Bradley conspiracy taking place in the world at large, it is not protecting him *but against him*. It is time for one of America's most beloved war heroes to finally have his day. And so it is that I present to you what one confidante has called America's best kept secret—the private life of General Omar N. Bradley.

Introduction

General Omar Bradley was one of the key military leaders of World War II. He oversaw the D-Day invasion of Normandy onto the beaches of Omaha and Utah, and his troops absorbed the brunt of a German defensive attack known as the Battle of the Bulge. At one time, he commanded the largest U.S. military force in history to serve under one commander: 1.3 million troops. Bradley was also one of only nine American generals ever to obtain a five-star ranking. In his later life, he became a celebrity, serving on the board of MGM, which placed him in regular contact with many famous actors and writers, one of whom he ended up marrying as his second wife, the talented Kitty Buhler. Yet for all of these accomplishments, few books have been written on his fascinating life. It seems that Bradley's status and achievements have been allowed to slowly slip outside the larger public memory, leaving a void in an otherwise popular stage of American history—World War II.

Several previous works have attempted to correct this issue, focusing mainly on Bradley's military achievements, including two that are semi-autobiographical. While a handful of other writers have researched Bradley's military exploits and the extraordinary feats of this American patriot, his personal life has always been left outside this discussion. This seems intentional, as few documents about the general's personal life have been discovered and it was assumed that he must have lived a rather boring and ordinary life ... until now.

This book presents compelling evidence of a man who was torn between his family, his job, and his own physical desires—a senior general whose public life was so separated from his private one that many of the details revealed in this work have never before been uncovered. It cannot be denied that Omar Bradley was a general who sacrificed many things for his love of country.

Introduction

During his postwar career, Bradley's life took many unique twists and turns as he became the head of the Veteran's Administration and the Chairman of the Joint Chiefs of Staff, making him the senior military commander at the beginning of the Korean War. Meanwhile, it seemed that his personal life was always subjected to his military service. He was a loving husband to his wife, Mary, but later on he would love another woman, Kitty Buhler—and who could blame him? His second wife, Kitty, was funny, charming, and beautiful. She lived an adventurous and exciting lifestyle, hobnobbing with the rich and famous. Their relationship could be viewed as their own real-life version of *An Affair to Remember*, which nobody has printed until now. This story is a biography on one of the highest-profile generals the United States has ever commissioned. It is a journey to understand the real Omar N. Bradley and thereby reveal "the best kept secret since the atom bomb"—the private life of this U.S. general.[1]

Key Source Discovered

Kitty owned the rights to Omar's life story, even if she never published any written work. There is a screenplay housed in the Special Collections Department at the University of Texas at El Paso, titled *The Omar Bradley Story*, that concentrates on his life during the Battle of the Bulge, but it was never formally published or circulated. Kitty further wrote a proposal for a "tell all" book about the life she and the general lived together, but that too never saw publication. That manuscript, which was procured directly from the estate of Kitty Buhler, reveals some intriguing new information about this couple and their early relationship and provides much of the new material expounded in this book. It presents to the public a more balanced view of this American hero, and it questions the longstanding "Boy Scout" image that the media has presented for so many years.

The Real Omar Bradley

Some have called Bradley's life seemingly too good to be true, crediting this as the reason that history has paid little interest to him. He is often criticized for being too conservative and for not taking enough risks.[2] To many people, Omar was not flamboyant enough to

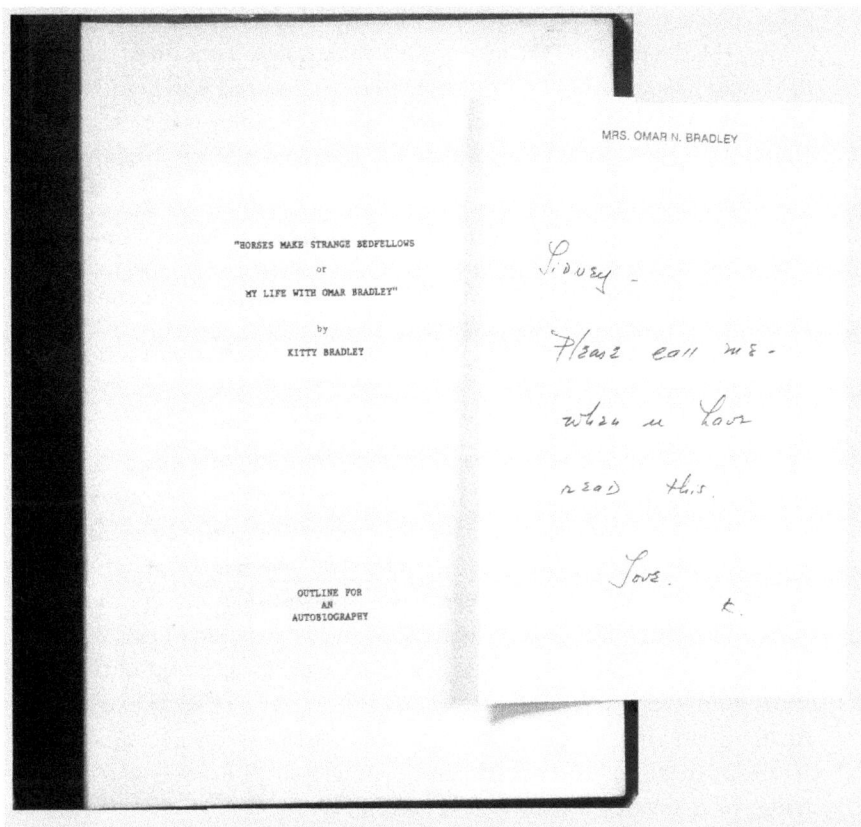

Picture of unpublished manuscript titled "Horses Make Strange Bedfellows" or "My Life With Omar Bradley" by Kitty Buhler. Note the title on the stationery of the handwritten note: "Mrs. Omar N. Bradley."

garner much interest; however, this biography will prove that this simply is not the case.[3] Previous writers have argued that it was Bradley's morality and matter-of-fact disposition that have made him uninteresting; however, he rubbed elbows with many movie stars and high-profile individuals and had his own indiscretions along the way. His life reads like a fascinating Hollywood novel, and this biography will reveal that Bradley's personal life was anything but boring.

Bradley was known by many different nicknames, including "The GI's General," "The Doughboy's General," "The Book General," and to some of his oldest friends, "Omar the Tent-maker" (likely due to his living quarters during the war). Most commonly, he was referred to as "Brad."[4] Dwight "Ike" Eisenhower, a classmate of Bradley's at West

Point, chose the following quote to represent him: "True merit is like a river; the deeper it is, the less noise it makes." He went on to suggest, "If [Omar] keeps up the clip he's started, some of us will someday be bragging to our grandchildren, 'Sure, General Bradley was a classmate of mine.'"[5] A more recent biographer, Jim DeFelice, summarized Bradley as a humble leader:

> ... a regular guy, somewhat soft-spoken and definitely shy. But one can't be too shy and become a five-star general. True, he clearly was reticent and self-consciousness [sic] when meeting people for the first time. But the overwhelming reason he didn't cultivate a media image seems to be one of values: his upbringing had taught him to perceive outward self-promotion as bragging and wrong, and as far as he was concerned, that's what news stories were.[6]

When Bradley's autobiography, *A Soldier's Story*, was published in 1951, it was met with mixed reviews. One *New York Times* reviewer noted that this work was valuable because it presented portraits of other famous commanders, but it did not tell the readers much about "who Bradley was." This review reveals the lacuna in history that this book attempts to fill: an examination of the private life of this famous general. Bradley's writings present a fairly accurate account of the war effort and are intriguing reads; however, they are also extremely detailed and lengthy, prompting the average reader to get lost in the details of these battles, which is unfortunate since Bradley was at the center of many key World War II conflicts.

Later in life, Omar gained celebrity status as he paired with his second wife, the famed Hollywood writer. It is this later stage in his life that has largely been ignored by the few biographers who have written about him. This time period is a thirty-year stretch of his life (1951–81) that remains largely undocumented that will be examined for the first time in this book.

Omar's Accomplishments

In his book *Bradley*, Alan Axelrod notes that there were four ideals that made Bradley a capable officer: (1) He understood that the terrain was an important part of any operation; (2) He looked at a battle from the point of view of the enemy; (3) He versed himself in the unglamorous art and science of logistics; and (4) He recognized the importance of the individual soldier.[7] Each of these traits would contribute to Bradley's legacy as one of the most efficient generals the U.S. has ever produced. Bradley's legacy has since become an important part of U.S. history.

In 1982, a middle school in San Antonio, Texas, was named after the general; in 1998, Bradley's image was cast into a twelve-inch collectable G.I. Joe action figure; and in 2013 a commemorative half-dollar was produced that bore his portrait and name. There is also an airport named after him in Moberly, Missouri, as well as a local holiday held in his honor. More impressively, an entire town, Bradley, West Virginia, was named in honor of this general of the army. Bradley's long-standing influence and reputation remain an integral part of history. As such, the aim of this book is to present the personal side of this American patriot and survey his life achievements and shortcomings, which will produce a more realistic image of a modern national hero. This biography will also include the forgotten years from 1951 to 1981 and will reveal many personal elements about his life that have previously been unknown.

This book is greatly indebted to Omar Bradley's and Clay Blair's book *A General's Life*. However, great care has gone into consulting previously unknown materials that reveal new details and stories hitherto unpublished. One of his earliest biographers, Charles Whiting, foreshadowed in 1971 Bradley's suitability as a role model by listing the limits of Bradley's example:

> But if Bradley cannot be regarded as a great captain, he will be remembered as a very able soldier, who grew appreciably in stature as the campaign went on and one who was a great advocate of the much maligned U.S. Army; a jealous guardian of its honour and its prestige ... he was very definitely a dedicated and highly professional American soldier, who did the best he could for his calling and his country, which I think, in the end effect, is all that such a modest person as Omar Nelson Bradley would profess to be....[8]

This seems true both professionally and personally, as this study will prove. It is unfortunate that his selfless personality was seen as a negative trait in his own generation. However, in this author's opinion, it is this very trait that separates a good man from a great man.

I. Prewar

1

The Early Life of an American Patriot

In the farmlands of Missouri in the early twentieth century, a young boy began his daily chores. Every day his routine was the same: He filled the woodbox with chips and kindling for the big kitchen stove, and he kept the buckets filled with water from the deep well out back. When there were cows in the barn, he helped with the milking. He also helped feed the chickens and keep the henhouse clean. At the end of the summer, he combed the backwoods in search of bee trees and their honey. One summer, he managed to accumulate two hundred pounds of wild honey, which he stored in the great earthen crocks that his mother gave him. Nobody knew that one day this boy would go on to become one of the highest-ranking generals in the U.S. Army while serving in the deadliest war.

Yet it was these childhood duties that prepared this boy to become a future national leader. These tasks gave him a sense of duty and personal fulfillment. After all, if there was no wood by the stove and no water in the kitchen, there would be no breakfast of home-cured ham, warm milk, and bright yellow-yolked eggs. If he didn't find the bee trees, there would be no honey bread after school. And if he didn't help Mother clean the lamps, there would be no light for the evening. These chores bettered his life, and they further instilled in him a strong work ethic and the sense of worth that goes along with hard work.[1]

* * * * *

This country boy was none other than Omar Nelson Bradley (1893–1981). Bradley would become the last of only nine generals in United States history to be promoted to a five-star rank, yet he had his humble beginnings in rural Missouri. He was born with military experience in his blood, as both of his grandfathers had served on opposing sides of the Civil War. His paternal grandfather (Bradley) was a Confederate soldier, and his maternal grandfather (Hubbard) served the Union.[2]

Bradley's integrity and morality can be traced back directly to his father, John Smith Bradley. In 1880, John Bradley, through perseverant self-study, discipline, and dedication was able to work his way into a teaching job in the rural school system. Bradley's father was an honest, hardworking individual, an eclectic combination of frontiersman, sportsman, farmer, and intellectual mixed together into one unique personality. John was powerful, fearless, and a crack shot with a rifle, which he often used for quail hunting. He was also known to hand-carve his own baseball bats and could throw a lethal curveball—a skill he would one day pass to his son, Omar.

John was an avid reader and knew the value of a good book. Through his teaching platform, he encouraged his students to read regularly while establishing libraries in each class that he frequented. John was especially known for his strength and resolve and was one of the few rural teachers who could effectively discipline the older, unruly farm boys when they misbehaved. One time, two troublemaking boys came at him with knives in hand, prompting John to pick up a stick and swing it at them. He managed to knock them both out, proving his resolve that he wouldn't allow anyone to intimidate him or manipulate his classroom.[3]

In his fourth year of teaching, at age twenty-five, John fell in love with one of his students, the lovely Sarah Elizabeth "Bessie" Hubbard.[4] Bessie returned these feelings and dropped out so that there would not be any talk about this teacher/pupil relationship.[5] They were married on May 12, 1892, at the Hubbard residence. It turned out to be quite a wedding celebration, because nine months later (to the very day) on February 12, 1893, Omar Nelson Bradley was born. Incidentally, this date coincided with the birthday of another great American leader: Abraham Lincoln.

Omar was named after a newspaper editor, Omar D. Gray, and his middle name paid homage to a local doctor. The name Omar was intended to be unique. There were many different John, Jim, and William Bradleys around, but John wanted his son's name to stand out. He never would have imagined that one day it would become a household name gracing the front pages of many national and international

1. The Early Life of an American Patriot

papers and publications.[6] The family grew in February 1900 when Bessie gave birth to another son, Raymond Calvert. However, his life was tragically cut short when he died from scarlet fever on January 18, 1902, just a few days before his second birthday. That was the extent of the Bradley family's immediate lineage.

Omar's father taught him the value of hard work. They spent most of their time together walking back and forth to school each day. Omar later described this one-on-one time with his father as being "spiritually reinforcing." The youthful Omar idolized his father as a strict disciplinarian who instilled in him a love of reading. He later jokingly remarked that "when you have your own father as your teacher, you always do your homework."[7] Omar devoured the classic works, filling his head with the chivalric acts of Sir Walter Scott's *Ivanhoe* and the antics of Mowgli in Rudyard Kipling's *The Jungle Book*. Omar was further fascinated with history and loved reading stories of the French and Indian Wars, the Revolutionary War, and the Civil War.

Folks of their era didn't have many forms of entertainment, especially in small towns such as Higbee, which had a population of only 1500. They didn't have radio, television, or any other electronic devices. Even if they did, it wouldn't have mattered, as the Bradleys lived on a modest income. Instead, Omar spent his time visualizing the battles throughout history and acting them out. It is an amusing mental picture to imagine General Bradley as a young boy reenacting these epic battles on his family's living room rug, using dominoes and elderberry sticks to build forts and utilizing empty .22 cartridges to represent the various lines of soldiers. He would whittle sticks into makeshift "cannons," taking special care to find the right "projectiles" that would fit inside their barrels. He would then proceed to blow into one end of the stick and propel out the projectile to simulate a cannon explosion. He utilized this cannon to knock down the dominoes and occasionally made use of a little brass tube, out of which he would shoot navy beans.[8]

A Death in the Family

One day, Omar's father came home after his daily six-mile walk to the school and was violently ill. He was later diagnosed with pneumonia, and after several days of resting in bed, John passed away. He was just two weeks shy of his forty-first birthday. Omar himself was not yet fifteen years old, a difficult age to lose one's father by any reckoning. Though John did not leave his family any large estate or inheritance, his legacy would carry on through his son's actions and ambitions, which included an insatiable thirst for education. This would eventually lead Omar to earn his nickname, "The Book General."

Following his father's death, the Bradley family moved to Moberly, a bigger city some fifteen miles north with a population of 10,000. The family rented a house on South Fourth Street, renting out rooms to two boarders in order to supplement their income. The family had also rented out their house in Higbee to pay the cost of their mortgage. It was at this time that Omar began a part-time job delivering issues of the *Moberly Democrat*.

Although not an overtly devout woman, Omar's mother was a faithful in church attendance. She joined a larger congregation in town called the Central Christian Church, which had a giant, looming steeple. It was here that Omar was baptized by immersion in a tank on February 14, 1909, within the church basement.[9] It was also here that Omar was introduced to Eudora "Dora" Quayle, a widow with two teenage daughters—Mary Elizabeth and her younger sister, Sarah (Jane). The Quayles happened to live across the street from the Bradleys, but it was at Sunday school where these families were first introduced.

Meeting Mary

Dora's husband had been Charles Quayle, a well-respected marshal who had served as the modern equivalent of a police chief. He died of tuberculosis in 1902 at age thirty-five, leaving behind a modest estate that included two small houses. Dora lived with her two girls in one of those domiciles and rented out the other one in order to earn additional income. Omar felt an immediate attraction to Mary Quayle, even though she was six months older than he was and a year ahead in school. He had been kept back a grade upon enrolling at Moberly High School despite the fact that he had shown an advanced aptitude for academics at his previous school in Higbee.

When Omar first met Mary, she was already in a committed relationship with an older boy who had graduated the year before. Omar did not date any girls during his high school years. He was admittedly shy and awkward around the opposite sex, and he was an outsider to the Moberly community. Therefore, he kept himself busy with his paper

1. The Early Life of an American Patriot 21

route and sports. In the fall of 1909, Omar entered Moberly High School and began his junior year. His teachers soon realized that he should not have been kept back a year and allowed him to skip ahead to the proper grade. He entered the Class of 1910, placing him within a closer proximity to Mary Quayle. Their original class had been together since grade school, and it became obvious to Omar that he was an outsider. Besides Mary and a few boys from the basketball team, he did not have many friends in his class.

There was not a lot to do for fun in Moberly, Missouri, during this time, but there was one winter activity that children of all ages enjoyed—ice skating. During the winter season, the lake in Forest Park would freeze over, providing an ideal location for ice skating and other winter activities.[10] Omar became quite adept at skating, but something occurred in the winter of 1909 that would have a life-altering effect on this would-be leader. That winter, Omar had a catastrophic accident when he suffered a violent collision with another boy on the ice. The boy's head smashed into Omar's teeth, knocking almost every single one of them loose and severely damaging his gums. Unfortunately, his mother did not possess the means to have his teeth fixed properly, and to his everlasting dismay they were never replaced correctly. This incident would lead to a future riddled with tooth and gum pain. Furthermore, this incident affected Omar's self-esteem, and for the rest of his life he rarely smiled with an open mouth and instead made a habit of closing his lips tightly to avoid anyone noticing his missing teeth. Because of this incident and a lack of dental care, Omar had his teeth pulled at a very young age.

Omar graduated in May 1910. In his high school yearbook, seniors were assigned a single adjective that was supposed to be descriptive of their personalities while foretelling their future greatness. Omar's word was "calculative," due to his math skills. This word is ironic, as Bradley's later moves in battle typified the phrase "calculated risk," which he applied in a military setting to determine the best course of action with a minimal risk. Mary graduated third in her class, and the word chosen for her was "linguistic," based on her early love of languages. Coincidentally, Mary's and Omar's senior pictures were paired at the bottom of the same page of their yearbook. Though these two were close to each other during these teenage years, neither pursued a romantic relationship.

Following his graduation, Omar was determined to pursue law, but he hadn't saved enough money to attend college immediately. He was also concerned about how his mother would fare without his continued presence and financial assistance. Because of this situation, Omar devised a plan to work at the Wabash Railroad in order to save enough money to attend the University of Missouri in Columbia. In the summer of 1910, he began working at the Wabash in the supply department, and due to his strong work ethic he was soon promoted to a repair position. Omar worked for nine hours per day, six days per week, and was paid seventeen cents per hour, which equated to roughly forty dollars per month.[11]

Across the street, Mary made plans of her own. She had a favorite aunt named Papita, who was a teacher at the State Normal School in St. Cloud, Minnesota. Mary decided to attend the school for her first two years of college, and then, if funds permitted, she would transfer to the University of Missouri. Following Mary's move to St. Cloud in 1910, Omar had very little contact with her. He felt chained to Moberly until a series of events occurred that would free him from his obligation as the family provider. That summer, Omar's thirty-five-year-old mother began a new relationship with John Robert "Bob" Maddox. Bob was a hearing-impaired farmer who had raised his two boys following the death of his first wife, Mary. On Christmas Day, 1910, Bessie and Bob were married, and Omar instantly obtained a new stepfather along with two stepbrothers. The boarders moved out and the three Maddoxes moved into the Bradley household. Incidentally, a month later, the Bradley house in Higbee was foreclosed on and was sold at auction for $441.20, which was enough to pay off the mortgage, thereby removing this burden from the struggling Bessie.

Change of Plans

Omar's initial plan was to attend the University of Missouri in the fall of 1911, but those plans were changed following a conversation with the Sunday School superintendent at his church—John Cruson. Cruson suggested that Omar apply to West Point. Omar knew very little about West Point and its admission procedures, and he replied naively that he couldn't afford the tuition if he was to be accepted. What Omar didn't realize was that the tuition to West Point was free and that each student received a small stipend. The main obstacle to overcome would be obtaining an appointment from a local congressman. This new information immediately changed Omar's career plans and no doubt evoked memories of the pretend battles of his childhood. Omar spoke to his mother about this newly forged plan, but she was not as enthusiastic. One of the main reasons for her dismay was that West Point, New York, was far away from Moberly, Missouri. But at this stage, Omar did not have many options.

He decided to "feel it out" and wrote a letter to his congressman, William M. Rucker, who lived about thirty miles away in Keytesville. It did not take long to receive a reply. The congressman explained that he had no vacancies left to fill at that time, as under existing laws he was able to recommend only one cadet every four years. Rucker's current appointment was in his third year and had one more year to graduation. This meant that Omar would have to wait at least one year more to apply, which seemed like a long time to the ambitious young country boy. He was ready to settle for the University of Missouri when something incredible happened—the rules for West Point recommendations were amended. Congressmen and senators were now permitted to appoint a new cadet every three years, which meant that Rucker now had an opening for 1911. But there was still one slight problem. There was a boy from Keytesville named Dempsey Anderson who was next in line for Rucker's recommendation. Omar knew that it was now a long shot, but he decided to take the entrance exams anyway in the unlikely event that Dempsey wouldn't pass them. This seemed even more unlikely, as Dempsey had been studying for these exams for over a year.

The exams that Omar took were administered at the Jefferson Barracks, near St. Louis, on an unusually warm spring day in 1911. The appointees and alternates from Kansas and Missouri assembled to take the entrance exam for the West Point Class of 1915. It was on this day that Bradley first encountered another perspective cadet with whom he would be associated throughout the course of his life and career— Dwight "Ike" Eisenhower (1890–1969).[12] Though they did not formally meet one another on this day, they were in the same large room taking the same tests. On that day, no one would have imagined that there were two future Generals of the Army in that room taking the same regional examination. This was a rank that had been attained by only a handful of officers over the entire course of American history. The odds of these two individuals being in the same room taking the same test were staggering.[13]

For Omar, West Point was a long shot, yet one that would ultimately pay off. A day or so later, he received a letter of congratulations from Congressman Rucker informing him that Dempsey had failed "some" of the examinations and that Omar had obtained the required grade, thereby becoming the "successful contestant." One can only imagine how Omar felt as he received this unbelievable news—his perseverance and hard work had paid off. He admitted to feeling bad for Dempsey, evidencing the empathetic attitude and integrity that he maintained throughout his lifetime.

2

Welcome to West Point

One bright summer day, as Omar Bradley and his fellow cadets left the mess hall at West Point, he managed to overhear the older boys talking among themselves. Though he couldn't make out the entire conversation, he heard enough of it: "Let's spigot the Augustines." Spigoting was a form of hazing that involved catching the victims and holding them under an opened water spigot, of which there were many around the campus. Since Omar had entered West Point in August, he was considered an "Augustine," and the other cadets resented the fact that he (and others) had missed out on seven weeks of hazing because he had reported late.[1]

That day, the "Augustines" scrambled as the older boys chased after them. There happened to be a good-sized sugar maple tree in front of Omar's tent, and in a split-second decision he decided to climb up it. He sat perched in this tree, where the thick leaves effectively hid him as he watched the goings-on from a safe altitude. He looked on as several of the older classmen searched all over the campus for him; he even witnessed several of his fellow Augustines getting dunked down the street. The stunt was soon over and Omar eventually climbed down, but this situation taught him resilience—a trait that would serve him well during his service in World War II as he fought against the Axis troops.[2]

Spigoting was not the only form of hazing at West Point during this time. While at the academy, Omar was also subjected to something called "dragging." In camp, most of the cadets slept on a canvas cot with a folded blanket for a mattress, with a mosquito netting hanging around it. This made it easy to "drag" the cot along with its sleeping occupant into the street. This rude awakening was occasionally intensified by someone throwing a bucket of water on the cadet. To lessen his chances of getting "dragged," Omar, along with his tentmate (who also happened to be an "Augustine"), slept on the floor. Omar surmised that by doing this they avoided having to fold and store the cot each morning and minimized their chances of getting picked on. After all, it was not as much fun to drag someone sleeping on the floor.[3]

Aside from this hazing, there were several other adjustments for the young Omar to make, including learning a whole new vocabulary. West Point had its own unofficial lingo, and several terms had new meanings. For instance, the word "beast" referred to a newly arrived "plebe," or what is commonly called a freshman.[4] Omar had to learn this social language, as did all incoming "plebes." To "max" meant to meet with maximum success; to "gum" meant to get emotional; to "speck" was to commit to memory; a "spoonoid" was a ladies' man; and "to crawl" meant to "chew out."[5]

Upon entering West Point, Omar became enamored with its stirring motto: "Duty, Honor, Country." Omar was athletic (like his father), and during his first year at West Point he gained twenty-five pounds, upping his weight to 173.[6] In the spring of 1913, he joined the varsity baseball team as a left fielder. One of his classmates, Red Reeder, commented on his appearance during this stage, suggesting that Omar looked a bit like Abraham Lincoln. He was six feet tall, "stringy," and lean with a tan and a well-built frame. "His shoulders carried the hint of success on future athletic fields."[7] He had a pleasant voice that people found appealing, and his arms had the "muscles of a 200-pounder," which he built by unloading forty-ton railroad cars with a shovel during his summer job. Omar proved to be an above-average, capable student. He was also a good shot, a skill that he seemingly had honed on his various hunting trips with his father.

It wasn't until 1913 that Omar's class was first granted a furlough. He decided to return to Moberly, where he spent several months with his mother and got to know his new stepfather and two stepbrothers.[8] Omar played baseball three times per week with a local semipro team, though he refused pay in order to remain eligible for West Point. Omar's skill at baseball would carry over into his military training, especially in his throwing accuracy. One such instance occurred while he was serving as the lieutenant range officer for combat in Douglas, Arizona. Omar was in a pit with several men, supervising them and timing their exposure. Live rounds were used in this training exercise, and bullets whizzed over their pit. All of a sudden, out of nowhere, a snake dropped into the pit. It looked like a rattlesnake, and Omar quickly became afraid that the men might jump out of the pit to get away. If they did, they would almost certainly be hit by the bullets flying overhead. Omar proceeded to pick up a small rock and fling it at the snake slithering down at the other end of the pit. The rock caught the snake just below the head and nearly took its head off. One of the men praised him, saying, "Thanks, Lieutenant. I was just about to go over the top. I would rather take my chances with the bullets than that snake in this narrow trench."[9] This story helps us understand the different skills and qualities that turned this country boy into a commanding officer.

It was also during this time that Mary's sister, Sarah (Jane), had graduated from Moberly High School. The plan was for Dora Quayle, Mary, and Sarah to move to Columbia so that both girls could attend the university. Mary taught in the town of Albert Lea, Minnesota, where she attended a teacher-training school in St. Cloud for two years and then taught for two more. She finished her two final years at the University of Missouri, where she graduated in 1916 with a major in English. When Omar was on furlough, Mary happened to have returned home for the summer months. Omar began romantically pursuing Mary, and the two began a courtship. This process included going on picnics with friends and relatives, attending church functions at Central Christian Church, and just sitting on Mary's front porch.

Mary returned to her teaching position to save enough money for further studies. During this time, Mary and Omar began corresponding, writing letters to each other once a week. This was Omar's first serious relationship, and this couple would continue to find creative ways of spending time together. Omar loved Mary. There is no denying this fact. Even years later, when Omar was on the front lines in Europe, he would greatly miss his first love. They decided they would get married as soon as possible; however, Omar's job would make setting any date complicated.

3

Groom-ing an Officer

Though Mary and Omar were engaged to be married, another girl caught Omar's attention while he was stationed in Arizona. This girl's name was Beatrice Dick. It was not uncommon for military men to keep an eye on their buddies' respective girlfriends and fiancées if they happened to be stationed nearby. In this particular situation, Bradley and a friend were looking after a girl downtown who was engaged to another lieutenant stationed in Alaska. Bradley and his friend took turns escorting Beatrice to different functions and dances that she would otherwise have missed. This occasional escort role would lead to an unhealthy obsession for one of the lieutenants, a soldier named Price. Price believed he had fallen in love with Beatrice and threatened to shoot her if she refused to marry him. He also threatened to shoot a dog that barked at him on the way to the streetcar one night. What made these reports so serious was that Price was known to carry his issued .40-caliber pistol into town with him whenever he went out.

Bradley eventually caught on to what was happening and reported the matter directly to Captain Harris, the post commander. The commander told Bradley to report to him the next time Price carried his gun off the army base. After several days, Price made plans to go into town that evening. Bradley notified Captain Harris, and he was in turn ordered to go downtown and escort Price back to the captain's quarters. Bradley felt a little uneasy about this order and was not sure how to handle this delicate situation. If he handled this mission in the wrong way, he could end up getting a bunch of innocent civilians shot along with himself. This was a sensitive circumstance. He finally devised an ingenious plan to "capture" this lieutenant. Bradley spoke with the company artificer, asked him to remove the powder from some bullets, and had them placed them in Price's pistol, rendering the gun harmless.

3. Groom-ing an Officer

Bradley knew that on this particular evening, Price would be calling on Beatrice, so he determined to get there at about the same time and inform him that Captain Harris wanted to see him right away. Bradley didn't know what his reaction would be, but he knew his gun was harmless provided that he had not discovered the substitution and replaced the empty bullets. Price came along without any argument or incident.

After interviewing Price, Harris decided that Price should be placed in the hospital overnight, and the next day he was sent with an officer escort to St. Elizabeth's Hospital in Washington, D.C. St. Elizabeth's served as a service hospital for "mentally deranged" military patients. After several months, Price was discharged from the hospital and retired from the service due to a physical disability. Several years later, Bradley heard that he had actually shot an African American man in Pittsburg, Kansas, and served five years in prison.[1] This unusual connection to Beatrice Dick revealed Bradley's quick thinking, his problem-solving skills in handling a volatile situation, and his ability to discern a dangerous situation. This discernment would prepare him for his future in commanding one of the largest armies in U.S. history to serve under one commander.

* * * * *

One of Bradley's fondest memories was his graduation from West Point in June 1915. Following this graduation, he was given a month's leave, during which time he went back to Moberly and lived with his mother on a farm just north of town. Mary visited him regularly, having completed her junior year at the University of Missouri. Their relationship continued to develop as they picnicked together, visited the Bijou Theater, and went on long walks. Bradley continued playing on a semi-professional baseball team in Moberly, again without pay. He had never dated during high school, and he had only one experience in college that could even remotely be considered a romantic encounter. By his own admission, he had "dragged" one girl to a dance and openly confessed to his deplorable inexperience "in matters of the opposite sex."[2]

There was one girl who caught Bradley's eye, but his loyalty to Mary stopped him from pursuing her—or so he claimed. This was Beatrice Dick, and many years later when writing his memoirs, Bradley stated: "Miss Dick was a very attractive girl. If I had not been engaged to Mary Quayle I could easily have fallen in love with her."[3] Later in life, Bradley occasionally wondered what would have happened if he had pursued Beatrice rather than Mary. He concluded that Beatrice's father would have persuaded him to resign from the service and become a banker. He noted, "I doubt that he would have succeeded as I really liked the service, and still do." Thus, it was a good thing that he chose Mary in the end.[4]

Despite his attraction to Beatrice, Bradley continued to pursue Mary. He even provided some "Freudian" explanation for this love, which he nonchalantly recorded in his autobiography:

> ... Mary was endlessly fascinating to me. She was pretty, bright, ambitious and domineering, like my mother. She did not hesitate to order Second Lieutenant Bradley around. She had strong likes and dislikes about people. Those she disliked got an icy shoulder. Her college and teaching experiences in Minnesota and a year at the University of Missouri, where she and Jane had joined the Kappa Alpha Theta sorority, had considerably matured and broadened her. She was no longer dependent on her Moberly roots and friends. She wanted to expand her horizons still more.[5]

This love-struck couple decided to take the "final plunge" and solemnize their love. In the summer of 1915, Bradley proposed to Mary. They set the date of the wedding for that next June, following Mary's graduation. However, a civil war broke out in Mexico that would serve as a major inconvenience for these young lovers, forcing them to reconsider their plans. This imminent conflict made any leave from the military impossible. It would be the first of many instances in which Bradley's army career negatively affected his family obligations.

When this situation arose, Bradley intended to write to Mary to alert her to the issue, but before he could do this, he received a phone call from his hometown newspaper, the *Moberly Democrat*. The paper had learned of his orders to go to the border and asked him a string of questions. Bradley became flustered and, before he informed Mary, inadvertently told the paper about his plans to postpone the wedding. The paper went ahead and printed its article with the headline: "War Orders Delay Marriage/Lt. Omar Bradley Called to Border/Was soon to Wed Miss Mary Quayle."[6]

Based on the way this article was written, it appeared that Bradley was the one who had postponed the wedding even though proper etiquette dictated that this decision was reserved for the bride-to-be. Mary, not one to hold back her opinion, was justifiably annoyed. However, their love survived this misunderstanding. They postponed the wedding until Bradley could go on leave. The postponement turned out to be a blessing in disguise, as a few days after her graduation, Mary came down with a case of typhoid fever so severe that it warranted her hospitalization.[7] Mary became seriously ill and felt very weak for many months following this incident. As a result of this condition, her hair suddenly fell out and she quickly lost weight. It took Mary several months to recover from this health issue, leaving Omar with a helpless feeling as he could only offer "sympathy and encouragement."[8]

Meanwhile, he had been assigned to the border town of Douglas, Arizona, strategically placed in the event that a Mexican civil war should break out (and where he met Beatrice Dick). Nothing ever came of this incident, and in October 1916, Bradley, along with all of his classmates at West Point, was promoted to the office of first lieutenant, after only seventeen months' service.[9] It seemed like the age old adage "timing is everything" rang true; Bradley had unwittingly entered the army at just the right time for advancement.

Back at home, Mary had recovered from her bout with typhoid fever, and the couple set the new wedding date for December 28. In order to prepare for this milestone event, Bradley applied for a month's leave from December to January. He then met up with Mary in Kansas City while she was visiting her cousins, but she was still pale and weak and her hair had not yet fully grown out. This reunion was a long time coming, as they had not seen each for fifteen months.

Finally, on December 28, 1916, Bradley and Mary were married in Columbia, Missouri. It was a small, low-key wedding, and there was one particular personal situation that seems peculiar: Omar's mother and stepfather did not attend. Bradley's hometown of Moberly was roughly thirty miles north of Columbia, and these two cities were conveniently connected by railroad. It seems unusual, given this surmountable distance, that Bradley's mother and stepfather would miss the wedding of Bessie's only son. Bradley claimed that their absence was due to the high cost of travelling, although this seems unlikely.

One recent biographer, Jim DeFelice, observed that this excuse seems to have been a "blatantly face-saving one though who it's sparing isn't clear." Local train fares cost two to three cents per mile at the time, and this travel along with the expense of room and board would have been somewhere between five and six dollars.[10] Though Bessie was in a difficult financial situation, Omar had been promoted to first lieutenant, receiving a raise in salary to $206 per month, which would have been considered a decent wage at the time. If Omar had wanted his mother to attend, he could have easily found a way to get her there. Yet the question remains, "Why didn't he?"

Another strange element to this wedding story was that Omar had no traditional best man at the ceremony. No close friends or relatives stood up at the altar with him as he bound himself in holy matrimony. Nor was there any maid of honor, as the intended individual, Jane Quayle (Mary's sister), missed her train connection for Columbia. Regardless, the pair was married by the Reverend Madison Ashby Hart of the Colombia Christian Church. Mary's hair was still too short, which prevented her from wearing the veil that her Aunt Papita had sent her, and she instead wore a hat along with a calf-length afternoon frock while her mother gave her away. Omar half-jokingly recalled in his autobiography that Mary had a "boyish haircut" during their wedding.[11]

Following the ceremony, the newlyweds honeymooned in Kansas City, Missouri, staying at the Muehlebach Hotel. Next they visited one of Bradley's West Point buddies, Jo Hunt Reaney, who lived in Texas, and checked into the historical Pasa del Norte Hotel. This encounter with Reaney served as Mary's first brush with army life, and this old friend welcomed them warmly, giving them a Navajo rug as a wedding present.

They stopped in Yuma on their way to California to pick up Omar's pay and continued on to meet Mary's two aunts, Papita and Maud, in Los Angeles. While in L.A., the couple saw an advertisement for some female English setters for sale. Later in their trips, Omar traded an old .22 rifle for a puppy, which they named Birdie. Omar described her as a "good and lovable companion," though she was always running away from them.[12]

Bradley had a soft spot for any type of canine. He continually kept dogs around him, even on the battlefield. In fact, following D-Day, his driver had picked up two terrier pups somewhere in France, and Bradley named them Omaha and Utah—the code names for two of the beaches stormed in Normandy.[13] Later in life, he and his second wife, Kitty, picked up two poodles that also bore these same proud names. It is not surprising that Bradley loved dogs given their general traits: loyalty, an ability to follow rank (i.e., listen to the master or alpha male), and their protective instincts—traits that Bradley held dear.

On January 11, 1917, the couple returned to Yuma and rented a small two-room house with a screened-in porch. Mary decorated the home in a modern style, using colored curtains and the Navajo rug that they had received as a wedding present. Their time at Yuma was miserable. The threat of impending war in Mexico had finally been squelched and life soon became "routine and boring" for the Bradley family.[14] Omar began applying for a transfer to Tanana in Alaska, and his request was soon approved—the Bradleys were moving again.

Telling the story of their relationship, Bradley noted that together they embarked on "forty-nine years of married Army life" but doesn't explain what a "married Army life" implies. Recent studies have attempted to define the meaning of a typical "army marriage," identifying key characteristics of military marriages. One such occupational hazard is that veterans and military personnel (males in particular) are more likely to have extramarital affairs than non-veterans. This characteristic would prove to be true of Bradley, as will be examined later in this book.[15] Undoubtedly, this statistic reflects the extensive social sacrifice that soldiers are forced to make and the fact that no definitive plans can be made outside active duty. Mary indirectly expressed a frustration with this very issue in an article written for the West Point periodical *The Pointer* in 1952:

> There is one more responsibility of the Army wife which cannot be abrogated. Army orders have priority over personal desires. First, last and always, your husband's job comes first ... when the orders come, and all has been done that can be done, they must be obeyed. Which may mean that the Army wife is left with the children and a move to make without the aid and assistance of her husband.... General Bradley has often told me that a good Army wife can do as much for the service and as much for her country as the officer himself. That's a big assignment for any girl in these difficult years. It's a challenge well worth accepting—but only if you really love the man who has asked you to marry.[16]

Mary was certainly a patient wife; yet even her patience would be put to the test over the next couple years, as the U.S. prepared to engage in a world war.

4

Close but No Cigar

America's involvement in World War I, called the Great War at the time, officially began on April 6, 1917, when the United States declared war on Germany. The U.S. called for a mobilization act, and all males age twenty-one to thirty were subjected to the draft. For Omar and Mary, this meant that their initial relocation orders to the 1st Battalion in Alaska were indefinitely canceled. Bradley desperately wanted to go out to the front lines in France and prove his worth on the battlefield, but it soon became obvious that this was not going to take place. Because of these aspirations, the next sixteen months would be arguably the most frustrating years in his early military career, and his frustrations were amplified by his own personal issues. Ultimately, Bradley was assigned to Command Company F in Butte, Montana, where he would sit on the sidelines during the course of World War I. He reached Butte on January 26, 1918, and Mary and her mother arrived there shortly thereafter.

Soon the Bradleys received some life-changing news—Mary was pregnant with their first child. If anything could lift their spirits, it would be the birth of their baby. Unfortunately, tragedy struck the Bradley family. Shortly after they arrived in Butte, Mary went into labor, but their baby boy was stillborn. The doctors believed that this complication was the result of Mary's earlier struggle with typhoid fever. In these days, infant deaths were more common, though the pain and psychological effects of giving birth to a stillborn baby are considerable and can include many long-standing emotional issues. The Bradleys were devastated with grief. For Omar, it brought forward depressing memories of both his little brother Raymond's death and his father's. Mary's mother, Dora, arranged for the body to be brought back to Moberly and buried in the Quayle plot in Oakland Cemetery alongside

4. Close but No Cigar

Mary's father. They bought a small gravestone to mark the grave and inscribed it: "Infant son of O.N. and Mary Bradley."

One of Bradley's assignments at Butte was policing the copper mines in Montana. Copper was a valuable resource, and the mines soon became the subject of labor unrest from the radical group Industrial Workers of the World (IWW). This placed Bradley into his first command post. On March 17 (St. Patrick's Day), this primarily Irish-immigrant organization planned a strike that quickly escalated out of control. In response to this protest, Bradley ordered his men to switch to live rounds, put on their bayonets, and go on patrol as a show of force that this sort of behavior would not be tolerated. Bradley was commended in the local papers for his effectiveness in the handling of this situation.

On August 18, 1918, Bradley was promoted to the rank of major. Soon thereafter, the Bradleys received word that they were being transferred to Camp Dodge and would become part of the newly formed 19th Infantry Division. It seemed that Bradley would fight in the Great War after all. On September 25, he arrived at Dodge and was merged into the 19th Division; however, something changed this trajectory. A violent case of the flu struck the camp; hundreds of men were infected and many died. This disease decimated their ranks as talks of peace began to emerge from the Kaiser in Germany. It seemed that any opportunity to fight had now passed.

During this time, Jane, Mary's sister, wrote to them about her forthcoming wedding, to be held in Moberly on October 12. She was to wed a rancher named Wayne Case Stewart from Dayville, Oregon. But even though Omar and Mary were only 150 miles from Moberly, neither of them attended this event. Omar was in the field, meaning he was not eligible for leave, while Mary sat out the flu season at home. Thus, as Jane had missed Mary's wedding, so too did Mary miss Jane's.[1]

That following month, on November 11, 1918, while Omar and Mary were in downtown Des Moines, they heard whistles blowing all over town. People were cheering and celebrating—the "war to end all wars" was finally over. Though Bradley was pleased that the devastation of this war had ended, inside he regretted that he was not able to participate in defending his country.

He believed this lack of experience would ruin him professionally. Not only that, he felt that the Germans had been let off too easily and that the U.S. should have allowed the war to reach Germany and given the Germans a chance to experience the devastation of war firsthand. He felt that the German people might not be convinced that they were licked, and he predicted that this would start another war in twenty years. Bradley's "prophecy" was off by only one year, for in 1939 Nazi Germany would invade Poland.[2] Little did Bradley realize that he would play an integral role in a Second World War, which would emerge out of the climate of armistice Germany, and that he would serve as one of the key players in this international conflict, leading the 1.3 million troops of the U.S. 12th Army Group.

On December 11, the Bradleys received orders to move to Camp Grant. When they arrived there, they rented a house in Rockford, Illinois, while Bradley worked at the base. He recalled that this camp was as disorderly as the previous one. The only upside to this move was that Mary's cousins lived in the area, and they would spend the winter together, primarily reading and contemplating their next move. Bradley wanted to return to the Northwest, ideally as a military instructor, but that seemed unlikely. He was then given his next assignment, to Vladivostok, Russia: Siberia. Bradley was appalled at this new assignment, but an issue soon arose that took his attention away.

In March 1919, he was placed on a disturbing court-martial case. The details concerned sixteen black soldiers who had allegedly gang-raped a white woman. The proceedings dragged on over the course of several months and into August. Though Bradley did not enjoy being on such an emotionally charged case, something positive did come out of this service. Due to his involvement in this court proceeding, he was made ineligible for the new Russian post. He was therefore reassigned on August 25 and was placed as an assistant professor of military tactics at South Dakota State College in Brookings. Bradley carried on his father's teaching legacy, instilling new cadets with a love of reading, science, and math. They spent one year at Brookings, which Bradley described as both "interesting and challenging."[3]

That summer, Bradley worked at an ROTC summer encampment in Michigan, and after that he went on a three-week camping and fishing trip in Minnesota. Again, fate smiled on the Bradley family. As Bradley was preparing to begin another year teaching at South Dakota State College, the news came that he had been reassigned: He would be a new math professor at West Point Academy—his *alma mater*. This was a very prestigious position, and there is no clear reason why he received such an ideal assignment, as he did not request it. The only logical explanation could be found in West Point's drastic need for teachers, as Bradley was one of thirty-seven math teachers.[4] On September 11, 1920, the Bradleys packed up their Dodge touring sedan and moved to West Point. Their dog, Birdie, who was always prone to wander, could not be found in time, and they had to leave without her. They would never see her again.

5

Here, There, and Back Again

More than 180 feet above the Hudson River, Bradley dangled on nothing more than a narrow cable. He had recently started working for a construction company on the new Bear Mountain Bridge for the wage of ten dollars for twelve hours of work. He probably wouldn't have needed this extra job if not for the drastic losses he and Mary had suffered in the stock market. Bradley hovered above the water on a 2,400-foot temporary walkway across the makeshift footbridge straddled between two 350-foot towers. The wind whistled through the narrow neck of the river, setting the cables swaying as he walked along.

Suddenly, a high wind bellowed through the air, snapping one of the smaller wires and transforming it into a deadly whip that struck Bradley's watch, cutting it in two. Bradley clung to the wires as he realized what had just happened and how close he had come to death. On that day, Bradley came to grips with his own mortality. He decided it was time to retire from the bridge-building business and stick to playing the stock market for additional income. This decision seems ironic, as Bradley would become a leading personality in the deadliest war in history, yet he quit this construction job because he considered himself a family man.

* * * * *

Omar enthusiastically returned to West Point in 1920, describing the experience as "coming home again."[1] One thing stifled the joy of this move: the Bradleys' mundane social life. Though Prohibition was the law of the land, there was no shortage of homemade alcoholic beverages available, ranging from bathtub gin to bootlegged whiskey. This era is known as the Roaring Twenties and was famous for its glamorous focus on celebrities, jazz music, and the rise of Art Deco.

At West Point, parties were held nightly, but the problem was that neither Omar nor Mary cared much for drinking or smoking. To Omar it was fine to just attend these parties without participating in these vices, but Mary was exceptionally sensitive to cigarette smoke. Also, she could not tolerate the obnoxious disposition of inebriated individuals, which made attending any social gathering very difficult. These hang-ups pushed the Bradleys to lead a low-key social life compared to their friends and colleagues. Their idea of a night out would be driving down to New York City for dinner and a show; however, in those days most people did not have much money to spend, and this was a rarity. Also, as part of Bradley's social life, in 1923, he joined the Freemason Lodge #877, a lodge that included other military personnel from the Highland Falls area (Joseph Stillwell among others). Though Bradley was a member of this fraternal organization, his level of involvement remains ambiguous.[2]

In the spring of 1924, Omar was given a raise from $300 to $350 per month, and the Bradleys lived a comfortable, moderate lifestyle—not lavish but certainly not poor. They had no children, and given their humble upbringings, they were used to living frugally. According to Bradley's own admission, he supplemented the family income through his poker winnings. He had developed a sure-fire system for his playing: He was a conservative player and would fold unless he calculated that he stood at least a 70 percent chance of winning. Bradley applied a systematic approach to gambling, as exemplified in the notations made in the various betting books and articles housed in his library at West Point Academy.[3]

The Bradleys desperately wanted to have children, but Mary had a difficult time getting pregnant again. Their return to West Point was followed by another unfortunate event in their personal lives—Mary had gotten pregnant only to miscarry. This was a depressing time for the Bradleys as they struggled to bear this grief, but something would soon lift their spirits. In March 1923, Mary became pregnant for a third time; thankfully, there were no issues or complications, and on December 3, 1923, she gave birth to a healthy baby girl—Elizabeth. Due to the many difficulties they experienced, they decided not to attempt to have any more children.

Bradley's teaching schedule became a point of frustration, as he spent time after school brushing up on his lessons in order to stay ahead of his students. As soon as he had developed a core curriculum, he was assigned a new class and the preparations began all over again. Their second year at West Point passed by rather unremarkably; in the third year, Bradley's teaching schedule changed yet again. In the spring of 1924, his four-year commitment was coming to an end, and he and Mary began discussing what assignment he should put in for next. They were thinking of going somewhere overseas. Bradley finally decided to apply for an advanced one-year senior officer's course at Fort Benning in Georgia, and not surprisingly, he was accepted.

Bradley spent the remainder of that summer working the stock market and fly-casting across the regional lakes. The Bradleys had spent four years at West Point, but their time was now drawing to an end. Bradley fondly recalled that this experience was among his most intellectually gratifying. It was during these years that he commenced serious study of military history and biographies, learning from some of the great generals and military leaders throughout time.

First Time at Fort Benning

Omar's next station was at Fort Benning, and the Bradleys decided to drive there in their old Dodge, though it was a slow process as the car wasn't very fast. Also, they were constantly stopping every few hours to warm up Elizabeth's bottles—she was about nine months old at the time.[4] Student housing was a rarity, compelling Omar and Mary to rent a house in the nearby city of Columbus. They rented a small framed house for the remainder of that year. Unfortunately, this house had no central heating system and maintained its temperature through the use of a coal-burning stove situated in the living room. The landlord assured them that the stove would be adequate to heat the house and that Columbus winters were mild at best. This would prove to be false information, as that following Christmas the temperature dropped drastically and the stove was grossly insufficient for the Bradleys' needs. Bradley recounted, "Night after night I huddled in the frigid kitchen reviewing my studies in extremely uncomfortable circumstances, silently cursing the landlord."[5]

Bradley commuted with several classmates to school each day, and even though Benning was a newer facility, its standards were still top-rate. During his studies, Bradley realized that his inability to fight in the First World War was actually not a negative mark on his record

5. Here, There, and Back Again

but a positive one. The newest methods of fighting utilized a more open warfare, and the next global conflict would become a "war of maneuver." Thus, the trench fighting in France became irrelevant, and many who had been exposed to that style were not able to adapt to this newest form of military tactics.

Following this training, it was time for the next assignment. The Bradleys decided it was time to put in for an overseas transfer. They chose the one location where every soldier longed to be stationed: Hawaii. Bradley's transfer was accepted, and they stopped over in Moberly to spend a few weeks with friends and relatives before they left. Omar visited his mother and stepfather, who appeared well aside from their financial struggles. Mary's mother, Dora, was now renting out both of her houses on South Forth Street and had been alternating between residing with Mary and Omar and the Stewarts. She would pay the Bradleys an extended visit once they had settled in Hawaii. It was also in Hawaii that Omar would reconnect with one of his early loves: golf.

6

Hello, Hawaii

Omar Bradley had a magnetic personality that attracted people toward him. He had a way of making a private feel like a general, and people generally felt comfortable around him. This dynamic was most obvious during his time spent on the Hawaiian Islands. Bradley made such a significant impact during his time there that even many years later this influence could be noticed.

One such example occurred on a follow-up trip to Korea in the early 1950s. Bradley and President Eisenhower had made a stopover in the capital city of Honolulu, where the city had decided to throw a parade in honor of their high-profile guests. President Eisenhower was in the second car, which was followed by Bradley's. Those in the crowd cheered for the president, but quickly turned their heads when they discovered that Bradley was trailing in the next vehicle. Bradley stole the crowd's attention away, as many of them yelled out, "There goes Omar!" Herbert Brownell, the future attorney general, was in the same car as the general and told Bradley, "Brad, I think you could be elected mayor of Honolulu if you should choose to run." Bradley's personality had won him many friends within the National Guard and reserves there, and it was this popularity and general likeability among his men that led to his unique nickname, "The GI's General."[1]

* * * * *

Japan was becoming a threat to the United States, as their cordial relationship slowly deteriorated. Japan's military power was increasing along with its stubbornness. Following World War I, Japan had been given several island groups in the Pacific region in an agreement known as the South Sea Mandate. During the 1930s, the Japanese navy began constructing airfields, fortifications, ports, and other military projects on the islands controlled under this mandate. In order to deal with this growing problem, the U.S. army and navy devised a strategy called "Plan Orange" for engaging a counter-attack against the Japanese should the need ever arise. One of the key elements to this plan depended upon an important naval base at Pearl Harbor in Hawaii.

Omar on the Links

The Bradleys' time in Hawaii was largely pleasant. The officers worked only half-days and rarely on weekends. This left Bradley with plenty of time for recreation, which included time with his family and many hours on the golf course. Bradley took a tactical approach toward golfing. As one friend commented, "The general gets the most pleasure out of a golf course the first couple of times he plays it. The first, because the terrain is new to him, and the second to cope with the terrain." Bradley also enjoyed the affluence of the game and the opportunities it provided him to meet with distinguished people, including golf pro Cary Middlecoff, Bing Crosby, Bob Hope, and William Mongey, the head of the Washington office of General Motors, with whom he would gamble at four dollars per game.[2] Bradley generally scored in the low eighties, occasionally managing a seventy-four. In fact, he had taken second place in the 1929 army-wide golf championship.

Bradley also participated in the National Celebrities golf tournament sponsored by the *Washington Post*. This event allowed him to play alongside some very famous individuals, including Arthur Godfrey, Edgar Bergen, Frank Leahy, Bobby Jones, Walter Hagen, Gene Sarazen, Sammy Snead, Lew Worsham, Tris Speaker, Dizzy Dean, Carl Hubbell, Jimmy Thomson, Lefty Grove, and Jack Dempsey, among many others. Major political figures also enjoyed this tournament, ranging from ambassadors to cabinet members to members of Congress as well as high-ranking military officials. This tournament was launched by Attorney General Tom Clark (who later became a Supreme Court justice) as a charity, with 100 percent of the profits going to juvenile delinquency programs and transitional housing.

Golf enabled the general to relax while providing him with physical exercise. It served as therapy not just for Bradley but for many veterans returning home from the war. He told a touching story of one such occasion. Sergeant Edward Beamon played in the first National Celebrities tournament in 1947. Before the war, he had been a talented golfer who considered going professional, but during the war he had lost both hands. The day before the tournament, he left the hospital and tried on a mechanical device that would allow him to hold a club with his artificial hands. The day of the tournament arrived. Beamon was given the spotlight in a fifteen-minute exhibition. Thousands of spectators crowded around the first tee, and the media focused its attention on the young veteran.

It was a tough spot for Beamon, who was not sure he would even be able to swing the club effectively, yet he was determined to at least try. He swung back and drove the ball with all of his might. The swing was incredible and the ball travelled over 150 yards—an impressive drive. The crowd went wild. Afterward, he addressed them on the PA system: "Thanks for inviting me. Guess I'd rather face a machine gun." That appearance began the rehabilitation process for Beamon and restored his confidence. He went out the next day and got a job in the golf industry. The next year, he returned to the tournament as a spectator "with a grin a mile wide," Bradley wrote. Bradley's opinions about golf as a therapeutic tool were validated through this beloved story.[3]

In Hawaii, Bradley played golf at the Schofield Barracks' eighteen-hole golf course four or five afternoons per week, bringing his handicap down to a four. He was thirty-three years old at the time. One day, he stopped in at the "nineteenth hole" and had his first taste of whiskey. He found it "pleasantly relaxing and thereafter made a habit of having a bourbon and water or two (but never more) before dinner."[4] Though his opinion on drinking had changed, Mary's hadn't, and she still remained abstinent.

Horsing Around

The Bradleys enjoyed numerous family outings, often driving the ten miles to the beach at Waianae to swim and enjoy the island's attractions. Occasionally, on Sunday afternoons, Mary and Omar drove to Waikiki Beach just outside Honolulu to listen to authentic Hawaiian music and gaze at the hula dancers at the historic Moana Hotel. Omar was earning about $300 per month, which was enough to hire a maid, making Mary's life easier and giving the couple the freedom to explore the islands with impunity.

It was during this time that Bradley became acquainted with the great George S. Patton, as they lived right across the street from each other. Patton at this time was a major and the chief intelligence officer of the Hawaiian Division. Despite living in relatively close quarters, the Bradleys never got friendly with the Pattons, probably due to their very different social lives. Patton was a dedicated horse trainer and polo player. Bradley would later take an interest in horse racing, though it seemed this hobby was based on his love of odds and mathematics. Aside from this later interest, Bradley did not seem very fond of horses.[5] Put simply, these two personalities had very little in common. Despite their differences, the two remained cordial to each other, and when Patton started a trapshooting team, he invited Bradley to join. Bradley impressed Patton with his shooting skills by hitting twenty-three out of twenty-five targets.

Bradley especially enjoyed the weather in Hawaii—"not too hot and not too cold."[6] Elizabeth was three years old at this time and, according to Omar, she caught many colds by playing in the sun and then sitting in the shade, thereby alternating between two extreme temperatures. The Bradleys would often drive down to the beach in their bathing suits. They bought Elizabeth some "water wings," which she used to paddle out to the raft. Sometimes people were startled to hear a small child's voice alongside them and were surprised to see a three-year-old child that far out in the ocean.

Before the Bradleys left Hawaii, Elizabeth had taken swimming lessons with a Hawaiian woman and had become an excellent swimmer.[7] As she was their only daughter, Elizabeth received all of her parents' attention—at least while Omar was home, which would become a rare event once the U.S. entered into World War II. Hawaii became a fond memory for the Bradley family.

Bradley served with the 27th Infantry for twenty months, until June 9, 1927, when he was relieved of duty and reappointed as the officer in charge of National Guard affairs for the Hawaiian Department. His responsibilities in this new post consisted of overseeing training standards and a number of other administrative duties, all of them mundane and not overly challenging. Following this assignment, Omar and Mary decided to return to the continental United States, and on April 28, 1928, he was ordered to become a student at the army's Command and General Staff School at Fort Leavenworth, Kansas. If he could successfully complete this class, he would be assured a promotion to colonel before his retirement. According to Bradley, to graduate from this course at Leavenworth was valuable professionally and was the modern equivalent to a master's or a Ph.D. "to some one in civilian life."[8]

The Bradleys packed their things and left on May 28, 1928. The future was bright for the family, but unfortunately for them things were heating up overseas. In 1928, the Nazi Party was beginning to gain influence.

7

Back to School

Hunting was one of Bradley's favorite pastimes. He had gone quail hunting with his father as a youth, and later, when he returned to Fort Benning in 1928, he was excited to find that it hosted an abundant population of both quail and pheasant. Every year when October rolled around, Bradley traded in his golf clubs for his guns. This was more than just a casual activity for him, as he invested countless hours and dollars into this sport. He even bought a young liver-colored, white-spotted purebred English setter for $65 and named him Tip. Tip was more than just a bird dog and became one of Bradley's all-time favorite pets. One day, he and Tip went out together to gather berries when, out of nowhere, a rattlesnake jumped out and bit Tip in the head. Bradley immediately picked up the dog and carried him to the car, rushing him to a veterinarian. The veterinarian injected Tip with an anti-venom serum that saved his life.[1]

This love of hunting brought Bradley into a close friendship with Master Sergeant Charles B. Copass, and the two became great hunting pals. Bradley even bought a Model A Ford and transformed it into an all-terrain vehicle in order to transport dogs, guns, camping gear, game, and other supplies. These two hunted throughout the South Georgia area, often successfully shooting and tagging the maximum numbers of animals allowed by state law. His ability to shoot accurately and under pressure thus served him well as both a military leader and a civilian hunter.

* * * * *

Omar had taken no vacation time or leave during his three-year active service in Hawaii and had accumulated three months of paid leave. During their transition to Kansas, the Bradleys decided to cash in this accrued time to spend the summer in Moberly. They thoroughly enjoyed their stay in Missouri, visiting with family and friends, picnicking, golfing, swimming, and reading. Bradley also enjoyed one of his other favorite activities—buying stocks and selling them at a profit. It was this thrill-seeking attitude mixed with his background in mathematics that would lead Bradley to the horse tracks later in life. Though he never really considered himself a gambler, he played poker with a 25-cent limit. He referred to gambling, by contrast, as "playing cards for more money than you can afford to lose."[2]

Bradley would typically begin his day by reading the morning paper, starting in the weather section and making his way to the stock market tables. Following the newspaper, he would next inspect the daily racing forms, where he enjoyed working out the probable winners from past performances. He noted, "I get almost as much fun out of that as out of going down to the track and betting them," but "not quite." Bradley believed that a man's character could be tested at the poker table and "that his temperament and moral courage will come to the surface."[3] Given his poker abilities, his stock market playing, and his tenure as a math professor, one has to wonder if these skills made Bradley a better gambler or if he merely justified his vice.

In September, the Bradleys arrived at the new assignment at Fort Leavenworth and took up residence in student housing right next to the golf course and the polo field. That first winter at Leavenworth was trying, and Bradley suffered from two serious medical conditions. The first was his recurring teeth issue, which by this time had become a serious problem. Ever since the earlier ice skating accident at age seventeen, Bradley's teeth were a mess. He had severe gum infections, which were the result of abscesses. This issue came back with a vengeance that first winter in Kansas. It became so uncomfortable and distracting that he visited the hospital, where he learned that if left untreated, the bacteria from these abscessed teeth could make its way into his heart valves and cause a heart attack. This prompted Bradley to make the difficult decision to have all of his teeth pulled. From that point on, he wore dentures.

Bradley was not the first American patriot to suffer from teeth conditions. America's first general, George Washington, suffered from a similar ailment. By 1772, at age forty, Washington's toothaches and issues had become a constant source of pain and frustration for him. He had them removed several at a time, until when he was inaugurated as the president in 1789 he had only one tooth left—a lower left premolar. That tooth served as an anchor for a pair of hippopotamus-tusk dentures that ultimately caused too much stress on the one tooth, forcing it to fall out.[4] Bradley was hesitant to have all of his teeth pulled at the young age of thirty-five, but the potential health risks of not having them pulled far outweighed his hesitancy. Over two sessions spanning two days, his teeth were pulled and he was fitted for dentures.

The second health issue that Bradley encountered was a violent attack of influenza, which was a very serious illness at that time. There was a minor epidemic in the school, and Bradley became one of its victims in early December.[5] He recalled:

> I went to bed in my quarters. When my temperature rose above 104 degrees, Mary became gravely concerned and called the hospital. An insensitive medic informed her that the hospital was full, the doctors were too busy to make house calls, and "not to worry," because a temperature of 104 was "quite common" among the influenza victims. Fortunately, my fever broke in a few days and by Christmas I was fully recovered. Mary was justifiably outraged at the hospital personnel for their disregard of me and she never forgave them.[6]

Bradley looked back on his time at Fort Leavenworth as generally positive, viewing it as a time of intellectual growth and the preparation of mental discipline. Again, the time came for him to start thinking about relocation. He was offered two positions: 1) to return to West Point and serve as the treasurer of the academy or 2) to become an instructor at the Infantry School at Fort Benning. Though Mary would have preferred to return to West Point at this juncture (likely due its location near New York City), Omar desired to return to Fort Benning because of its outdoor atmosphere and for the potential to his career. Ultimately, Bradley opted for Benning. This turned out to be one of the most fortunate decisions of his professional life, because it was there that he was introduced to George Catlett Marshall (1880–1959). Marshall's influence would forever change Bradley's life and the trajectory of his career, though he wasn't always an easy person to please.

Back to Benning

When they arrived at Fort Benning in 1928, both Omar and Mary were pleased with the updates that had occurred during their four-year absence. Benning now possessed the appeal of being a fully settled army base rather than just a transitory location. The Bradleys lived in a duplex unit on campus, which was conveniently located next to a new nine-hole golf course. They had taken quite a beating in the stock market crash of 1929, losing around $5,000 (approximately $70,000 in 2015 money), and needed to take out a loan to cover their losses.

The catalyst for the positive changes at Benning was primarily one man—George Marshall, who at this time was a lieutenant colonel and the assistant commander in charge of the academic department at the school. Bradley referred to Marshall as "one of the greatest military minds the world has ever produced."[7] Marshall was one of the main forces pulling Bradley up the ranks, and he would give Bradley various opportunities to prove his abilities.

One of Marshall's new rules was that no teacher was allowed to lecture from notes. The lectures had to be delivered impromptu, so for his first lecture Bradley "cheated" by reading off several notecards placed on the floor by his feet, though no one seemed to notice. Bradley admittedly was not a gifted orator. His speaking skill was one of his weak spots, but at the same time his voice was also an asset—"hesitant, slightly rustic"—and it compelled "the hearer to listen hard for the next phrase and at the same time convinc[ed] him of the General's candor."[8]

The Bradley family maintained a comfortable lifestyle at Fort Benning. The quarters were heated and well insulated during the colder months. They were even able to hire a maid who was an excellent cook. They coordinated meals based on Bradley's health needs. After his teeth were pulled, he developed allergies to certain foods, including corn, wheat, seafood, and chocolate. If he ate any of these foods, he would break out into painful hives and his face would swell up. This did not prohibit Omar from enjoying his favorite foods, which were a choice cut of roast beef and a good piece of filet mignon cooked medium-well.

He also enjoyed calf's liver and bacon, corned beef and cabbage, minute steaks, applesauce, green beans, and navy beans. For breakfast, Bradley largely ate cereal, but he preferred scrambled eggs (American style) with bacon or, curiously enough, prunes—a preference that his men would constantly tease him about. For dessert, Bradley's favorite was apple pie, but nothing could top ice cream; his favorite flavor was vanilla, although pineapple sherbet was a close second.[9]

Bradley's daughter, Elizabeth, was now six years old and entered first grade at the post school. Mary oversaw the household and enjoyed playing bridge. She also began quilting, an activity that she had taken up at Fort Leavenworth and continued with great skill for many years.

7. Back to School

Omar joined a poker club that met once per the week and continued his method of playing, which allegedly made extra money for the family. After his first year of teaching, Marshall chose Bradley to take the position of chief of the Weapons Section, becoming one of Marshall's four chief assistants at the Infantry School.

The Great Depression

This time also coincided with a tragic event in American history. The Great Depression was a widespread financial disaster that began with plummeting stock prices around September 4, 1929, and came to a head with the stock market crash on October 29, 1929, also known as Black Tuesday. The effects of this crash were widespread, ranging across various socioeconomic classes. The greatest nation on Earth had been effectively brought to its knees, but not by any outside threat.

At Benning, Bradley commenced his duties as chief of the Weapons Section working under Marshall. He also organized a trapshooting range and began a new relationship with the staff officer, Walter Bedell "Beetle" Smith (1895–1961), a World War I veteran. Smith captivated Bradley, who claimed that he possessed a brilliant and analytical mind and was a gifted communicator.

In May 1931, following the end of that first school year, Omar received the news that his mother, Bessie, had suffered a stroke. He was granted a ten-day leave and took the train to Moberly. His mother, though just fifty-six years old, appeared ill and a full recovery seemed doubtful. Omar stayed in Moberly as long as possible visiting his sick mother, relatives, and friends before finally returning to Fort Benning on June 2. Three weeks later, on June 21, Bessie suffered another stroke, and this time it was fatal. She was buried in the Log Chapel Cemetery and laid to rest next to Omar's father and his deceased brother Raymond. Omar and his stepfather were never very close, and following Bessie's death, when Bob moved out of Moberly, the two never spoke to each other again.

From 1932 to '33, as the Bradleys finished up their final year at Benning, Omar started contemplating his next career move. His education made him an ideal candidate for the Army War College. There was a widespread belief that when and if the U.S. engaged in war, graduates of the War College would become field staff officers rather than serving as line officers or troop commanders. Bradley struggled with his next move, but he ultimately applied to the college. The education route had served him well so far, and he decided to keep on it even if it could prove to be a risky move. He felt certain that if a war ever did arise, he could work his way into a field position. Not surprisingly, his application was approved.

During the Depression, more than five thousand banks failed, the unemployment rate peaked at 25 percent, and hundreds of thousands of U.S. citizens were homeless. As a result, there was a pay cut even among military personnel; each soldier lost one month's pay, yet was still expected to work during this "payless furlough." This cut was spread over a twelve-month pay period, which helped to soften the blow, though it was still inconvenient. For Bradley, this meant his monthly pay was reduced to $290, although he was fortunate compared to many of his peers and colleagues. Given their other benefits such as housing, medical and dental care, groceries, and other items, the Bradleys' standard of living was not drastically impacted. Their one major financial obligation was paying back the loan they had taken out to cover their losses following the stock market crash.

In the fall of 1933, the Bradleys left Fort Benning and headed to Fort Humphreys, the home of the Army War College, located along the banks of the Potomac River. Professionally, the previous four years had been a constructive period in Bradley's military career, preparing him to become an efficient commanding officer. He had also networked with some major figures who would become leading officers in his immediate future, including George Marshall, Joe Stilwell, Bedell Smith, and many others. These personalities would become important to Bradley when the U.S. entered World War II on December 11, 1941.

The Army War College

The Army War College was located at Fort Humphreys along the Potomac River in Washington, D.C. The Bradleys had to rent an apartment in the city because there was no student housing readily available. The 84 students who enrolled that year were divided into teams of six, and each was assigned a research topic. Once they had adequately researched a given subject, they would present it to their classmates, who were then invited to critique their findings and methodologies. Bradley described it as a laid-back environment where grading was obsolete and where there was no need to try to impress one another.

His biggest complaint was that these projects and scenarios were based on hypothetical situations, thus making their work of little value outside the walls of the institution.

One project deserves mention for its foreshadowing of world events. A group of students was given an assignment to monitor a radical named Adolf Hitler in Germany, a country that was rapidly rising in power. In its presentation, this group flat-out dismissed Hitler as unimportant and called him "mentally unstable."[10] Within a few short years, this "mentally unstable" leader would command a deadly army bent on world domination and establish the Third Reich. Many of these students would face his army on the front lines of battle.[11]

Bradley began pitching for the school's softball team practices until they saw how few hits he gave up. He was permanently barred from the mound once they realized his skills. The Bradleys' first year was largely uneventful, and they spent much of their time visiting such famed sights as the Capitol, Washington Monument, Smithsonian Institution, Mount Vernon, and Arlington Cemetery. On February 6, 1934, the family was invited to a reception for senior army officers, where they met President Franklin D. Roosevelt along with the first lady.

At this time, the Bradleys rarely entertained visitors at their apartment, but Mary socialized with the other army wives through her bridge games. Their daughter Elizabeth was now ten years old and went to a public school, where she was permitted to move ahead a half-grade. In the spring of 1934, it was time again for Mary and Omar to discuss their next move. A senior position in the tactical department had just become available at West Point, a position that appealed to the teacher in him. This would give Omar an opportunity to influence countless soldiers over the years. Mary had always loved West Point and their time together there. It was an easy choice.

Returning Home to West Point

In 1934, after ten years away, the Bradley family returned to West Point. Omar referred to this school as "a place of unparalleled beauty and solidarity. I again felt like I was coming home."[12] Many changes had occurred since their last tenure there. There were more spacious academic buildings and cadet quarters, a new mess hall, the new Thayer Hotel, and a post school for staff-dependent children. There was also a new ice skating rink, and the Bradleys lived a mere three hundred yards away from it. It was there where Elizabeth spent most of her afternoons ice skating after she had finished all of her homework.[13] After completing the eighth grade, Elizabeth attended high school in Highland Falls, the town adjacent to West Point. There she was taught to memorize formulas for algebra, and as a former math teacher, Omar took a great interest in his daughter's homework.

Bradley was in the tactics department, where the main goal was to develop character, discipline, and gentlemanly conduct in the cadets, as well as physical strength, stamina, and combat skills. In other words, the purpose of "tacs" was to turn cadets into soldiers. Bradley trained the cadets in all manner of weapons, including the ones he had mastered at Fort Benning, such as machine guns, mortars, and artillery. He introduced them to sand tables (which are exactly what they sound like), allowing them to examine a number of different types of terrain.

During the next four years, West Point graduated roughly 1,110 cadets. Bradley personally influenced a great number of these soldiers and officers, many of whom would go on to fight in World War II, Korea, and Vietnam. That same year in July, Bradley—who had been a major for twelve years—was promoted to the rank of lieutenant colonel. This made him second in command at West Point and gave him additional responsibilities and duties. His final year teaching at West Point was 1937–38.

Across the pond, war clouds were gathering. Benito Mussolini, the dictator of Italy, successfully invaded Ethiopia, and Hitler began assuming dictatorial powers in Germany. Hitler had begun a massive rearmament program, and in 1936 his troops occupied the Rhineland. Japan was also arming its people in an obvious attempt to take over China.

In 1936, the U.S. Army was increased to around 167,000 men, though it was still grossly understaffed and this number was much less than would ultimately be needed. In 1938, events occurred like a chain of dominos falling over: Hitler staged a bloodless coup and absorbed Austria into the Third Reich, while Japan made a move on China.

At this time, the Bradley family relocated yet again. Bradley had no more schools to attend and was reassigned to Washington on the War Department General Staff. He had been a teacher for the first thirteen of his eventual twenty-three years as a commissioned officer. His role in the army was about to change drastically.

8

WAR-ning

The summer of 1939 was another time of transition for the Bradley family. Omar was now an assistant to Brigadier General Lorenzo D. Gasser. This time the Bradleys rented a two-story brick house in the northwest section of Washington; it had a large fenced-in backyard where Tip and his offspring, Mollie, could frolic, exercise, and bury bones. This ideal location provided Bradley with an easy commute to and from the War Department, which was in the process of being moved to the Munitions Building on Constitution Avenue, near the Lincoln Memorial. It was also in close proximity to Elizabeth's school, Western High School, where she was presently in her junior year.

By September 1938, three months after Bradley began his duty in Washington, Hitler had allied with Mussolini in Italy and begun his takeover of Czechoslovakia. This pushed a sit-down between Hitler, Mussolini, British Prime Minister Neville Chamberlain, and French Prime Minister Edouard Daladier to work out a peaceful arrangement. The British and French leaders gave in to Hitler's demands in favor of a resolution. Though some believed this "Munich Pact" meant peace in Europe, Bradley knew that it had only managed to stall a European war.[1] As usual, Bradley had an uncanny ability to interpret world events, but it seems unlikely at this stage that he foresaw how large a role he would play in this impending war.

Hitler's takeover prompted a hawk-like response from the U.S. armed forces and its president, Franklin D. Roosevelt (1882–1945). President Roosevelt began talking about mobilization, emphasizing the importance of sea and air power. This meant that Bradley's office was buried in paperwork, attempting to keep up. For one year straight, Bradley and his team focused solely on requests from Generals Malin

Craig and Marshall; they drafted congressional legislation while dealing with numerous other related items.

In the spring of 1939, Hitler began breeching the Munich Pact by enlarging his territory in Czechoslovakia. On April 27, 1939, General Craig, the chief of staff, was replaced by Bradley's mentor, George C. Marshall. Marshall would prove to be a very useful boss to Bradley, continually providing opportunities for him to excel. At this time, Bradley was just forty-six years old and a rising star. Marshall talked to Bradley's boss, Lorenzo Gasser, and requested that Bradley join Marshall's own team. This provided Bradley with a golden opportunity; if he succeeded in this position, it would guarantee his advancement and a bright future.

Bradley had worked closely with Marshall at Fort Benning for three years, and the two seemed to work well together. He personally knew Marshall's wife, Katherine, and his stepchildren, yet Bradley remained "in awe and some fear of the man."[2] This "fear" seemingly came from Marshall's outspoken personality. At one point, Marshall had sixty or more men reporting to him, and he expected them to be both prompt and succinct. Those who did not follow this expectation or found themselves unprepared were quickly reassigned to new posts and forgotten. This was not the case with Bradley, who was a hard worker and climbed his way into Marshall's good graces; he was soon promoted for his loyalty and dedication.[3] Bradley gave presentations and served as Marshall's assistant. This included writing most of his outgoing letters along with a host of other duties. Marshall was a tough but fair supervisor and encouraged independent thought among his men. He did not micro-manage, though often he made unrealistic demands and expected immediate results. War was now imminent for the U.S., but the army was still small, ill-equipped, and vastly underprepared.

One fateful day, the event that many American leaders feared came to fruition. On August 23, 1939, less than two months after Bradley commenced his duties in Marshall's secretariat, Hitler signed a nonaggression pact with Russian leader Joseph Stalin (1879–1953). One week later, on September 1, Hitler's forces invaded Poland. This prompted France and Great Britain to declare war on Nazi Germany, and so began the greatest conflict in the history of the world.[4] At the early stages of this war, Roosevelt explained that America would remain politically neutral, though he authorized some minor increases in the number of U.S. soldiers just in case.

8. WAR-ning

Dora Quayle, Mary's mother, who had been living with the Bradleys off and on, died at age sixty-nine on September 3, 1939, the very day Great Britain and France declared war on Germany. This death occurred as Dora was visiting the Stewarts in Dayville, Oregon. Jane, Mary's sister, brought her body to Moberly, and the service was led by the Reverend C.W. Cornn of Central Christian Church. Dora was buried in the Quayle plot at Oakland Cemetery alongside her husband, Charles, whom she had survived for thirty-seven years. Both had been buried next to the Bradleys' infant son. Sadly, due to the nature of Omar's job, neither he, Elizabeth, nor even Mary, was able to attend the funeral services. Dora did leave behind a small inheritance: her two properties and some stocks, which were divided between Mary and Jane.

The 1940 U.S. Army budget did not reflect the fact that the U.S. would soon be at war. The staff became unrestrained in their demands, which translated into more paperwork for Bradley and the office of the Chief of Staff. The army did not yet seek large-scale mobilization, settling on a budget of $853 million.

On April 9, Hitler began taking over Denmark and invading Norway. A month later, the Germans worked their way across the Low Countries and into France. The Dutch fell in five days and the Belgians in nineteen days. On June 10, Italy invaded France from the south and the Germans occupied Paris. On June 22, France signed an armistice. Over the span of two and half months, the Nazis had conquered Western Europe and were now a threat against Great Britain. This methodical capture of these countries was a bold and impressive feat, evidencing the efficiency of the German army.

Bradley's work became all the more pressing, and he poured himself into it. Meanwhile, over a two-year span, his daughter Elizabeth transformed from a girl into a woman right underneath his eyes. For her senior year of schooling, she transferred from Western High School to a private all-girls school in Washington, an institution called Holtan Arms located at 2125 S Street. Bradley had just returned home from maneuvers in Louisiana in time to be present for her high school graduation. The impact that his military service inflicted on his family was great, forcing him to miss important events.

Omar was undeniably proud of his daughter. He described her as "a striking, tall blue-eyed blonde, with exquisite manners, a becoming modesty and a deep Christian faith."[5] Elizabeth decided to attend Vassar College that fall. Vassar is a private college that still ranks as one of the top liberal arts schools in the country. It is located in Poughkeepsie, New York, though it was not coeducational at the time Elizabeth attended. Due to its reputation and private nature, the cost of tuition was higher than most lieutenant colonels could afford, but Omar and Mary had been fortunate in their investments; they had even paid off their 1929 debt, managing to save some money on the side.[6]

After Elizabeth's high school graduation, Mary and Omar took three days leave, from June 8 to 11, to attend Omar's twenty-fifth college reunion. During this celebration, the Germans were in Paris and the French capitulation was only twelve days away. In the summer of 1940, Hitler launched an air and U-boat invasion against England, hoping to force surrender. He maintained this vehement attack through the summer and fall months of 1940. By this time, he had also absorbed Hungary and Rumania into the Third Reich. The Russians were equally aggressive, acquiring the Baltic States. In late September, Japan allied with Nazi Germany and Italy to form a Tripartite Pact (also known as the Axis Pact). As the war expanded into a world war, the U.S. Army added millions of men, preparing for the worst.[7]

This war placed America on edge. Bradley had been working in the War Department for two and a half years, and it was time for him to start transitioning to a troop command. His duties would soon change following a visit from Brigadier General Robert L. Eichelberger, whom he had known at West Point in 1934–35. Eichelberger bluntly asked Omar, "How'd you like to be a commandant of cadets?"[8] This would have been a lateral move, as there was no promotion involved in it, but this job offer gained Bradley an even better position. Marshall offered him command of the Infantry School at Fort Benning. Unbeknownst to Bradley, he would also be receiving a new promotion. His rank was raised to brigadier general.

Two days following this development, Omar woke up from a nap with a severe earache. He called the Water Reed Medical Center and was instructed to come in and be seen by the doctors. Bradley complied and was diagnosed with the ear condition mastoiditis. He was given some drops and ordered to check into the hospital the next day.

This was unsettling news, as it seemed he would need to undergo an operation. Fortunately, this was not the case, and he was prescribed a new drug called sulfa. However, the drug itself posed a serious problem. It seemed that the newly promoted general was allergic to this medicine, and he came down with severe hives, causing his head to swell. The days dragged by, and Bradley began to worry that he would not be allowed to carry out this new assignment due to these health issues. Surely they would not appoint a sick man to such an important position. For a short while, it seemed that he would lose everything that he had worked so hard for.

On February 15, 1941, three days after his forty-eighth birthday, Bradley talked his way out of the hospital. A week later, on February 23, he was ordered to report to Fort Benning and take up the position of commandant of the Infantry School. By this time he had nearly recovered, and he along with Mary and the two dogs, Tip and Mollie, set off in their Hudson. When they arrived at Benning, they received a telegram from the War Department that officially promoted Bradley to brigadier general, at least on a temporary basis. He had bypassed the rank of colonel, going from lieutenant colonel straight to general, and was the first in his class to receive such an honor. Bradley relieved Courtney Hicks Hodges (1887–1966), who went on to become one of the unsung heroes of the Second World War. Hodges arranged for Bradley's swearing-in ceremony to brigadier general, and Mary herself pinned the one-star insignia onto his collar. He assumed his duties in early March 1941.

During his time at Benning, Bradley improved Marshall's Officer Candidate Schools. The OCS was essential to filling the junior ranks in the rapidly expanding army. Bradley expanded the program twenty-four fold without much added cost or a large demand for new instructors. He first brought this plan to Marshall, who was impressed with it and gave him the green light to move forward. The Fort Benning OCS program became the standard model and turned out thousands of junior officers who filled in the ranks at both the European and Pacific fronts.

This OCS program became one of Bradley's major accomplishments in the army and pointed to one of the traits of good leadership as he himself would later come to define it. In 1975, Bradley published an article titled "Leadership" that broke down his tough but polite leadership style into ten main elements: (1) A good leader inspires his staff and subordinate commanders to do the job and (2) recognizes that they do not know everything. (3) A strong leader should have self-confidence and not be intimidated by his staff, but rather encourage them to speak up, especially if they think the commander is wrong in his decision-making process. Once a decision has been made, each person must support it 100 percent; there should be no division. (4) A good leader produces and trains up other leaders. (5) A capable leader must possess human understanding and consideration for others without coddling. "Men are not robots and should not be treated as though they were machines." Strong leadership requires mental and physical energy and a strong work ethic. (6) A strong leader must also be stubborn at times, (7) Have self-confidence, and (8) possess imagination. (9) A capable leader must delegate and not micro-manage. (10) Finally, the main element a leader must have is character. Bradley claimed that a "man's character is the reality of himself." There was one more trait Bradley threw in as a leader—luck! A good leader must have opportunity on his side.[9]

Bradley firmly believed that leadership could be developed and improved by training, as evidenced by the brilliant success of his OCS program. Though not as flamboyant as either Patton or MacArthur, Bradley knew what it took to get the job done effectively and efficiently. It is with this practical approach that he earned his place among America's greatest heroes.

Marshall visited Fort Benning several times during Bradley's tenure as commandant and was generally pleased with the direction he had taken it. One visit in particular stood out for Bradley. Marshall had asked him, "Bradley, do you have a man to take your place when you leave here to command a division?"[10] This caught him by surprise, as he did not think he would be eligible to command a division. This is just one more example of Marshall's support. Commanding a division would mean another star and a promotion to major general. Bradley immediately began training Colonel Leven C. Allen to relieve him in the event of his promotion, which would come sooner that anyone would realize.

On December 7, 1941, atrocity struck the nation. At 5 p.m., as Mary and Omar were at home tending to their garden, a colleague stopped by and told them the horrific news: Pearl Harbor had been bombed by the Japanese.[11] They were both stunned. Bradley put on his army uniform and hurried to his post headquarters, where his staff had already started to gather, speaking to each other in quiet, somber voices. Fort Benning had an important duty to perform in such emergency situations—to protect key facilities in the state of Georgia, such as electrical generating plans, bridges, and dams, a procedure named "Emergency Plan White." Bradley ordered and executed Plan White, and troops soon deployed to the key facilities and secured them. America was shocked. The war had made its way stateside, and all eyes turned to Washington for its response.

9

There's No Place Like the 82nd Division

Omar Bradley stood at the starting line of an extremely difficult and elaborate obstacle course that he had designed himself. It boasted high walls, deep ditches, log barriers, culverts, rope swings. Several months had passed since he had revamped the process for new draftees coming into Camp Claiborne. Bradley had pushed for a renewed emphasis on physical fitness that went over and above the daily calisthenics and sporting events—thus this new, rigorous obstacle course. All the men in the division were required to participate in this new fitness program, which included the occasional running of this course.

Up to this point, Bradley had prided himself on keeping fit, but time wears on every man and he was no exception. He had just turned 49 years old a few days before. Bradley looked up and began running the course, and he was actually making good time until he encountered the rope swing. As he pushed off the swing, his hands began to slip. He finally lost his grip altogether and was unable to pull himself up. He plunged headfirst into a pool of raw sewage beneath him. One spectator recalled that the "sight of a two-star general in such a predicament was a vast delight to all ranks" and that "the incident became one of the memorable highlights of the training period."[1] Bradley could do nothing but laugh at himself, showing that he didn't take himself too seriously, as others in his position may have done. This lighthearted sense of humor carried with him throughout his entire life and made him a pleasant companion both during the war and afterward.

* * * * *

The Japanese began infiltrating the Western Pacific and Southeast Asia following the attack on Pearl Harbor. On the home front, the U.S. Army had activated new divisions and reactivated former ones such as the 82nd, which Bradley would command. He was the second general in his class to make two stars and the first to command a division.[2] Bradley pulled together his division staff and picked an aide, Lewis D. Bridge, who had been in his April 1942 OCS class at Fort Benning. Bridge recommended bringing on an additional staff member from the same class: Chester B. (Chet) Hansen. Hansen was a graduate of Syracuse University, where he served as the editor of its daily newspaper. He kept a detailed diary of his wartime experience, which became invaluable for piecing together the wartime events of Bradley's life. Parts of his diary were published indirectly through Bradley's first "autobiographical" work, *A Soldier's Story* (1951), but unfortunately much of it remains unpublished. Bradley recounted that Hansen was "an artist at putting words together," making his diary an important piece of U.S. history.[3]

In late February 1942, Bradley and his three dogs—Tip, Mollie, and a newly acquired hunting dog named Pete—moved stations. Mary came later, traveling in their new 1941 blue and white Buick, which they had bought at the Detroit factory to replace their aging Hudson. When Mary arrived, they rented an unfurnished house in Alexandria, Louisiana. By this time, gas rationing was in effect, and Bradley commuted to Camp Claiborne in a carpool. While traveling on base, Bradley was driven around in a fancy division car—a luxurious Packard Clipper.

The 82nd Division had been created during World War I. It had fought through some major campaigns including Lorraine, Saint-Mihiel, and Meuse-Argonne. One of its most popular soldiers was a sharpshooter from Tennessee named Sergeant Alvin C. York (1887–1964), who broke up an entire German battalion singlehandedly and earned the Medal of Honor. He was portrayed in the 1941 film *Sergeant York*, starring Gary Cooper.[4]

The new 82nd became an experiment in mobilization. It sprang to life almost overnight and consisted of seven hundred officers, twelve hundred enlisted men—most of whom came from the 5th Division at Fort Bragg, North Carolina—and about sixteen thousand draftees who came directly from the reception centers. Another of Bradley's many contributions to the military system was his approach toward recruits. He noticed that for many of these new draftees, their most desolate hours immediately followed their arrival to the camp. They were thrust into a strange, impersonal world and were pushed to "hurry up and wait." Because of this drastic change, many quickly became homesick. Keeping the morale positive was becoming a real problem.

Bradley did everything he could to make the draftees feel at home and that they belonged to something important. They needed to understand that their new "family" really did care about them as individuals. This is not to say that Bradley coddled these recruits. He was still tough on them, "but in an intelligent, humane, [and] understanding way."[5] Officers were sent to the reception center to greet, interview, classify, and assign each draftee to a specific unit and duty, according to his civilian background. When the trains arrived at Camp Claiborne, they were greeted with a brass band, categorized into their preassigned units, and marched to preassigned tents, where they found their equipment on a cot with bedding. A hotel meal was waiting for them in the mess tent. They even developed a rush cleaning and laundry system so the draftees could refurbish their travel-stained uniforms. It was these little touches of home that were extremely effective, and within a short while all the new divisions adopted Bradley's system.

Bradley continuously evoked the rich history of the 82nd to inspire his soldiers and commanders to greatness. He took the inspiration one step further by arranging for Sergeant York to come and address them personally. During his stay, York was a houseguest of the Bradley family, giving Omar the opportunity to spend some one-on-one time with this historic figure. York's appearance was an effective morale booster for the troops, but before he left, York said something to the general that discouraged him. On his departure, York bluntly told Bradley that he would not get very far in this world because he was "too nice."[6] Despite the criticism, the under-appreciated general would prove to the Western world that one could be "nice" and "polite" and yet still climb the ranks and become an effective officer and leader. Bradley always believed it paid to be polite. This polite disposition became such a part of his nature that in Sicily in 1943, when an aide accidentally fired a pistol as the general was handing it to him, Bradley shouted, "Put that damned thing down, Chet! Please."[7]

Noting the success Bradley had achieved with his command, Marshall sent a request for him to accomplish the same thing with the 28th National Guard Division, which desperately needed assistance. This reassignment was disappointing for Bradley, and he didn't know whether to laugh or cry. Reluctantly, Bradley turned command of his pride and joy, the 82nd Division, over to Matt Ridgway and took over the 28th National Guard Division on June 26, 1942. This new post was ten miles north of Alexandria, and Bradley brought six men from his previous division, including his aides, Chet Hansen and Lew Bridge.

The division made incredible progress under Bradley's leadership. This success made Bradley a focal point for the media, which hovered around him and his division searching for stories. They were hoping to discover another George Patton, and Bradley always thought they were just a little disappointed with his unassuming personality, as he was not as outspoken as other leaders. Certain journalists fueled these sentiments by writing bittersweet reviews about the general, such as:

> He is not showy enough to become legend. He is not mystic enough to cause wonderment. He is tough but not cussed enough to provide narrative. In a service where personal conspicuousness is regarded with awe and something of disfavor, Bradley appears solid and stable. He'll take his Army straight, thank you, and leave the color to the sideburn boys. But don't confuse glamour with leadership. Bradley is preeminently a leader.... The general doesn't only command respect; he wins devotion. That perhaps more than anything else is responsible for the heated loyalty to his command. That more than anything else is the key to his character.[8]

The media was always pointing out Bradley's normalcy and ordinary nature, but regardless of their opinion, none could deny that he was an effective leader.

Once the 28th National Guard Division had been cleared for its final maneuvers, Bradley knew he would be going overseas. At home, Mary was preparing for this inevitability. They packed up their household items and shipped them in boxes to Moberly, where they were then placed into storage, though each kept one footlocker full of personal effects. When the time came for Omar to go, Mary would be moved into the Thayer Hotel at West Point, where she (along with many of the officers' wives) would live throughout the duration of the war. Entering her junior year at Vassar College, Elizabeth would be only thirty miles from her mother. By this point, Elizabeth was getting serious with a West Point cadet named Hal Beukema, the son of one of Omar's classmates who now served as a professor of government, history, and economics. Elizabeth would spend weekends at West Point and visit her mother and Hal in the same trip.

Just after New Year's Day in 1943, following Christmas leaves, Bradley's division made the move to Camp Gordon Johnston in Carra-

9. There's No Place Like the 82nd Division 65

belle, Florida. Mary and Omar found temporary quarters in a hotel in Wakulla Springs, fifty miles from the camp. During this transitional phase, Omar spent most of his time with the troops and saw Mary only on Sundays. This must have been a trying time in their relationship, as intimate moments were getting rarer and rarer. On February 12, 1943, Omar celebrated his fiftieth birthday at Camp Gordon Johnston.

Daily newspaper reports highlighted the campaign in the North African city of Tunisia, alerting Bradley to the fact that he would not be in the States much longer. Then, on February 16, secret orders arrived assigning him to command x Corps, which was based at Temple, Texas. Bradley had no sooner finished reading these new orders than he received a phone call from Alexander R. Bolling. Bolling told "Brad" that he was going overseas on extended active duty—not his division, just him. Bradley asked how he should dress for his new duty, as he attempted to figure out where he was headed—Africa or the South Pacific. As it was against regulations to give out specific details over the telephone, Bolling replied: "Remember your classmate; you're going with him." The classmate to whom Bolling referred to was Dwight Eisenhower, and Bradley's new destination was Africa.

Bradley and his aides flew to Washington on February 17. He took only one footlocker with him, along with a Valpak suitcase. He sent a second footlocker down to Africa by ship, but he would not receive that luggage until several months later. In the meantime, Mary, with Marjorie Hansen (Chet's wife) and the Bradley dog, Mollie, drove the Buick to West Point and settled into the Thayer Hotel for a long stay. For the first time in his thirty-one-year career with the army, Bradley was finally going to fight in a real war, and it meant that he would not see his family for more than six months. In Africa, Bradley would receive some amazing firsthand experience, as he led his men through some of the most horrific battles in history. Unfortunately, his command began following a U.S. defeat in a conflict known as the Battle of Kasserine Pass.

II. WAR

10

We Missed the Bombs Down in Africa

Bradley prided himself on joining his troops on the front line of battle. In Northern Africa, he joined the 9th Division assault battalion, trailing behind them in order to see how they would act under fire. The problem was that he had run a little late getting there and watched from behind as his men deployed into a skirmish line some three hundred yards ahead. As he impatiently drove toward the battlefield, he heard a loud voice coming from a vehicle behind him; it was the sergeant of engineers warning him to be on the lookout for enemy mines. Bradley acknowledged the man with a nod, but he kept his jeep moving at full pace, as he was anxious to catch up to his men. He went another forty yards when suddenly he heard a scream over the sound of the jeep engine; it was a lieutenant warning him that he had almost run over a land mine.

Bradley jammed on the brakes and got out of the vehicle to inspect the surrounding terrain. He suspiciously eyed the fatal explosive. It was an Italian mine, about two and a half feet long with eight sticks of dynamite in each end. The enemy had placed them on the slope with about two inches of their black cover showing from the enemy side but completely covered from the approach side. The lieutenant exclaimed, "There is another one right over there—that jeep just ran over it." As Bradley turned his head, he realized that the jeep to which the lieutenant was referring was his own. No one could figure out why the device had failed to detonate; the mine should have exploded but didn't.[1] This experience unnerved Bradley, but upon later reflection he concluded that God must have spared him for the important tasks ahead. Given the number of close calls that Bradley would experience throughout

10. We Missed the Bombs Down in Africa   67

his lifetime, it seemed to some that a higher power was watching out for and protecting him throughout the war.

* * * * *

In Northern Africa, the Germans were being led by the "Desert Fox," Erwin Rommel (1891–1944). Rommel, a World War I hero from the Battle of France, was considered a humane leader (even toward Jews). He led the attack on Poland at the beginning of the war, and in 1942 he was on his way to Libya with a small force. Rommel was a brilliant tactician who had orchestrated some astonishing victories in North Africa, defeating the British on several occasions. Bradley had a deep respect for this German field marshal, referring to him as a "brilliant commander." This campaign would also allow Bradley to come into close contact with the U.S. general and future president Dwight Eisenhower. Marshall had originally sent Bradley with orders to Eisenhower for a covert operation known as "Husky D-Day." Even though Omar and Ike had graduated from the same class twenty-eight years previous, they had seen each other "fewer than a half-dozen times."[2]

Bradley flew from Natal, Brazil, to Dakar in North Africa. He landed on a cold morning just after daylight. The wind was blowing, it was cloudy, and their runway was just an open field. The Allied forces had just suffered their first major defeat. The Germans had effectively repelled them in the Battle of Kasserine Pass. This battle began when Ike first arrived in the African continent on November 8, 1942, and was under pressure from his superiors to push the Allied forces to capture Tunisia. Tunisia was an important port city in Northern Africa. If the Allies could seize it, they could effectively cut the line of supply to Rommel's *Afrika Korps*, which was off in Tripolitania.

By the end of January, approximately 74,000 Germans and 26,000 Italians were in Tunisia, and by February 16 the U.S. had lost 2,546 men. On February 19, the 8th Panzer Division overran a platoon of Sherman tanks from the 13th Armored Regiment. Several Americans abandoned their vehicles and retreated into the hills; others stayed and were either killed or captured. On that day, the Germans successfully captured twenty tanks and thirty armored personnel carriers, most of them equipped with 75mm guns.[3] By February 20, the Allied forces had nearly collapsed. The next day, Rommel's forces cracked the defenses of Kasserine Pass, though he was later forced to withdraw due to dwindling resources.[4]

Dress for Success

When the war first began, Bradley had packed 77 pounds of "useless blouses and pink trousers" at the insistence of his Washington friends. His bedroll, which contained a down sleeping bag, an air mattress, and a waterproof L.L. Bean pup-tent, was delayed in shipping and left on a pier on Brooklyn. This was the last time during the war that he parted company with his bedroll. Bradley didn't have pajamas in Africa and instead slept in his underwear and a wool shirt, due to the frigid conditions in those military tents.[5]

On March 11, a few days after Bradley had arrived at the front, he was appointed the commander of II Corps. This new assignment was made at a meeting of several minds, including Eisenhower, Marshall, and Patton, who was presently the commander of that unit. Patton, who knew his role in leading the division was a temporary position, concurred with Ike's decision for Bradley to replace him. The decision came a little sooner than Patton had anticipated, but this enabled him to travel to Morocco in order to plan an invasion into Sicily. Patton seems to have preferred to have Bradley as his understudy in Tunisia rather than as his stand-in in Morocco.[6]

Bradley was forthright in his personal opinions of Patton. He explained that there was no "professional rivalry" or jealously between the two, as later rumors have suggested. Bradley described Patton as a superb field general and leader, though he admitted that Patton "had many human and professional flaws. Those flaws held the potential for danger, even disaster so much so that Marshall and Ike felt Patton had to be continuously watched and tethered."[7] Bradley shared these same reservations. The two would become close as the war waged on, but at this early stage Bradley was leery of this outspoken (and at time obnoxious) leader. Bradley took command of Patton's II Corps. His mission was to defeat the Axis forces as quickly as possible without risking more casualties than necessary and without allowing any enemy forces to escape.

Near-Death Experience

Besides the Italian land mine, Bradley experienced another brush with death on April 1. He returned again to the front lines, this time to witness the jump-off of a division known as "Benson Force." As he

10. We Missed the Bombs Down in Africa

stood on the platform, a dozen twin-engine Junker bombers hit their observation command post, and for the second time in Northern Africa, Bradley was almost killed. He took cover in slit trenches, but the bombs killed three men within close proximity to him, including Patton's aide Richard N. Jenson, who was standing just fifteen feet away. The attack also killed one of Bradley's jeep drivers and wounded several others, including a British field liaison officer and Bradley's aide, Lew Bridge. As a result, Bridge was taken out of action for a month while Bradley's other aide, Chet Hansen, quickly recovered from the shock. Fragments from the bomb had ripped apart his jeep and his .30-06 Springfield rifle, but again fortune smiled on the general.

The Allied victory at the final battle of Tunisia seemed apparent. The Allied army had effectively trapped and besieged its enemy. Meanwhile, Rommel had been reassigned by Hitler, replaced by Colonel-General Hans-Jürgen Bernhard Theodor von Arnim. After a noble triumph at Hill 609 and the efficiency of the tanks and flanking maneuvers, an Allied victory was within reach. On May 9 von Arnim finally surrendered, and over the next week 250,000 Axis military personnel laid down their arms. The Allies were not without their losses. For the U.S., 2,715 soldiers were killed, 8,978 were wounded, and 6,528 were reported missing. Bradley's II Corps played an important role in this attack, and on May 9 Omar proudly sent a two-word cable to Eisenhower: "Mission accomplished."[8]

This victory received media attention, and Bradley became the subject of praise for his daring leadership and the victory it had ensured. Though this did not yet turn "Omar Bradley" into a household name, it was the beginning of a steady stream of coverage that would continue long after his retirement from active duty. Bradley recounted in his autobiography that it was during this stage that Eisenhower:

> ... told war correspondent Ernie Pyle to "go and discover Bradley." In time Pyle followed that advice. Locally however I apparently became well known. On what had to be a very slow day, an OSS agent in Morocco filed a report to Washington stating that the Arabs, believing my Christian name, Omar, to be Moslem, were "proud to believe that a man of their own religion" was rising to high command in the U.S. Army. So much for fame![9]

The name that Omar's father had intentionally picked out for its unique qualities had become an intriguing subject for the U.S. media to latch onto.

In 1972, when asked by a reporter for the *Armed Forces Journal* what his proudest memory of the war was, Bradley referred to this victory at Tunisia:

> When I drove out from my command post at Mateur in Tunisia in early May 1943, and met 41,000 German prisoners, II Corps was marching into our prisoner of war compounds. We fought from April 23 to May 8 with 97,000 men in the corps. We took less than 5,000 casualties—killed, wounded, and missing. But we'd been fighting hard: before that if we could get 12 prisoners a day, we'd be doing well.[10]

This was a major victory for the Allied forces, but it was only the beginning. Larger and better-equipped forces awaited them in Sicily and beyond. As the Allies made their way into the European front, they would face some of the most deadly battles in modern history.

11

Sicily or Bust

Operation Husky was the code name for the British proposal to capture Sicily. Given the city's unique geography, it would be a difficult place to launch an assault. Eisenhower came up with the idea to make a small, quick thrust to grab the island immediately following victory in Tunisia. However, through a series of miscommunications and bad weather, the planning for the attack on Sicily was postponed.

On May 13, Bradley left Tunisia and was given a promotion to the three-star rank of lieutenant general effective June 2.[1] After securing the town of Relizane, II Corps set up headquarters in a set of school buildings surrounded by barbed wire. Bradley still had what he considered his small "family"—Chet Hansen and Lew Bridge, who would remain with him for the duration of the war. Bradley was then assigned another mission with Patton. By this point, they had come to an understanding and "worked in complete harmony" with each other.[2] The final days of planning blurred together for the general, and on July 4 he drove to a French naval base and boarded his amphibious forces command ship, the *Ancon*, a 493-foot prewar luxury liner. There he settled into his relatively comfortable quarters and enjoyed a dish of ice cream—his favorite dessert.

The battle for Sicily finally began with an air attack from the Allied forces. The Americans bombed Sicily by day while the British bombed it by night. Despite its consistency, Bradley concluded that "the air support provided us on Sicily was scandalously casual, careless and ineffective."[3] One trump card that the Allies held was their ability to crack the secret codes of Germany's messages. Many of the Allies' successes were based on the British intelligence known as "Ultra" that intercepted and read the German codes and radio communications. This gave the Allies a great advantage and figured into their planning where to invade and when. It would also play a crucial role in timing Operation Overlord and the Normandy D-Day invasion.

The *Ancon* departed on the afternoon of July 5. It led a host of other transports to Sicily as the Allied aircraft flew overhead patrolling the skies. Even though the seas were moderate, Bradley endured a touch of seasickness. The voyage to Sicily took five days, but during this time he had developed a personal health issue, a sickness much worse than seasickness—hemorrhoids. The pain was excruciating, and no painkiller could numb it. Bradley knew that if the pain persisted, he would have to leave his post in order to recover. He consulted with the *Ancon*'s physicians, and they recommended local surgery.

As the vessel approached the darkened beaches of Sicily, Bradley stumbled down to sick bay. Following the operation, he returned to his cabin feeling worse than he ever had in his life. His aide Hansen recorded the following remark: "The general is ill in his room, confined there by an inopportune local operation. Compelled to lie in bed, he soon became quite ill in the pitching sea. Chafed because he has been confined to his quarters and is unable to view the start of the campaign."[4]

The Allied forces landed as scheduled early on July 10. Many of the Sicilian coastal divisions surrendered, fed up with Mussolini (and Hitler) and the personal and economic privations that the war had caused for them and their families. Countless numbers of Italians either surrendered or retreated into the surrounding countryside. Many were taken to a prisoner of war camp in North Africa or worked as laborers for the British army. Several Axis aircraft appeared overhead at dawn and managed to sink the destroyer *Maddox* and a U.S. minesweeper while just missing the British submarine *Safari*.[5] Later that day, several hit-and-run bombing attacks inflicted damage, yet overall there were no serious setbacks. All of the Allied forces had made their way ashore with minimal casualties.

Not surprised by the Allied assault, the Axis forces soon began retaliation. It was during this time that Bradley frequently clashed with Patton and his proposed strategies. In at least two instances, Patton deliberately countermanded Bradley's orders to his troops. The details are irrelevant for the purpose of this biography; however, these conflicts directly affected their relationship at this time. Nevertheless, the Allied forces pushed onward. As they made their way further inland, thousands of weak and tired Sicilian and Italian defenders surrendered; they were so tired of the war that many were even willing to provide the

11. Sicily or Bust

Allies with valuable top-secret information. In all, 33,000 Sicilians were paroled to their homes, allowing the Allies to move forward without having to police them.

It would be an understatement to say that the final chapter in the Sicily operation was not a pleasant experience for Bradley. The Allies had managed to corner the Axis troops in a narrow triangle-shaped, thirty-mile beachhead, with Messina at the vertex. However the enemy achieved a clean getaway right under the Allies' noses. This escape began on August 10 and spread out over a six-day period. In all, the Axis evacuated 110,000 men, 10,000 vehicles, and roughly 17,000 tons of supplies and equipment.

The campaign finally came to an end on the evening of August 16, 38 days after the Allies had landed on the southern beaches. The 3rd Division entered the city of Messina, where civil dignitaries came out attempting to surrender. However, the men were under strict orders not to agree to anything until Patton arrived—he was to negotiate the terms. The next day, Patton arrived, leading a motor cavalcade into the city—Sicily was successfully captured. This victory came at no small cost to the Allied forces, involving a total of 22,811 casualties; 5,532 were killed, 14,410 were wounded, and 2,869 were missing. Yet for all of those losses, they had managed to kill only a few thousand Germans; it was a "pyrrhic victory" for the Allied forces.

Bradley found this hands-on experience invaluable, as he learned firsthand about practical warfare and battlefield management. The Allies had also accomplished a major goal: permanently knocking Italy out of the war. The "tripartite" was no more. It was during this time that columnist Ernie Pyle caught up with Bradley at Nicosia. Pyle was an American journalist who traveled with various soldiers, reporting the news directly from the front lines. He would go on to win a Pulitzer Prize for his efforts, but his bravery would ultimately cost him his life when he was hit by a Japanese machine gun on the Pacific island of Iejima on April 18, 1945. The general was initially hesitant about publicity, but his aide Hansen convinced him it could be beneficial to cooperate with the media and Pyle specifically. Pyle shadowed Bradley for three days, writing a six-part series that was published and circulated widely in the U.S. Pyle's reports were largely positive; he observed that Bradley looked more like a schoolteacher than a soldier. Pyle also focused on the general's morality and positive personality, noting:

> ... he didn't smoke at all. He took his cigarette rations and gave them away. He drank and swore in great moderation. There was no vulgarity

in his speech.... He could be firm, terribly firm, but he was never gross nor rude. He always put people at their ease.... He still had the Middle West in his vocabulary—he used such expressions as "fighting to beat the band" and "a horse of another color." There was absolutely no pretense about him, and he hated ostentation.... [He] was not what you would call easygoing. Nobody ran over him. He had complete confidence in himself, and once he made up his mind nothing swayed him. He was as resolute as rock, and people who worked with him had to produce or get out.... He had a nice quality of respecting other people's opinions and of paying close attention to other people's conversation.[6]

This was Bradley's first taste of real fame and publicity. Following this interview, Omar had the opportunity to fly from Sicily to England, where he stayed for a few days. He then returned to the United States for two weeks and picked up some additional personnel, during which time he saw his family. He would not see them again until June 1943.[7]

12

Operation Overlord

Winston Churchill and President Roosevelt met with the "Combined Chiefs," a military staff made up of high-ranking officials from Allied nations that included General George C. Marshall and General Henry H. Arnold, among others. They met to determine the best strategy for defeating Hitler and his Nazi regime. In May 1944, they came up with a strategy called "Roundup," which was later changed to the code name "Overlord," although they were reluctant to implement it due to its potential risk for high casualties.

It was therefore determined that the 1st U.S. Army would be established in Britain, as there were no American Army headquarters or commander there yet. Bradley was handpicked to lead this command.[1] This pushed Eisenhower to commission Bradley as a leader for one of the most important U.S. Army combat missions in World War II: D-Day.[2] He was to leave as soon as possible, returning to the States to recruit a full army staff.

On September 8, Bradley formally took leave from his command of II Corps, installing John Lucas as his replacement. The men of II Corps held a moving ceremony for their departing leader. They formed a semicircle while Bradley made a goodbye speech in a few simple words. The officers then proceeded to form into a single-file line to shake hands with him. As he walked to his car, the band started to play "Auld Lang Syne," and as he drove to the airfield, troops lined the road shoulder to shoulder, presenting their arms in salute.

The first stop was England, where Omar spent a week, and on September 14 he flew to the U.S. to assemble his 1st Army personnel. The trip ended in Washington, D.C., where Mary and Elizabeth met the plane. Though Bradley had been gone for only eight months, it felt more like eight years to him.[3] The Bradleys celebrated a brief but much deserved reunion and talked about Elizabeth's future and her recent engagement to Hal Beukema. Their plans were to get married in early June following her graduation from Vassar (and Hal's from West Point).

Bradley nonchalantly noted in his autobiography that due to security he could not be present for any of the ceremonies. When asked by his family and friends if he would be able to attend the wedding, his response was, "We'll see if I can get it off." However, he knew full well that he would be in the middle of leading the Normandy D-Day invasion at that time.[4] Thus the father missed his only daughter's wedding.

Bradley returned to England on October 2 and commuted in a Cadillac limousine back and forth between his two posts—Bristol and England. He assigned aide Lew Bridge to London and Chet Hansen to Bristol. In London, he lived in the Dorchester Hotel, and in Bristol he stayed in a spacious country house along with certain staff members of the 1st Army. One day while Omar was in the middle of his three-hour commute from London to Bristol, he suffered another close call. His driver entered a dense fog near Slough, creeping behind a long line of trucks. The driver thought he would be able to pass this line of traffic easily, but when he pulled out, the car ran head-on into a British command car. As Bradley was thrown against the rear of the front seat, his glasses broke and he gashed one of his cheeks. Amazingly, no one else was injured, but Bradley was rushed to a hospital despite his insistence that he wanted to continue on to Bristol. He was physically exhausted and suffered from a nasty cold. He used these five days in the hospital to recuperate from his illness.[5]

Some confusion arose over who would be the commanding officer of Operation Overlord—Marshall or Eisenhower. On December 6, a letter was taken to Soviet leader Joseph Stalin that had been written by Roosevelt and approved by Winston Churchill. It read as follows: "The immediate appointment of General Eisenhower to command of Overlord operation has been decided upon. Roosevelt."[6] Bradley himself had a mixed reaction to this news. He was pleased that Marshall would remain at his "vital post" in Washington, meeting with the Combined Chiefs, but on the other hand he was sorry that Marshall was denied the fame and prestige of a high-profile operation such as Overlord.

By early 1944, Hitler realized that an invasion of France was inevitable, expecting it to come in either May or June. It would be an impossible task for the Allies to completely disguise such a far-reaching assault, so instead they used their forces to spread disinformation, misleading the Germans to believe that this attack would be coming from a different direction. Their ability to break the German code that was used in top-secret communications allowed the Allies to confirm that the Germans had taken the bait. The Allies put out false information that the 1st Army Group would be striking at Pas de Calais in northern France and that this army would be led by none other than General Patton himself. The Germans accepted this disinformation, which greatly contributed to the eventual Allied victory.

Overlord planners had assigned Bradley's 1st Army three U.S. Army corps for the Normandy assault: V, VII, and XIX. This operation was an essential step toward winning this war, but if it failed the consequences would be dire. It could be at least another year before the Allies could launch a second invasion of this magnitude, and by that time Hitler might have sufficient forces and "secret weapons" to make any campaign futile. Also, if this operation failed, it seemed likely that the Russians could lose faith in the Allies and would negotiate a peace treaty with Germany. It seemed to be all or nothing.

D-Day was postponed from May 1 until the first week in June in order to accumulate more supplies. As planning for this monumental attack proceeded, Bradley's responsibilities increased. The general found himself drawn in closer to a tight-knit circle of British intelligence that included government and military leaders such as King George VI, Churchill, and many others. Bradley first met King George, along with Churchill, at a dinner party held at 10 Downing Street. Bradley was a bit standoffish at first, but as the evening progressed, he was able to loosen up and enjoy himself. He recorded the occasion, noting that "for the first time I realized how dreadfully lonely and isolated the life of a monarch must be, how difficult it must be for him to have any sort of life outside of the royal family. He seemed to take great delight in signing my 'short snorter' ... and produced his own, as did others."[7]

That evening Bradley started a new "short snorter," a term used to describe a banknote that was circulated during World War II upon which signatures were exchanged between soldiers (and other participants) traveling together. On that occasion, Bradley assembled the signatures of all present and later added Hodges's and Patton's to the list. Even many years after the war, Bradley still considered this bill one of his prized possessions.[8]

Defining Leadership Traits

In the final days leading up to D-Day, Bradley and other high-ranking leaders did some last-minute preparation work including going over their plans, attending meetings, and coordinating with each other. It was around this time that the media showed an intensified interest in Bradley and his life story. He became a national celebrity, gracing the cover of *Time*, which labeled him "The Doughboy's General," and was featured in magazines such as *Life* and *Newsweek*, among others. Bradley felt funny about his newfound fame, as he considered himself a private person and wanted to remain that way, but he soon realized that this was an impossible feat. America was at war and the public wanted to know who was leading its military. Bradley's aide Chet Hansen convinced him (as he first did in Sicily) that the public had a right to know about his life. Bradley explained that the only satisfaction he received from these stories was that they mostly expressed his love for the soldiers and reiterated the fact that he would not spend their lives recklessly. Thus, if these writings increased the morale of his men (and his country), he would continue to participate.

This sentiment separated Bradley from other generals such as Britain's Bernard Montgomery ("Monty") and Patton, both of whom were considered "glory hounds." They enjoyed the media attention and publicity, and they made sure everybody knew it. Bradley was more reserved and genuinely concerned for his men, which earned him the title "The GI's General." He wore the regular GI clothing and traveled in a jeep with no escort vehicles. There was only one privilege afforded to Bradley that he graciously accepted—his own personal bathroom.

At first, Omar was a little embarrassed by this gesture, claiming it was not necessary, but since he was the commander, the troops believed he should have his own toilet. Thus, they carried with them a little one-seat toilet with some stars painted on the side of it.[9]

Hunkering Down

On June 3, Bradley and several key members of his staff drove to Plymouth, England, to board the cruiser USS *Augusta*, which would serve as their headquarters during the invasion. Bradley stayed in the skipper's quarters during this time. Each soldier brought with him some standard gear, including a waterproofed gas mask, life preserver, pistol, web belt, helmet, and vitamin pills. After getting settled, the men enjoyed some ice cream together and Bradley added a French note to his "short snorter," collecting signatures on it and giving some out in return. He soon learned that the weather was not conducive to the upcoming invasion, which posed a potential problem and delay.

On June 5, Bradley awoke to a teletype message from Ike: "D-Day stands as is, Tuesday, June 6." That same day, the *Augusta* embarked on its journey in a procession with twenty-one convoys headed for the Omaha and Utah beaches. There were five localities for the D-Day operation—Juno, Gold, Omaha, Utah, and Sword beaches; the U.S. would concentrate on Utah and Omaha, along with Pointe du Hoc in between. Bradley crawled out of his bunk at 11 p.m. after only four hours of broken sleep.

Suddenly, Bradley experienced another untimely personal issue— a gigantic boil appeared on his nose. The doctor told him that boils so close to the brain could quickly become a very serious health issue. This boil turned out to be so painful that he had to have it lanced in the infirmary. The Navy medic insisted that to prevent further infection, Bradley should wear a bandage over his nose for several days. He reluctantly complied, not wanting this minor issue to grow into a major one, yet he felt ridiculous keeping that large, awkwardly placed bandage on his face. Though he refused to let any photographers take his picture during this time, several photos were leaked. As these pictures circulated, rumors began to fly that the general had been wounded in battle based on this large bandage on his face.[10]

At 3:35 a.m. on June 6, the *Augusta* bells rang out, calling the men to their quarters. Bradley appeared on the bridge while Hansen recorded his every movement in his diary (out of respect for the general, he did not include the boil on his nose), noting that Bradley smiled very lightly as though it was "good to be near the coast of France and get the invasion under way. The waiting was difficult and the moments of decision on postponements were telling on the other commanders, Bradley, however, does not reveal any concern or worry whatsoever. He looks quite optimistic about the entire operation."[11] Bradley revealed that he was not as optimistic as he appeared because he knew Omaha could be a bloody battle. He had no idea how bloody it would actually turn out to be.

13

Today Is D-Day

It was a cold, dreary morning on June 6, 1944. In a drafty, metallic war room that had been improvised on the afterdeck of the cruiser *Augusta*, the caged lights shivered under the concussion of its naval guns. The blackout tarp over the thin, steel door to the deck closeted the oily smell of their GI clothes.

Seven army soldiers were on board, including Bill Kean, Bradley's chief of staff, and a handful of principal planners. All of them showed the fatigue of a winter and spring of nighttime planning. Tubby Thorson, Bradley's operations chief, had grown gaunt in his hard-lined face. He leaned wordlessly against a desk. Colonel Benjamin A. "Monk" Dickson, Bradley's chief intelligence officer, had put on the worn-out suspenders he had donned in Sicily and before that in Tunisia. They hung over his sharp shoulders to the faded pistol belt that circled his waist. To Monk, the belt and suspenders were a sign that they were in the field again. No one had much to say. They were neither nervous nor relaxed, but relieved that the Channel had been crossed, apparently without any detection.

From opposite walls of the tiny war room, the Omaha and Utah beaches stared at each other in a profusion of colored maps. Crayoned lines split the beaches neatly into their narrow sectors, each with a letter and a color. From behind the beaches, a sharp, red line marked the German defense.

Printed across the face of each map was the angry, black warning "Top Secret." These were the words that had shielded those maps from the world at large. They looked bolder in the bright, unshaded light. On the deck, the big guns of the *Augusta* thundered out to the world that the secret was out. Bradley pushed through the canvas tarp and turned his glasses toward the Normandy coast.

13. Today Is D-Day

Gen. Bradley at his desk with portraits of his daughter and wife close at hand (Joseph Fansler Petit Collection, West Point Academy).

At that point, there was nothing for him to do. The plan had taken over and, for better or worse, the invasion was on. For the moment, there was nothing any officer could do except trust in the plan and in the men who were carrying it through. Not until later in the day could Bradley hope to control or influence the forces ashore. The attack was in the hands of the assault platoons.

All that morning the men waited. And yet even during those crucial hours, Bradley never detected the slightest suspicion that they would not get ashore. The invasion had been built on confidence—on confidence in the plan and in their ability to make it work. It was won on faith, on the faith of commanders in the courage of their troops and on the faith of those troops in the skill of their leaders. Though Bradley had considered calling off the invasion, he believed his men would be successful, though this success would come at a high cost.[1]

* * * * *

The two main U.S. targets on D-Day were the Utah and Omaha beaches.[2] Utah was taken with little resistance from the Germans, but

Omaha was not as easily secured. Though the troops were successful in their mission, very little went according to plan. The Germans relentlessly defended the beach, firing from well-fortified stations with rifles, machine guns, and anti-tank guns that covered the shoreline.

Bradley later confessed that he privately considered evacuating the beachhead after getting scattered negative reports that made him rethink. He agonized over the withdrawal decision, "praying that our men could hang on."[3] This uncertainty was based on the severe communication issues between the commanders and the forces fighting on the beach. From the few scattered messages they had received aboard the *Augusta*, it seemed that this attack was going to be an utter and catastrophic failure.

In spite of all of the tactical failures and outright blunders, D-Day proved to be a major victory for the Allied forces. They were able to make it over the Atlantic wall and landed over 156,000 men onto French soil, although more than eight thousand U.S. soldiers were killed, wounded, or missing. Behind these soldiers came a large number of reinforcements and supplies. Hitler had one main opportunity for victory, but unfortunately for the Axis forces he was basing his next move on the false (dis)information that pointed to Pas de Calais as the Allies' next target. Hitler sought to defend that area rather than Normandy—a move that would prove to be a fatal error and would ultimately contribute to the defeat of Germany.[4]

Wedding Day Blues

On June 8 (D-Day plus 2), Omar visited Omaha Beach, although his mind shifted to other things. This was the day that Elizabeth and Hal Beukema were to be married in the West Point chapel—they were both twenty years old at the time. It was announced in the States that Elizabeth was getting married, and because of Bradley's position it received some media attention. Hal had graduated two days earlier—on D-Day itself. He and Elizabeth had grown up with each other and attended the seventh to ninth grade together until Hal went off to prep school.[5]

Bradley told the deputy commander, "You people are going to have win this war in a hurry if I'm going to make my daughter's wedding." "When is it?" he was asked. "Tomorrow," Bradley replied, "D plus two." The commander threw up his hands and laughed. Bradley recounted

13. Today Is D-Day

being "very disappointed at having to miss the wedding of my only daughter (another grudge I have against Hitler)."[6] In his stead, an old friend of his, Colonel Harris Jones, who was the head of the West Point mathematics department, gave Elizabeth away. A special report of this wedding was made through NBC channels by broadcaster Mary Margaret McBride, a former sorority sister of Mary's who attended the wedding. McBride went to the wedding and recorded a broadcast of it, which she graciously sent to Bradley in Normandy. A transcript of both the broadcast and the wedding was dispatched on June 10, a few days after the event. It was noted: "To be handed personally to General Bradley if [you] should meet him!" Bradley emphasized that it was a "very human descriptive account and I almost felt as if I had been there."[7]

Following this wedding, Mary gave up her room at the Thayer Hotel (at West Point) and moved into an apartment on Connecticut Avenue in Washington, D.C. Hal entered the Air Corps flight training program upon his graduation and learned to fly the latest and greatest B-29 heavy bombers.

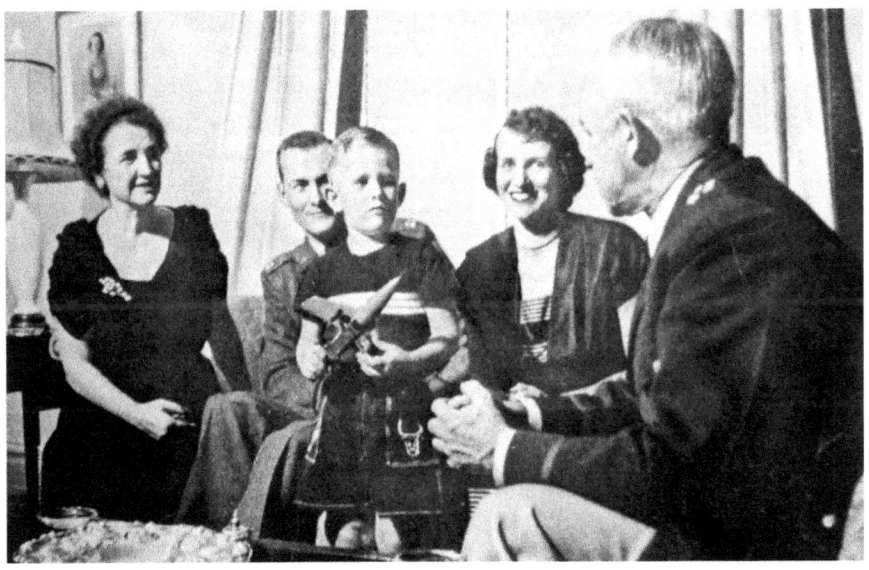

Omar N. Bradley and his entire family on June 8, 1944, two days after Bradley landed his D-Day forces in Normandy. Pictured here are Bradley's only child, Elizabeth, and her first husband, Henry S. Beukema. Holding model plane is Omar's grandchild Henry Jr., and at left is Mary Bradley (taken from *Magazine Articles By and About General of the Army, Omar N. Bradley: 1970–1971*, vol. 4, 43).

Gas Attack

Back on the European front, the Allies were in danger of entering a stalemate. They attempted to push through the German lines as the Nazis desperately held and defended the French city of Caen. The Allies had to break through. Bradley recalled that a few days following D-Day, an incident occurred one night while the soldiers were camped out along the beach. A lone shout echoed through the night, yelling out one word: "Gas." The Allied soldiers repeated this word, yelling it to spread this warning of impending calamity to their fellow soldiers. It was well known that the Germans utilized poison gas as one of their offensive fighting strategies. Bradley heard the ruckus and stepped out of his tent. He asked the guard what this commotion was all about; the guard replied that he didn't know, only that someone had yelled out "gas." Bradley turned his head and sniffed the air but couldn't smell anything. He asked the guard if he smelled anything abnormal, to which the solider replied in the negative. Omar decided to go back to bed.

Meanwhile, all across the camp, men began scouring the beach looking for gas masks, but few could be found. The gas mask was a standard item issued to each individual soldier. However, these masks quickly became a nuisance to carry, especially in wartime, so many men had discarded their masks early on.[8] In the end, it turned out that there was no gas attack, sparing the lives of the unprotected.

Entertaining the Men

After the Allies had taken these beaches, the men began to settle into camps. It should be noted that there were no officer clubs for the higher-ranking officers in this location and the troops didn't have radios. All they had were signal radios, but these could not be used to play music and there was little entertainment for men on the front. However, a nonprofit group was founded in 1941 called the United Service Organizations (USO), which would provide programs and entertainment for the troops abroad.

"Camp Shows," as they became known, began in the States and soon traveled worldwide. In fact, the USO daringly traveled to Normandy within one month after Operation Overlord had been successfully implemented. These shows brought famous stars and starlets to the front lines in order to entertain the soldiers. Many major figures in the entertainment industry participated in these events, including Bing Crosby and Bob Hope (both friends of Bradley), Judy Garland, Bette Davis, Humphrey Bogart, Frank Sinatra, Laurel and Hardy, Jack Benny, Lucille Ball, and Marlene Dietrich, among many others. These entertainers greatly increased the morale of the soldiers by reminding them what it was they were fighting for.

Everyday Life in a War

The troops lived with whatever they could carry in their bags or fit into their jeeps. Given these restrictions, the living conditions were very primitive. Most of the men had no shelter except the small "pup tents" that they were issued. It took two men to pitch a full pup tent, which housed two soldiers, and if they could find a little "lean-to," their tent was considered a palace by fellow soldiers.[9]

Most soldiers used their helmets as portable sinks. In Tunisia and Sicily, the army had purification units, also called shower companies, that provided showers with hot water. These consisted of pipes with small showerheads along with a few boards placed on the ground so the soldier's feet would not get muddy. Each shower had a canvas surrounding it that was roughly six feet high. The problem was that these purification units didn't come around very often. These units would also do laundry for the troops, washing and steaming the uniforms, though these were not in France before the Battle of the Bulge—only the essentials were dragged across the channel and brought across the beach.[10]

Some officers preferred taking over local farmhouses from the French villagers, though Bradley rarely (if ever) did this, even though he had the rank and ability.[11] Instead he lived in a nine-by-nine tent. When the troops arrived in France, Bradley built a frame onto a six-wheeled truck, to which he added a bed, a desk, a small closet, a map board, and a little washbasin in the corner. A field telephone in a leather case was positioned on one end of his desk, and a big calendar hung on the wall.[12] Omar had positioned a ten-gallon container over the basin that he filled with water, giving him the luxury of "running water." He had only one change of clothes and one change of boots, which he alternated from day to day.

Throughout the war, Omar also utilized several trailers as his headquarters. One was equipped with map boards on each side of the wall, stretching some twenty feet long and eight feet high. There were even fluorescent lights at the top of the maps so the soldiers could easily read them. One of these trailers also functioned as a living and sleeping quarters for Bradley. It had a bunk over one end, a comfortable armchair with a reading light, a small closet (in which he kept his one change of outer clothing and paratrooper boots), and some drawers under the bunk.

The third trailer was similarly equipped for guests, such as Eisenhower, who frequently spent the night at Bradley's headquarters. These three trailers were parked with the rear end of each next to a platform so that the general could move from one to the other without descending to the ground. This made for more comfortable living and working arrangements, at least until colder weather made a hotel room more attractive.[13] Bradley described his typical daily routine and the schedule that he kept during the eleven months of this European campaign:

> My day consisted of arising at six on my way to the hotel for breakfast. I usually stopped by the war tent to see if anything of importance had

Gen. Bradley in his headquarters in one of his three trailers (Joseph Fansler Petit Collection, West Point Academy).

happened during the night. At seven we held a briefing in the war tent attended by all the staff officers and any visiting senior officers. At eight I left by car or plane to visit subordinate units. All Army Corps and division headquarters had a landing strip for L-5 planes. The Army headquarters usually had an airfield that would take my C-47. I carried a jeep in my C-47 so I would always have transportation where we landed. I usually returned to my own CP about five in the afternoon. My senior officers most of whom had visited other units during the day would assemble in my trailer and we would each report what we had seen during the day while we had one, and only one drink. At six, we had dinner. After dinner I repaired to my desk in my trailer, and did paper and administrative work until eleven. Then to bed. It made for a rather full day, five a.m. to eleven p.m. day in and day out, seven days a week.[14]

Speaking of Family

As to Omar's family situation during this time, all military operations were classified and kept confidential even among military officers and their families. Americans knew an attack against the Germans was forthcoming, but they did not know when or where it would take place. Bradley was concerned as to what the ramifications of D-Day would be on the continental United States. Following June 6, the D-Day invasion was highly publicized and no longer a secret, but how would the enemy retaliate? Every American, including Bradley's wife and daughter, knew the importance of the D-Day invasion. If the U.S. failed in this invasion, what would that mean for the Bradley family and the rest of the world?

Omar received the occasional letter from Mary and Elizabeth while in the field, but these letters became more infrequent following D-Day. Written letters were the only form of communication that Bradley was permitted to have with his family, as he was not allowed to make any visits or even call them on the phone. Additionally, any letter that he wrote had to be censored and couldn't contain any details about his location or any future military plans or destinations. Once he wrote and told Mary that he had been to a party celebration and had seen a lot of people there whom they had both known, but he couldn't tell her who these people were. Bradley explained, "When you censor your own letters it is worse than if somebody else was going to [censor] them."[15] The general told his men one story of how during the last campaign he wrote to Mrs. Bradley using a typewriter. One time she "took him to task" for the brevity of his letters. His reply was direct. He proceeded to take the letter in which she had complained, retyped it into a single paragraph, and sent it on to her. "She still takes me over the coals for that one," he said as he laughed.[16] Thus, even though Mary often complained because Bradley wouldn't tell her anything, the truth is that he couldn't.

14

Cherbourg and Alcohol in the Army

Following the Normandy landings, the Allies needed to secure a deep-water port to allow reinforcements to be brought directly from the United States. Cherbourg happened to be both the largest and most accessible port from the landing spots, and it soon became a priority for the Allied forces. The Battle of Cherbourg represented not just a military battle but a psychological one as well. The Allies took advantage of their position knowing that the enemy was trapped inside with no chance of escape. For this reason, the Allies distributed a large number of leaflets across the city.

This booklet told the Axis troops that they had fought well but that there was no longer any reason to continue: "Our bombers have destroyed your cities. You are faced with overwhelming strength. Surrender now and return safely to the loved ones you left behind. If you don't surrender and come over, we have no alternative but to give you more and more of this"—this cued a forty-eight-gun "salvo" into the German position to show that they meant business. These leaflets concluded with the tagline, "And don't forget your mess kit."[1]

The Germans responded in kind by circulating their own booklets to the Allies, which they fired across the lines. They played on the American reputation for "fleshy sex interests and dislike of war," and one of them featured the following:

> "All Quiet on the Home Front" with [a] naked woman having intercourse with Jew[s]. Crude and pornographic. Caption on back—"Hey Kid from the USA. This is what it's like at home. Do you think they want to end the war. Do you think anyone gives a darn what happens to you. While FDR and the rabbis make their dough, do you think they care if you get killed."—"Hey Kid from the USA—are you from the

wrong side of the street. FDR's sons are in the army, parading down the streets of London with uniforms and fancy buttons. They come from the right side of the street."[2]

Though an edited and briefer version was reprinted in *The General's Life*, the full version evidenced the anti–Semitism that was deeply rooted in Nazi ideology.

On June 26 the Allies successfully captured the port city of Cherbourg. The Germans, led by General von Schlieben, surrendered the city, but before they did they set booby traps, sabotaging the vicinity. This plan destroyed much of the city, including the various port facilities, bridges, power stations/transformers, and buildings. Rumors circulated that the Germans had also placed time bombs around the area, though this was later proven to be false information. After the surrender of eight hundred German soldiers, the captured commanding officer, von Schlieben, requested to dine with Bradley.[3] Bradley flatly refused the commander's request, stating that he "would not eat with that bastard for anything." Instead, von Schlieben was given a K-ration just like the rest of his eight hundred fellow soldiers, who were now prisoners of war.[4]

There was one "silver lining" in the capture of Cherbourg: The Allies discovered a large supply of liquor in the vaults underneath the old Fort du Roule.[5] There was everything from French wines to five-star cognac, but unfortunately for the U.S. soldiers there was no Scotch or bourbon. Once word got out, every officer in the immediate area was sending representatives to grab some of these war "spoils." Even Monty sent a messenger to pick up a truckload of the cognac.[6] Though Bradley wouldn't allow his men to take any alcohol from this site, he did personally stash a half-case of champagne, which he opened at his grandson's christening a few years later.[7]

Drink, Drank, Drunk

Bradley claimed that no soldier ever got drunk while on his command—in fact, there was just about no drinking at all according to his report. Occasionally at night, an officer might share a drink with his men, but drinking was a rarity. When the men did drink, they would typically enjoy a homemade version of an "old-fashioned" made with marmalade. This recipe was published in *Time* magazine, but Bradley had his own unique substitute recipe for this famous drink.

14. Cherbourg and Alcohol in the Army

A typical "old-fashioned" contained bitters, orange slices, sugar, and bourbon. Since there were no oranges or bitters in the field and bourbon was a rarity, the soldiers would instead use a half-teaspoon of orange marmalade, which was more easily obtainable. They would then dissolve the marmalade in the water and add ice and bourbon, making a good "old-fashioned" substitute. This drink became especially popular toward the end of the war when Bradley had made it to Verdun in 1944. As to whether the men drank on duty, Bradley's remarks that it never occurred seem unrealistic. Rather, it appears he was attempting to protect the reputation of his men.

Eisenhower served Scotch, but he could get away with it as the commanding officer. During the war, officers had no entertainment allowance, but they were still expected to continually entertain visitors. Bradley had visitors nearly every night, and in the interest of being cordial, he served them drinks. They often went through four or five cases of Scotch per month. The U.S. officers were buying it for $18 a case or $1.50 a bottle through the embassy in London. Bradley had to pay $80 or $90 a month out of his own pocket just to entertain these high-level visitors, who included senators, congressional committees, labor leaders, industrial leaders, etc.[8] Even after the war, it was not uncommon for Bradley to enjoy a Scotch or bourbon, and he "developed a reputation in Washington as a man who makes one drink, usually bourbon-and-soda, last all evening. When he drank two, it was seen as a sign of great internal jubilation."[9] Bradley's view on drinking alcohol reflected his military strategy—moderation.

Cobra

By July 10, Bradley developed a plan to break out that was known as Operation Cobra. Cobra called for major bombing of a rectangle three and a half miles long. If it was successful, it would increase morale and build a momentum that would help finish the war. On July 20, the original day set for the operation, it was reported that a cabal of German generals had unsuccessfully attempted to assassinate Hitler. The Allies viewed this as a positive sign that an organized revolt could occur among Hitler's high-ranking officials. Incidentally, one such high-ranking general who was caught up in this Nazi revolt was none other than the Desert Fox himself—Erwin Rommel. Hitler subsequently forced Rommel to ingest a cyanide pill in return for assurances that his family would not be persecuted. Thereby Hitler removed one of his most capable generals. Time was certainly of the essence, and Cobra needed to be executed as soon as possible.

Heavy rains pushed Operation Cobra back one day, until a break appeared on July 24. Despite the generally clear weather, a heavy cloud moved over the target area. According to Bradley, a cancellation notice was sent to the pilots, though it came a little too late—only three of the six fighter-bombers received this recall order before they attacked. Furthermore, no radio channels had been designated for emergency communication with these bombers, and the only way to reach them was to broadcast on frequencies on which they might be listening.[10] Regardless of these attempts, some four hundred bombers reached France and dropped their bombs. Through a combination of human error and bad weather, some of these bombs fell behind Allied lines, killing twenty-five soldiers and wounding 131. It transpired that the planes had flown perpendicular to the lines they were given rather than parallel, as Bradley had initially insisted.

There was plenty of blame to go around. Martin Blumenson, very critical of Bradley, claimed that the general was fully aware of the risks and the potential casualties of his troops. Yet he also noted three different causes for this drastic operation, including (1) None of the ground commanders or staff officers involved in this operation read the air forces' orders for the strike; (2) Many of the men on the ground were vulnerable because only a few of them had dug foxholes for protection; and (3) "Some of the problem lay in the Army-Air Force relationship" and their long-standing suspicions of each other.

This mistake cost the lives of U.S. soldiers, and Bradley was infuriated. Not only that, but this misfiring could have tipped the Germans off to their future plans of attack. It was an all-out disaster. When Bradley investigated how a mistake this major could occur, he claimed that he was fibbed to by members of the air forces, who told him that they had never agreed to fly parallel to the road in the first place.

Blumenson suggests that this might not have been the case and makes an incriminating speculation about Bradley: "Were Bradley on the one hand and the air forces on the other building a case to absolve themselves of responsibility for the short bombs?"[11] Still, it seems in the end that the truth was that this was a risky operation and everyone knew it, yet it was one that Bradley deemed worth the risk. The air forces then refused to launch a second attack unless it was perpendicular to the road. Fearing that the Germans would soon catch on to

14. Cherbourg and Alcohol in the Army

his plans if they hadn't already (and they hadn't), Bradley reluctantly agreed to this new course of action and reset the jump-off for the next day, July 25.

On that day, the weather cleared and the planes arrived on schedule. Fifteen hundred heavy bombers, 380 medium bombers, and 550 fighter-bombers flew perpendicular to the target, dropping some four thousand tons of bombs and napalm. Unfortunately, again to the terror of everyone involved, the bombs hit Allied forces, resulting in another eleven casualties and 490 wounded. The commander of Company B, 8th Infantry was an eyewitness to this incident, which he described in detail:

> The dive bombers came in beautifully, dropped their bombs right in front of us just where they belonged. Then the first group of heavies dropped theirs in the draw several hundred yards in front of us.... But then the next wave came in closer, the next one closer, still closer. The dust cloud was drifting back toward us. Then they came right on top of us. At least three plane loads fell in the next 10 or 15 minutes right on the first and second platoons. We put on all the orange smoke we had but I don't think it did any good; they could not have seen it through the dust.... The shock was awful. A lot of men were sitting around after the bombing in a complete daze.... I called battalion and told them I was in no condition to move, that everything was completely disorganized and it would take me some time to get my men back together, and asked for a delay. But battalion said no, push off. Jump off immediately.[12]

To make matters even worse, the Allies were met with heavy resistance from the Germans. However, the bombings were generally effective in severing Nazi communications, and they killed thousands of enemies and destroyed three battalions of Panzer Lehrs.[13] Despite this setback, General George Patton wrote to Eisenhower about this operation on July 28, 1944: "Bradley certainly has done a wonderful job. My only kick is that he will win the war before I get in. However, nothing can be done about that."[14] At the end of the day, the Allies had broken through and the Germans retreated. Cobra went down in history as the "Saint-Lô breakout." The war was still far from over and Hitler still had the opportunity to turn the tide. The Allies and Germans were soon about to meet head-on in a conflict known as the Battle of the Bulge.

15

Bulging Out

Bradley's jeep engine hummed as he drove along the countryside. As his eyes were fixed on the road ahead, he noticed a man darting across the road and running into the hedges on the other side. Though the man did not have any noticeable weapons, Bradley believed it was a German soldier trying to flee across the lines. As he reached down to pull his firearm, he realized that he had left it at his headquarters. For a moment, Bradley considered chasing after the man on foot and trying to tackle him, but logic soon took over. This was the only day throughout the entire war that Bradley had ventured out without his pistol. When he arrived back at headquarters, he realized that this may have been a blessing in disguise. After all, if he did have his gun on him, he would have jumped out of his vehicle, chased after the soldier, and perhaps have gotten himself shot and killed. For many years, Bradley didn't tell a soul about this story because he was embarrassed about leaving base without his firearm. However, it reveals yet another possible near-death story in the general's life—and it certainly wouldn't be his last.[1]

* * * * *

After the assassination attempt, Hitler became wary and began taking direct control over the Western front. Against all of the advice of his military advisers, he refused to allow the troops to withdraw to the Seine River, which was a logical move given that it would provide a natural defense barrier. Bradley referred to Hitler as his "very fine friend on the German side" because he was always interfering with the decisions of his own generals.[2] Hitler made the decision to fight the showdown battle for Germany in Normandy rather than take the home-field advantage, a choice that would prove to be one of the greatest

15. Bulging Out

blunders of World War II. Bradley devised a plan to encircle the entire German army in Normandy, which would prevent a retreat to the Seine if the Germans ever did decide to withdraw. This next move could potentially end the war.

By this stage of the war, it was believed that high-ranking German commander Gerd von Rundstedt was leading the Nazi Western front. This was unfortunate for the Allies since von Rundstedt was a methodical leader as opposed to the erratic and unstable Hitler. Von Rundstedt also had at his disposal a strong Panzer reserve—the 6th Army. The obvious move would be for the Germans to launch a counter-attack once the Allies had crossed the Roer River. The British believed that von Rundstedt was the one calling the shots and maintained that all future engagements would be calculated with textbook precision. Though "Ultra" allowed the Allies to crack the German codes, they were now headed into Germany, where there would be less radio communication since the Germans utilized secure and uninterceptable landlines. The playing fields were now leveled, and the Allies had to depend on good old-fashioned military strategy.

The Allies made a grave mistake in assuming that Hitler was not leading the German forces. The truth was that he was still fully in charge and that von Rundstedt was merely a front man chosen intentionally to mislead them. Behind the scenes, Hitler was the one pulling the strings, and he was preparing a vicious and "desperate strategic counter-offensive of massive proportions."[3] Four armies made up of forty divisions would *blitzkrieg* through the Ardennes, led by seven armored divisions. The goal behind Hitler's strategy was to split the Allied forces in two, seize their supply depots, and close off Antwerp, encircling and destroying their forces. Hitler had identified the weakest link in the Allied front, Ardennes—an eighty-five-mile stretch between General Hodges and Patton. This attack would go down in history as the Battle of the Bulge, the battle fought in the Ardennes region of Wallonia in Belgium, France, and Luxembourg on the Western front.

This particular section of the line was guarded by Troy Middleton and his VIII Corps. Bradley and Eisenhower decided to visit Middleton and tour this front line. They inspected several of his divisions, and both determined that four divisions could adequately hold this position. This was a risky decision to be sure, but it was not uncalculated, for at this stage an attack was only a remote possibility. These plans were based on a limited German attack of four to six divisions, and Bradley later wrote that he believed this plan could even contain "the full weight of the 6th Panzer Army."[4]

On December 16, 1944, Bradley visited the Supreme Headquarters, Allied Expeditionary Force (SHAEF), in Versailles. He left early, traveling the icy roads, and stopped for lunch at the Ritz Hotel in Paris. When he arrived at Eisenhower's headquarters, the commander was in an elated mood—he had just been promoted to the rank of five-star general. Later that day, Eisenhower promised that he would recommend Bradley to be promoted to the four-star rank of full general, which would place him one star above Patton and Hodges. Bradley was both "flattered and pleased" at this positive news.

Later that afternoon, Bradley received reports that earlier that morning the Germans had launched their counter-attacks at five separate points along the 1st Army front. Bradley and Eisenhower were astonished at the magnitude of this offensive attack. This was not the "spoiling attack" that they had expected; rather, this was an all-out offensive move. It wasn't until dawn of December 17, following the interception of von Rundstedt's attack order, that the Allies realized how fanatical their enemy had become. This order revealed an unusual combination of nationalism and religious terminology, reading: "The hour of destiny has struck. Mighty offensive armies face the Allies. Everything is at stake. More than mortal deeds are required as a holy duty to the Fatherland."[5]

On December 16, Bradley went to bed at midnight but could not fall asleep. He spent the night thinking about this offensive attack—they had not been prepared for a counter-attack of this caliber. The Allies had to regroup and reorganize their strategy. They still held the possibility of destroying the German army west of the Rhine, but they needed to head the Germans off west of the Roer River if they hoped to turn this battle around. The next morning, Bradley received even more discouraging news—his men had been hit hard again during the night.

Bradley, Eisenhower, and General Bedell Smith agreed that their first objective would be to hold the north and south shoulder of penetration; the second objective was to block the westward rush; and the third was to defend the Meuse River.[6] This setback placed Bradley's "Eagle Tac" Luxembourg headquarters in certain jeopardy. Eisenhower tried to convince Bradley to relocate his headquarters to Eagle Main at Verdun (France), but he refused to comply. Bradley revealed his resolve and determination, declaring, "I will never move backwards with a headquarters. There's too much prestige at stake."[7] He believed his retreat would be viewed as a sign of weakness both by the Germans and his own troops. He would not let that happen.

The German attack was powerful, incorporating the 6th and 5th Panzer armies along with the 7th Army. It also included 25 to 30 divisions, along with some aircraft and V-1 missiles. The following day on December 18, Patton paid Bradley a visit. Patton had previously set up his 3rd Army headquarters in Luxembourg and moved into Bradley's hotel. During the Battle of the Bulge, these two patriots worked together closely, seeing each other daily, dining, and planning together, working in harmony to win the war. On December 19, Eisenhower held an emergency meeting at Bradley's headquarters in Verdun. They met in a stone barracks heated by a potbelly stove. By this time, the German "bulge" in the line was growing in size and depth. There were two choices: (1) a withdrawal to the Meuse River or (2) Bradley's plan—a quick attack in the southern flank led by Patton.

Patton believed he could orchestrate this attack by December 22, and Eisenhower approved it, though he believed a more realistic time frame would be by December 23 or 24. On December 23, the weather cleared and the sun peeked out for three days. Fighters and bombers flew in to support Patton's forces, and transports dropped supplies in Bastogne. The next day was Christmas Eve, and a violent German counter-attack pushed back. Meanwhile, that same afternoon, Bradley and Patton attended the Christmas Eve services at an Episcopal church in Luxembourg. Bradley prayed for the souls of all the American GIs whose courage in battle had already doomed the German army. To him, it was not a matter of "if" but "when."

The Beginning of the End

The Battle of the Bulge was not solely a military battle, as there was also a battle of personalities taking place behind the scenes. One such battle was waged between Bradley and British General Bernard "Monty" Montgomery. In war, timing is everything, and the two disagreed on the best times to strike, among other things. Bradley wanted to exploit Hitler's "blunder" of the Bulge and proposed that the Allies concentrate their efforts on the center. Pursuit without pause would place great pressure on the German forces, denying them the opportunity to build up a defensive line against the Allies. The decision rested on Eisenhower's shoulders, and he decided on December 28 to consult with Monty. Monty explained that Bradley's offensive was a waste of resources and insisted it be canceled; he believed that all fronts other than his own should go on the defensive so that he could lead an assault into the heart of Germany. This request was not surprising, as Monty had been proposing for months that the entire U.S. Army should be placed under his command.

On January 5, an unauthorized leak of a SHAEF announcement noted that the command of Bradley's two armies had passed to Monty because the communications with his armies had been cut.[8] This was not entirely true, but two of Omar's armies were temporarily reassigned to Monty. There seems to have been two reasons for Eisenhower's decision to reassign these troops: (1) Arguments poured in from the British that there was no contact between the 12th Army Group and the 1st and 9th armies, and (2) Eisenhower believed that the situation was far worse than it actually was at this time.[9] Regardless what the actual reasons were behind this situation, it was still a shock to the general. Bradley was not an irrational person, and he could see the logic in a temporary arrangement, but this would forever strain his relationship with Monty. Furthermore, this was a clear sign of Eisenhower's lack of confidence in him, which was probably the most hurtful part of this whole ordeal. Also, in the leaked SHAEF message, the word "temporary" was left out along with the fact that the 1st Army would revert back to Bradley's control in the immediate future.

Additionally, at this time there was a media battle waged between Britain and the U.S. over much the same issue. One BBC broadcast expressed a pro–British tone, claiming that Monty's British forces "saved the day" and thereby bailed out the U.S. troops, a misleading statement that outraged Bradley and his men. This was one of the few times Bradley allowed his men to see his anger.[10] In response to these remarks, Bradley held his own press conference on January 9 and explained why his actions at Ardennes were a carefully calculated risk. Bradley did not sink to Montgomery's level and instead gave him credit for the "notable contribution" he had made to the battle. Eventually, Churchill interjected himself into this media frenzy and used his influence to begin smoothing things overs. This indirect feud between Bradley and Montgomery began to cool down as the two armies came together. On January 16, the forces met at Houffalize, effectively cutting the Germans at the waist. The Allies were now closing in on the Nazi troops.

Monty's Revenge

Montgomery had devised two defensive strategies—"Veritable" and "Grenade," which were designed to clear out all of the Germans west of the Rhine River and set up a thrust into the heart of Germany. On February 5, Eisenhower arranged a meeting with Montgomery at Bradley's headquarters. Montgomery was commanding many different U.S. divisions, and his megalomaniac attitude deeply concerned Eisenhower. When Montgomery arrived at Bradley's headquarters, he was coldly received. Bradley reluctantly ate lunch with him, but he soon dismissed himself to go on a tour of the fronts with Eisenhower. In his memoir, Bradley called Montgomery an "arrogant egomaniac" who had publicly demeaned him and attempted to destroy his usefulness as a commander.

Eisenhower and Bradley drove to Bastogne to confer with Patton. Patton had plans to move toward the Rhine River, but Bradley and Eisenhower insisted he keep a low public profile during Veritable and Grenade. Veritable began on February 8, and its purpose was to seize the Roer dams so the Germans could not flood the river and impede an Allied crossing. The second part of this operation was for the 1st Canadian Army, with 400,000 men, to attack from the southeast and work its way in. It started off slowly, and as a result the Allied troops failed to take the Roer dams. This gave the Germans adequate time to demolish the floodgates and cause a worst-case situation. This flooding meant that the 9th Army could not swing across the Roer River for at least two more weeks.

Grenade, which was set to begin on February 10, consisted of linking the 9th Army of 303,000 men with the 1st Canadian Army. Additionally, VII Corps, with four divisions totaling 100,000 men, would simultaneously jump off, with the 9th Army covering the right flank. On February 23, after a two-week delay, the troops crossed the Roer. The Canadian Army drew the Germans on them as the 9th Army, supported by VII Corps, attacked. Over a two-week period, the 9th Army drove down roughly 53 miles of the west bank of the Rhine from Düsseldorf to Wesel, managing to capture 30,000 Nazi soldiers. This attack enabled the British and Canadian armies to drive forward another 23 miles and capture another 22,000 troops. The tide of the battle had turned.

The next move, a battle plan that Bradley had labeled "Lumberjack," was intended as a follow-up maneuver to Veritable and Grenade.

Lumberjack was designed to advance Hodges's and Patton's armies to the Rhine River, thereby clearing out the Germans north of the Moselle and west of the Rhine. On February 20, Eisenhower authorized Bradley's plan, which was to commence on March 3. Lumberjack was a great success. Bradley called it "nearly flawless ... the kind of campaign generals dream about but seldom see."[11] All the corps advanced according to plan with great speed, completely uprooting the German forces and causing them to fall back in confusion, leaving a trail of abandoned weapons and equipment in their wake. It was during this time that Eisenhower began pushing for Bradley's promotion to four stars and the rank of a full general. Bradley's name was sent to the Senate for a four-star promotion, and it was approved on March 29, 1945.[12]

The Rhine, the longest river in Germany, provides a natural barrier between France and most of Germany. By this stage, Hodges had already crossed this massive river, and the new plan was to exploit the Remagen beachhead. From March 9 to 16, Bradley and his men concentrated on enlarging the Remagen bridgehead, and the rest of the plan depended on Patton and his men. On March 18, Bradley flew to Reims to meet with Eisenhower. They talked about Bradley's right-hook offensive, a plan now called "Voyage." It was during this time that Bradley told Patton to keep driving and cross the Rhine to link up with Hodges. The following day, Bradley took a brief vacation, which he spent with Eisenhower and Kay Summersby at an incredible $3 million seaside villa. He enjoyed 48 hours of rest and relaxation before returning to his headquarters on March 22. The next morning, while Bradley was eating breakfast, Patton called, informing him that he had made it across the Rhine—he had snuck across the night before. The Allies were now entering the heart of Nazi Germany.

At first, Patton didn't want anyone to know about his covert operation in order to maintain the element of surprise, but that evening he called Bradley and said: "Brad, tell the world we are across. The Germans know it now. We shot down several of their planes today while they were trying to knock out our bridge. I want everyone to know that I beat Monty across."[13] Bradley decided immediately to act on this information, holding a press conference and letting the world know of this incredible U.S. achievement. The main objective of this conference was to steal Montgomery's thunder, as the American army had crossed the river before Monty and his British troops. Bradley stressed the fact that Patton had made it across the river without any artillery preparation.

15. Bulging Out

It was then Montgomery's turn to cross the river, and he did so with the typical pomp and flash that the media had come to expect of him. A final plan to defeat Germany was created with Bradley's input, prompting one military historian to call it the "Bradley Plan," though Bradley in his modesty insisted that he could not be credited as the sole author. This plan consisted of two main elements. The first was working with the Russians. In six weeks, they had swept to the Oder River and to Neisse in the south. It was inevitable that the Allied forces would meet with them head-on in the immediate future. The second part of the plan centered on Hitler's potential escape. As the war came to an end, it was believed that Hitler and his high-ranking officials would retreat to a "redoubt" in the Australian Alps. It was rumored that this Berchtesgaden would serve as his final command post. This meant that Hitler and other Nazi leaders might escape the justice of the Allied forces, "bringing the war to a murky end with no formal surrender."[14]

It became imperative to drive through to the center of Germany and link up with the Russians in order to cut off any chance of escape. This new focus mandated a shift in priorities, meaning that Berlin could no longer be a main concern for the Allied forces. Bradley met with Eisenhower, and these two leaders determined that the final plan must contain the following two elements: (1) Completely encircle and destroy the German forces in Ruhr and (2) Drive through the center of Germany toward the Leipzig-Dresden area, meeting the Russians at the Elbe River. The British were wary of this and did not want to leave Berlin for the Russians to take over, but for the sake of winning the war they went along with it.

A Day to Remember

Bradley's men began speaking about an unimaginable horror in a slave-labor camp at Ohrdruf. Bradley had heard the rumors about the ruthlessness of the elite German SS division, but nothing could prepare him for what he would see there.

*****

As Bradley and the U.S. forces advanced from Kassel to Elbe, they came upon something more despotic than they could ever imagine—concentration camps. They liberated a slave-labor camp near Nordhausen that was run in an underground V-weapons factory. The treatment of these "slaves" disgusted the Allied soldiers. Bradley kept pushing until he and his troops reached the Elbe. On April 11, Eisenhower flew to Bradley's headquarters at Wiesbaden. The next day (April 12), Eisenhower and Bradley flew to Patton's headquarters at Herzfeld to discuss a new mission. He also visited Ohrdruf concentration camp that day. As he entered this "camp," the smell of death overwhelmed him even before he had passed through the stockade. As he looked around, he saw thousands of naked, emaciated bodies that had been flung into shallow graves on both sides. Others lay in the streets right where they had fallen. Lice crawled over the yellow skin of their sharp, bony frames. A guard showed him how the blood had congealed in coarse black scabs where the starving prisoners had torn out the entrails of the dead for food. Omar was too revolted to speak and wrote in his diary, "For here death had been so fouled by degradation that it both stunned and numbed us."[15] These unspeakable crimes confirmed the insanity of the Nazi ideology and confirmed how far-reaching the Allied victory really was for the future of humanity.

Bradley would never forget that day, for two main reasons. One was his visit to Ohrdruf, and the other was the Allies' discovery of a hidden Nazi treasure deep in a salt mine near Merkers. This treasure consisted of more than $250 million in gold ingots and coins together with various bars of gold, silver plates, $2 million in "greenbacks" (with lesser quantities of British money), and art treasure that had been looted from museums and homes in Nazi-occupied territories.[16]

On April 16, the Russians began their assault on Berlin. Their two armies converged on the city, isolating and encircling it. The Russians made their way to the center with their artillery, reducing the Third Reich to a pile of rubble. By this time, most of the high-ranking Nazi officials had fled the city. Hitler himself had made plans to escape on April 20, his fifty-sixth birthday, but at this juncture no Nazi general would take his orders seriously. He had become maniacal in those final days of the war and decided that as a soldier he should obey his own commands and defend Berlin to his death. On April 30, as Russian troops closed in on his bunker, Hitler and his wife, Eva Braun, committed suicide. Braun swallowed poison, while Hitler shot himself in the head using a Walther pistol. The war in Europe was finally over. The Third Reich had been decimated.

This was a tremendous victory for America, but it came at a high cost. Bradley recorded that a total of 586,628 U.S. troops had fallen,

15. Bulging Out

Luxembourg Eagle Tac Off Dance: Gen. Bradley dancing with Mary Lee Pitcairn, Red Cross, taken on November 2, 1944 (Joseph Fansler Petit Collection, West Point Academy).

and out of that number 135,576 would never rise again. He noted, "The grim figures haunted me. I could hear the cries of the wounded, smell the stench of death. I could not sleep; I closed my eyes and thanked God for the victory."[17]

Omar and Marlene Dietrich: Friends or Lovers?

Throughout the war, especially through the USO, Omar met several actors and actresses, including Marlene Dietrich and Dinah Shore.[18]

Shore came over to entertain the troops late in the summer of 1944 after they had passed through Paris. She saw Mary's and Elizabeth's picture on Bradley's field desk and began telling him about her own new husband, Robert Montgomery (or so the story goes). Rumors have recently surfaced about the connection between Bradley and Dietrich. Marlene was a beautiful and captivating leading lady, a German-born American actress and singer.

Dietrich had been naturalized in 1939 and assisted in war bond drives following Pearl Harbor. She was also vehemently opposed to Hitler and the Nazi movement. As further evidence of her widespread popularity and fame, in 1999 she was voted by the American Film Institute as the "ninth-greatest female star of all time." Her movies, such as *Shanghai Express* and *Desire*, were legendary, and she was one of Hollywood's most elite stars.

Bradley first went to Dietrich's show on November 19. His aide, Hansen, described that particular show as just "moderately entertaining" due to the "exceedingly unhappy" supporting staff. Following the show, they had champagne in the royal box with the Bridgemeister and his wife along with Dietrich and another lady from the show. Dietrich

Omar N. Bradley with members of the Women's Army Corps aboard the USAT *Edmund Alexander*, August 15–16, 1947 (courtesy Carlisle Military Museum, USAHEC).

Lt. Gen. Bradley, Twelfth Army Group, with movie actress (and likely lover) Marlene Dietrich, who was touring to entertain troops on November 21, 1944 (Joseph Fansler Petit Collection, West Point Academy).

spoke lavishly about the 5th Army, whom they had entertained before their dreary trip across Iceland and Greenland.

Dietrich had her own "short snorter"—a (typically) dollar bill set aside to gather up signatures and autographs of the people she came across. She unrolled her "snorter," which Hansen described as a magnificent specimen, crammed with signatures. He also recorded that Dietrich looked "well in her heavy gown—she hadn't shown her legs in the show and she sang badly—yet she was far more personable in the salon afterwards where she really appeared quite vivacious."

On November 21, Bradley went to a cocktail party with Dietrich and they had a private dinner afterward with his aide. Hansen wrote that Marlene "had a gay time and the General enjoyed having her there. 'A lady in the mess makes a whale of a difference once in a while, doesn't it,' [Omar] said and laughed. When the photographer came around, Brad told [Hansen], 'Well, for once you don't have to ask me to edge a little closer,' and he moved in with a chuckle. Dietrich came afterwards for dinner—a good one with filet mignon and ... the works." Hansen also reported that on that day, "The old man was in a jolly mood."

On the morning of May 7, 1945, Marlene Dietrich left with the air crew for Belsen, Germany, where she hoped to locate her sister who was reportedly being held under suspicion at a concentration camp. She did eventually locate her and returned to camp later that afternoon unnerved by what she had seen. She also wondered about the fate of her mother, from whom she had not heard anything in the previous six to eight years. Dietrich continued to entertain the troops while also working with the American Red Cross in the 3rd Army. Hansen remarked about Dietrich's disposition that "occasionally she is quite temperamental and infuriates us to the extent where we might delight in kicking in her teeth in but these periods are short lived and result largely from an impetuous dramatization of her part."

On May 12, 1945, later in the evening, Dietrich landed at Erlanger for a party. She didn't arrive until after the reception had started and then immediately upbraided Hansen for the "old dirty plane" they had sent to pick her up. Hansen recorded: "I hurried her to a room, thrust a Martini into her hand and asked her to please hurry and dress. She reappeared an hour later, ten minutes late for dinner in a stunning gown that infuriated the other Red Cross girls and charmed the men." At this party, Bradley danced every dance, each with a different lady—as was customary—yet still the question remains: Were they just friends or something more? One of Bradley's more recent biographers, Jim DeFelice, asks the question bluntly: "Did the general and actress have an affair?" He answers emphatically "almost certainly not," justifying this by pointing out that Omar had missed his wife and daughter "terribly."

DeFelice does note that the opportunity existed, but concludes that there is "no evidence that he bedded the actress, and the crisis during the Bulge cut short most socializing. Most important, given everything we know about his personality, an affair seems unlikely."[19] DeFelice's conclusion seems solid enough, but does it hold up to recent evidence? In a recently discovered document written by Omar's second wife, Kitty Buhler, the following personal information is divulged:

> [I] ... will tell you something about the German actress with the sultry lisp and legs [presumably referring to Dietrich], the buxom flaxen-haired Countess from New Jersey ... as I discovered them I added their names to our Christmas mailing list.
>
> Each of them before my time, but in her own time, had contributed to Omar's knowledge and well-being. I owed them a debt. Once, one of Omar's ex-mistresses and I lunched at the Four Seasons in New York. We had Eggplant Parmesan and a marvelous time. I never did understand why Mamie got upset over Ike and Kay Summersby.[20]

Kitty indirectly implied that Omar entertained more than one mistress throughout his lifetime, seemingly including Dietrich. Kitty should certainly know—she was one of them! Omar's romantic relationship with Kitty will be examined later in this work, but there are other important events surrounding the end of the war that deserve discussion first.

16

Partying with the Russians

At the Fürstenhof Hotel in Bad Wildungen, last-minute preparations for an intercultural luncheon were under way. Actor Mickey Rooney and composer Glenn Miller, along with his fifty-man orchestra, had been flown in from Paris for this very occasion. Violinist Jascha Heifetz was also scheduled to appear, but he missed his connecting flight. More than thirty different senior officers gathered together and began preparing batches of martinis for their guests. After all, "they had gotten Vodka hangovers on the Russian grounds and they expected the Russians to return this courtesy."[1] The tables were set with every conceivable delicacy, somewhat braced by K- and C-rations. Heifetz finally arrived and was rushed into uniform. Meanwhile, Rooney directed traffic on the stage, getting Glenn Miller's boys into uniform and into position to perform.

When the Russians arrived, the 12th Army Group was ready for them. The instant Marshal Konev and his troops stepped through the doors, the Glenn Miller Orchestra burst into a rousing, soul-soaring rendering of the Russian National Anthem. The Russians stood frozen until the song was over and broke out into a thunderous ovation.

"Excellent," Konov murmured through his interpreters.

Bradley's shrug was nonchalant and he responded, "Just a few soldiers from the American army."

The toasts got under way and the Russians sampled the martinis—a new experience for them.

Then Jascha Heifetz took the stage, "silencing the celebrants with the enthralling virtuosity of his violin. The last exquisite notes of the violin fade; the thin khaki-clad figure on the stage bowed his head. The room was hushed with awe."[2]

Konev was moved to comment, "Magnificent!"

16. Partying with the Russians

Gen. Bradley in his office at Namur on April 1, 1945. The office was formerly occupied by the Namur Governor (Joseph Fansler Petit Collection, West Point Academy).

The Americans and Russians resumed the business at hand. Each attempted to drink the other under the table, but this time the Americans had the hometown advantage and they were winning.[3] This would be the first of many future celebrations toasting the Allied victory and the defeat of the Nazi regime. However, this truce between the U.S. and the Soviet forces would soon come to an end due to a crisis in Berlin.

* * * * *

In May 1945, the party described above was thrown for the purpose of bringing together some of the officers from both the U.S. and Russian armies; this party was scheduled as a meeting of commands. Before the fall of Berlin, Bradley and his men had been invited to the Russian headquarters, but he was aware of their custom of drinking hard liquor. Thus, in preparation for this meeting, he drank a shot glass of olive oil—an old technique used to inhibit the amount of alcohol the body consumed.[4]

The Germans hadn't even surrendered yet when Bradley first sat down with Soviet military commander Marshal Ivan Stepanovich Konev.

Gen. Bradley toasting with Marshall Konev of the Russian Army during a luncheon held in the latter's honor at Bradley's headquarters on May 7, 1945 (Joseph Fansler Petit Collection, West Point Academy).

The two leaders sat at a table about fifteen feet wide and sixty feet long and dined together. Konev sat at the head and Bradley at the middle with his chief of staff, General Allen, across from him. The line around the massive table alternated from Russian to American as it wrapped around the corners and circled around the ends. The table sported rows of wines and decanters filled with Russian vodka.[5]

There were also all types of unique food items, including huge loaves of black bread, butter, whole roasted pigs, geese, caviar, veal, beef, cucumbers, and clear broth with whole fish floating in it.[6] It was enough food to feed an army—two armies, to be exact. As soon as Bradley and his chief sat down, Konev grabbed a bottle of vodka and began filling up his glass. Konev next proceeded to fill Allen's cup and so on down the line; then he put the vodka down and filled his own glass with white wine. The interpreter translated Konev's remark, explaining: "The Marshal has stomach troubles and he can no longer drink vodka."

16. Partying with the Russians

Konev began by toasting the American army, and Bradley responded in like kind, toasting the Russian army. Then the Russian artillery toasted the U.S. artillery, and the toast was returned. Each of these toasts was followed by sips of vodka; on and on, this custom continued down the table. Bradley came to the realization that if they kept up this frequency, everyone sitting at the table would soon be inebriated. By the time the toasts came to air commander Vandenberg, his toast marked an unspoken transition from sipping to gulping (i.e., bottoms up).

Bradley had sipped the first glass, but decided to switch to the smaller glass in front of him that held about half an ounce. He also began pouring his own drinks, and after his first vodka shot he filled his glass with white wine instead. Thus, he made it through the lunch without any complication—the olive oil had been effective. Meanwhile, the aides were further down the table. There were preliminary toasts and local toasts in honor of staff officers of various branches of service. Bradley made it a point to clarify that neither Russians nor Americans got drunk during this gathering, but that seems difficult to believe given the amount of alcohol each soldier must have consumed.

Following the lunch, the Americans were brought into another room that had a small stage at the front with an orchestra set up. A mixed choir of roughly thirty Russians in uniform began singing the "Star-Spangled Banner" in perfect English.[7] They went on to serenade the soldiers, singing the humorous American song "There Is a Tavern in the Town" followed by "It's a Long Way to Tipperary." Next they performed a Ukrainian *gopak* along with a folk dance in the native Russian style.[8]

The men then left the building and gathered in front of a large audience, where Konev awarded Bradley an honorary red flag. Bradley in turn presented Konev with a brand new jeep that included an American carbine attached to it. Konev responded to this gesture with his own personal gift, presenting Bradley with a war horse—a Don stallion complete with saddle, bridle, and accessories. Bradley was flattered and decided to have the horse flown back to his headquarters.

However, surmising that his busy schedule with the VA would not permit him much time to ride this beautiful animal, he quickly gave up on the idea of bringing it home. It remains doubtful as to whether he would even have been permitted by his superiors to transport this horse back home to the States. Bradley at first wanted to turn him over to the Remount Service as a stallion, but he soon concluded that for the amount of room the horse would take up, he could bring back two veterans who were anxiously waiting their return home.⁹ Yet again, Bradley put the needs of his men over his own desires. He finally decided to leave the horse in Europe, contenting himself with receiving occasional reports on its well-being.

Ten days later it was the Americans' turn to reciprocate and host the Russians at their headquarters in Kassel. This raised an immediate problem—how on earth would they get enough vodka for an entire Russian army? It then occurred to the general, "Why give them vodka?" Vodka is a Russian drink and they were coming to an American base for a cross-cultural experience. After some discussion with his men, Bradley determined that he would serve them martinis instead. Five parts gin and one part vermouth created a strong enough drink suitable for the Russian Army, or so Bradley thought.

The next day, Bradley sent his plane to Leipzig to meet Konev's party and fly them the rest of the way.¹⁰ When nearly forty Russians

The horse that was gifted to Gen. Bradley from Marshall Konev following a luncheon (Joseph Fansler Petit Collection, West Point Academy).

arrived, Bradley offered Konev a martini, which he ladled from a huge brass pot into a soldier's cup. Konev drank about half of it and immediately his face changed—"too strong," he claimed in broken English. This reaction prompted Chet, Bradley's aide, to get into a drinking bout with Konev's aide; even Bradley's German translator decided to enter into a drinking contest with Konev's guard. That day, the Americans stood up well against the Russian forces.

The Americans even taught the Russians their own cultural dance—the jitterbug. In preparation for this event, the U.S. Army held an unofficial jitterbug contest with a group from the Women's Army Corps and nurses; the top five were picked to perform in front of the Russian army. Bradley recounted that the Russians seemed to enjoy this most because it reminded them of their own energetic dances, although it seems more likely that they enjoyed the women performing it. Regardless of the reason, this performance received the loudest applause.[11] The luncheon ended promptly at 3:00 p.m. Though the two leaders could only speak to each other through an interpreter, Konev later wrote down his personal reflections on this experience and on Bradley's suitability as a general. He called Bradley:

> A professional soldier, he was strong, calm, and reserved.... He understood the nature of modern warfare well and accurately differentiated the primary from the secondary. I felt he also had a profound understanding of artillery matters and appraised our tanks, their armament, armor, engines, etc. with a knowledgeable eye. In sum, I both felt and could see that the man beside me was well oriented in the use of all arms of the service, and this, in my opinion, is the primary mark of a highly qualified commander. I had the impression that here was a military man in the full sense of the word, an army leader worthy of representing American troops in Europe.[12]

Thus, the war ended on a positive note for Bradley and his men. Despite the many lives that were lost in this horrific conflict, it was finally at an end. The world was safe again thanks to the bravery and valor of the Allied soldiers.

Home Again

Bradley was scheduled to return to the States on June 2 in order to participate in a multitude of victory parades. This would be a temporary leave, as he needed to return to Europe for several weeks so he

Above and opposite: Gen. Bradley autographing a "short snorter" for Pct. Madge B. Conyers at a dinner party on April 1, 1945 (Joseph Fansler Petit Collection, West Point Academy).

could relieve Eisenhower. Following his return home, Omar took a month's leave to spend some much needed time with his wife Mary and to report to his new position at the VA. Bradley desperately wanted to transfer to the South Pacific and assist General Douglas MacArthur (1880–1964) in fighting the Japanese; however, Marshall suggested he

16. Partying with the Russians

take this position. As Bradley well knew, any suggestion from Marshall was an order in disguise, and he obeyed it.[13]

On June 2 and 3, Omar flew into New York from Paris with layovers in the Azores and Bermuda. Mary had come from Washington to meet him and was waiting anxiously at the airport. They had not seen each other in twenty-one long months, and they went directly to the Waldorf Astoria Hotel downtown. Given this long absence and Bradley's large role in the war, they had a lot to talk about, including his new top-secret appointment to the VA. Within an hour, they had to leave the Waldorf and return to West Point for the thirtieth reunion of the Class of 1915. During this time, they stayed with their daughter's in-laws, the Beukemas.

On June 4, Omar and Mary flew to Philadelphia to participate in a victory parade. Afterward, they returned to West Point to attend the graduation ceremonies on June 5. Bradley was asked to be the keynote speaker and presented diplomas to 852 graduates. The next day on June 6, for the one-year anniversary of D-Day, they traveled to New York to conduct a radio interview with Mary's friend, the same former sorority sister who had attended Elizabeth's wedding—Mary McBride.

116   II. WAR

After that, the Bradleys took some much deserved R&R, taking in an Olsen and Johnson show and going to see Hildegarde at the Plaza.

The following day, Bradley flew to Washington to meet with Marshall and President Truman about his new job. He learned that the VA was under serious attack. He was assured that this would be no longer than a two-year appointment and that it would greatly enhance his career. Bradley was even allowed to retain his four-star rank along with the commensurate pay, as well as keep his place on the army's seniority list.

On June 9, he and Mary flew to Missouri for a statewide celebratory tour. His first stop was his hometown of Moberly, where he hadn't visited for twelve years. Hal Beukema flew from his post in Roswell, New Mexico, to join in the celebration and was even authorized (by Marshall) to bring his wife, Elizabeth, with him.[14] Hal and Elizabeth had just celebrated their first wedding anniversary three days before, and it was Bradley's first opportunity to really get to know Hal as his

A picture taken of Lt. Gen. Bradley autographing programs for a few congressmen who visited his headquarters. Senator Cliff Davis (1897–1970), an outspoken member of the Ku Klux Klan, looks into the camera (Joseph Fansler Petit Collection, West Point Academy).

16. Partying with the Russians

son-in-law. Omar wrote that he was "very much impressed—even if he had chosen the Air Corps over the infantry."[15]

Moberly went to great lengths to welcome Bradley as they landed at what would one day be named the Omar N. Bradley Airport (1964). It was declared "General Bradley Day," and all of his extended family and distant relatives showed up for this momentous occasion, welcoming him home like a long-lost son. Even the governor of Missouri, Phil M. Donnelly, made an appearance at Moberly with other dignitaries, putting on a parade and giving extended speeches at Tannehill Park. In his own brief speech, Bradley described the terrors of war and bluntly communicated that he hoped never to see them again. He heartily endorsed the new United Nations as a feasible method of preventing future wars.

In the evening, Moberly High School Class of 1910 held a reunion in Bradley's honor, and a fried chicken dinner was served at the Masonic Temple, to which all the Bradleys and their relatives were invited. This reunion revealed that all of the members of the Class of 1910 were still alive and well; they attributed this to a "hearty Missouri stock."[16] The next day Omar, Hal, Mary, and Elizabeth attended services

General Omar N. Bradley, CG, 12th Army Gp., shown speaking over BBC, giving his V-Day message to the people of the world on May 5, 1945 (Joseph Fansler Petit Collection, West Point Academy).

at the Central Christian Church, where both he and Mary had been baptized many years earlier. That Sunday proved to be a quiet and reflective day for the Bradleys as they went to visit the Oakland and Log Chapel cemeteries, paying their respects at the graves of their departed loved ones.

They continued on to St. Louis and attended another victory parade on June 11. The city even declared a school holiday in Bradley's honor. On June 12, they returned to Washington, where Bradley visited President Truman and other key political leaders to prepare for his new position in the VA. Bradley met with Marshall and received some great news—he had been designated a house on "General's Row" in Fort Myer, Virginia. It was an old brick house on a bluff overlooking the majestic Potomac River. This was not just a luxury for the obvious financial reasons; it was also a symbol of prestige, as these houses were coveted by every high-ranking Washington-based army officer. Off-base housing was very expensive and difficult to find, but official housing was both free and staffed with orderlies and servants. Fort Myer also had a commissary, laundry, movie theater, and other amenities, making it an ideal home for the Bradleys. Several of Bradley's close friends lived in this same post, and he knew that from this point on in his career their private life would be comfortable. America was now at peace and he could finally relax. Or could he?

III. Postwar

17

Omar the Entertainer

During his postwar Washington life, Omar acquired the habit of throwing parties and other social gatherings. On October 25, 1950, he opened up his home for an official U.S. Army soirée with a guest list of some eight hundred attendees. This party had been preceded by an elaborate amount of staff work. To preclude the possibility of any of the foreign guests getting lost on the grounds, military police personally routed each car entering Fort Myer. Receiving guests at the general's side that evening was his small-framed wife Mary, a merry woman with ginger hair. In the front of the house, guests were assisted out of their cars, which were then parked by army personnel. Cars for departing guests were called for using a radiotelephone. This system was so efficient that one lieutenant colonel and his wife who were trying to reach their own quarters were firmly waved from their vehicle, guided up the front steps, and introduced to the Bradleys. This couple was given a drink and a plate of Smithfield ham and turkey by one of Bradley's aides before they could explain that they hadn't been invited—they were embarrassed and hoped the general wouldn't remember who they were.

Guests at these parties included a wide range of leaders, including Fleet Admiral Lord Fraser of North Cape and Field Marshal Sir William Slim from Britain as well as Lieutenant General Efisio Marras, the army chief of staff of Italy. This list also included all of the ambassadors of the twelve Atlantic Pact countries and top-ranking army, navy, marine, and air force officers and their wives. A long buffet table held hams, turkeys, shrimp, hundreds of hors d'oeuvres, and sandwiches, made to order by the Bradleys' white-capped chef.[1] Following the war, Bradley began to entertain more, and this new social life seemingly contributed to his likeability as he started his new position as the VA director. Or would it?

* * * * *

Omar and the VA

On August 6, the United States dropped an atomic bomb on Hiroshima and on August 9 dropped another one on Nagasaki. August 14 was officially "Victory over Japan Day" (V-J Day), as the Japanese formally surrendered and entered into peace negotiations. The following day, Bradley was sworn into his new position as the VA administrator. Mary, President Truman, and several senators and generals were at this brief ceremony. Bradley later told the press: "I don't think there's any job in the country I'd sooner not have nor any job in the world I'd like to do better. For even though it is burdened with problems, it gives me the chance to do something for the men who did so much for us."[2]

There were many issues that he had to tackle, such as the GI Bill educational program, which covered a certain amount of tuition for all veterans, as well as job training, disability pensions, loans, and insurance. From 1945 to 1947, the number of VA employees increased from 65,000 to 200,000, reflecting the influx of veterans returning home from the war. This growth presented some unique problems for Bradley and the VA, which often translated into a seven-day work week for the general. Through his resolve, passion, and perseverance, he unwittingly antagonized some powerful leaders on the Hill, and for a while Bradley thought the VA job would become the ruin of his professional career and force him into an early retirement.[3]

During this time, Bradley also developed a fondness for President Truman, meeting him several times and believing him to be an impressive leader. Truman was well versed in U.S. history and attempted to learn from past mistakes; he was also not afraid to take charge. He had a sign on his desk that would soon become a national catchphrase: "The buck stops here." This evidenced Truman's integrity, a trait that Bradley highly regarded. It seems likely that these two men got along so well because they held similar interests, morals, and personalities.

Even though Truman was ten years older than Bradley, they came from similar backgrounds. Truman's ancestors (like Bradley's) had migrated from Kentucky to Missouri, and he had grown up in a small town not very far away from Higbee and Moberly. Truman had also served as a captain in World War I and experienced front-line action in France. Together, they also shared respect for General Marshall. Though Bradley had never registered to vote and identified himself neither as a Republican nor a Democrat, he took a liking to Truman and his Democratic policies, especially his concern for the "little man."[4]

Throughout his work in proposing new and radical policies, Bradley discovered a new ally—the national media. His job had elicited interest from many different press corps and writers for national magazines, who more often than not supported his changes and decisions. Flattering stories about the general appeared in *The Saturday Evening Post, Look, Parade,* Ingersoll's *PM,* and elsewhere. Even *Time* magazine, which placed Bradley on its cover three times, supported the general.

Bradley was passionate about rehabilitating wounded and disabled veterans instead of just warehousing them. This largely referred to physical issues, as post-traumatic stress disorder was not officially recognized by the American Psychiatric Association until 1980. Bradley knew that without encouragement and opportunity, most of these injured men could become inured to institutionalization. His emphasis on rehabilitation within the VA encouraged corporations and private companies to hire disabled veterans.

The Bulova School

One of the most successful of these programs was the Joseph Bulova School of Watchmaking, which was founded in 1944 by Arde Bulova, who would become chairman of the Bulova Watch Company of New York. This Bulova School was tuition-free and designed for veterans who had suffered at least a 70 percent disability. It provided paraplegics, people with polio, and leg amputees with a new skill, as many could not return to their previous professions following the war.

The school was founded by Arde Bulova immediately following World War II and was established specifically for paraplegic veterans, though it later opened its doors to handicapped civilians as well. It offered a rehabilitation environment complete with sports and medical facilities. One study proved that Bulova graduates fared as well or better than other non-handicapped men employed as technicians or watch repairmen and even typically earned over 15 percent more than the national average.[5] It also provided job placement within the Bulova Watch Company. Because of the success of this program, Bradley frequently highlighted it as a prime example of government and industry working hand-in-hand together to effectively rehabilitate returning veterans. He visited the school often and handed out the diplomas to the twenty members of the first graduating class in 1946, and he became close friends with Arde Bulova and the vice president, Harry

D. Henshel. This close association led Bradley to join the Bulova Watch Company following his retirement from public life in 1953.

Two of the biggest battles that Bradley fought during his time with the VA were (1) his resolution in finding qualified doctors to come into VA service (he pushed Congress to pass a law taking doctors out of civil service), and (2) he strove to get new VA hospitals built near major medical schools. Bradley had made some constructive changes in the VA, but he was destined for other things. He would soon succeed Eisenhower in his position as the chief of staff of the U.S. Army.

Passing the Torch

Following the war, Eisenhower and his wife, Mamie, moved into their quarters at Fort Myer. The Bradleys lived right across the street from them. For the first time in their careers, these two leading generals were neighbors, though they saw little of each other. The reason for this was probably because Mary and Mamie didn't get along very well and the men were busy in their own respective jobs. Rarely would their paths cross. Bradley recounted that from time to time he and Eisenhower would work on their golf drives around the parade flagpole, but that seemed to be the extent of their relationship.

During this time, the Eisenhowers lived at house No. 1, which the Bradleys would later occupy when Omar transitioned into the new chief of staff position. This house was a big red mansion located on the Army Post; it stood on a tree-shaded street with a wide, wooden veranda. Bradley paid only a hundred and fifty dollars per month for it—the maximum sum allowed for quarters to a general. This house had a historical lineage of its own. The Eisenhowers had resided there for three years before the Bradleys, and before them General and Mrs. Marshall had lived there for a record tenure of six years. The MacArthurs had also lived there from 1930 to 1935. When Omar was promoted to chairman, the Bradleys moved into No. 1. It had a large living room, furnished mainly with pieces out of the quartermaster's stores, and resembled a Washington hotel suite.[6]

It was during this time that Truman laid out a unification plan for the armed services, while Eisenhower figured out his own personal goals. He managed to avoid being roped into the 1948 presidential race and accepted a position as the president of Columbia University. The goal was that he would leave the army around November 1947 and

17. Omar the Entertainer

Bradley would then relieve him as chief of staff—with the blessing of President Truman, of course. Beginning in April 1947, Eisenhower prepped Bradley for this position. On April 17, Eisenhower made Bradley a permanent four-star general. On May 23, he further decorated Bradley with his third Distinguished Service Medal and arranged for him to be recalled to active army duty for a period of six weeks so that he and Mary could make an extended inspection of the U.S. Army forces in Europe. Omar and Mary were very enthusiastic to take this trip for both professional and personal reasons—Hal and Elizabeth had recently given birth to a son, Henry Jr., who was their first grandchild. Hal was stationed in Berlin, so it would give Mary and Omar the opportunity to see their grandson for the first time.

They commenced their trip with a weekend at the socialite Perle Mesta's Newport, Rhode Island, mansion, called Midcliffe. Perle held various gatherings at her Washington home. She was the U.S. ambassador to Luxembourg and famous for her incredible parties. She invited only the elite of high society to these gatherings, which further attested to the celebrity status that Bradley was achieving.

From Newport, the Bradleys traveled to New York, where they met up with some friends. On August 15, they sailed to Germany and reached Bremerhaven on August 26. They spent six days in Berlin learning about the condition of the troops and contemplating the future Russian threat. Over the next several weeks, they traveled throughout Europe, Austria, Italy, Sicily, Switzerland, France, and England. While there, they made plans to visit the British Isles, which included a trip to the Isle of Wight, a place to which Mary had traced some of her distant cousins. On September 25, they flew home via the Azores and Bermuda.

Bradley returned to the VA for another eight weeks while Truman searched for a replacement. Ultimately, Carl R. Gray took Bradley's place as the administrator of the VA, and Truman announced Bradley's new appointment as the army chief of staff on November 21. Though Eisenhower intended to step down at that time, he still had some issues to resolve before a smooth transition could be made. He pushed back the change until February of the next year, which left Bradley with nine weeks of free time.

Bradley took this opportunity to relax with his wife, spending three weeks at Fort Benning, where he golfed and hunted. They then took a round trip by train to Los Angeles with Chet Hansen and his wife, where on January 1, 1948, Bradley was made grand marshal of the

Rose Bowl Parade. He was installed as army chief of staff on February 7, and Truman insisted on being present. They all gathered together in the office with Truman, Ike, Mary, and Army Secretary Kenneth Royall. Mamie Eisenhower, ill with the flu, was not able to attend, but her mother was present. Truman decorated Eisenhower with the Distinguished Service Medal and awarded him a silver cigarette case. Eisenhower then administered the oath of office to Bradley and said, "You have the job." The whole ceremony lasted no more than five minutes.

The Joint Chiefs of Staff consisted of several members: the chairman, who presided but did not have a vote; the chief of staff of the army; the chief of naval operations; and the chief of staff of the air force. The National Security Act defined their role, declaring that they were "the principal military advisers to the President, the National Security Council, and the Secretary of Defense."

When Bradley took up the post of chief of staff, he envisioned retiring after his four-year term in 1951, though it turned out he would be promoted again within eighteen months. When he began his duties, it was indisputable that the Soviet Union had become the next foreign threat to the U.S. Three weeks after Bradley assumed office, Stalin and his political operatives seized control of the Czech government, a takeover that was reminiscent of the Nazi regime. This new Cold War represented a different type of threat to the American people, yet by this time the army had been scaled down to 552,000 men and was rapidly shrinking.

It was at this point that the Soviet authorities in Berlin started to become difficult to deal with. They began restricting U.S. access to Berlin and seemed to be forcing the Allies out of the city altogether. Moscow also shut off most of the electrical power in the city, sealing Allied forces and Berliners in with only a thirty-day supply of food. This procedure was designed to push the Western occupation forces out of the city.

Bradley's daughter, son-in-law, and grandchild were in Berlin during this conflict. He made the decision to remove them from danger, calling in a favor with the air force and requesting that Hal be moved back to the States. The air force brought Hal and his family stateside to the Pentagon. Mary was ecstatic to have her daughter and grandbaby home in Washington, but Hal did not appreciate being pulled off the front lines for a desk job in Washington. This appeared to be one of the drawbacks to marrying a general's daughter, but the obvious benefits far outweighed the detriment.

Bradley maintained that the most difficult period of his postwar years was the eighteen months from March 1948 to October 1949. The Joint Chiefs drew up a "unified" war plan that quickly led to a revolt of the navy and a near revolt of the air force. The negativity and disagreements from these military leaders were so harsh that they even pushed one leader, James Forrestal, to commit suicide (though this death has led to numerous conspiracy theories). The controversial issues that Bradley dealt with ranged from budgetary items, including the navy's purchase of a "supercarrier," to the availability of atom bombs to the establishment of Allied organizations, such as the North Atlantic Treaty Organization (NATO). It seemed that for every decision he made, someone opposed him, but fortunately for his career, he wouldn't be in this position for very long.

Omar's Aide: George H. Waple, III

One of the fringe benefits of being a general was that Bradley amassed a small personal staff that helped him run his house and keep him organized. He always strived to treat each staff member fairly, and whenever one of them had a birthday he would throw a small party, after hours, of course. One such subordinate officer was George H. Waple, III, who was assigned to the Bradleys in August 1948 and whose autobiography sheds some light on the Bradleys' daily routine and relationship.

Waple had fought under Bradley from Omaha Beach to the Elbe River. He was transferred to the office of the Chief of Staff. Waple had the pleasure of joining one of his close friends, Sergeant Henry Pickerel, in this post, and together they alternated days working for the general. During the years 1948 and 1949, Waple helped the Bradleys with their typical routine tasks, such as chauffeuring them to various parties, taking Mary shopping, bartending on occasion, and driving them to the racetrack.

On one occasion, Waple drove and personally accompanied Bradley to the Laurel Park race track in Laurel, Maryland. On this particular occasion, Waple's brother had a horse named Tumble Boy running in the fifth race. Waple's brother assured the general that his horse had a decent shot at winning, and as the odds on the tote board were 10–1, the general decided to take this gamble. Tumble Boy won his race, and Waple returned to the box in excitement, exclaiming, "We won!" The general looked at him and smiled, saying, "Yes, I bet two dollars on him." Waple in this later writing (1998) confirmed what Bradley had written in *A General's Life*, where he admitted having a passion for horse racing even though he rarely won. Waple exclaimed, "I could see why; he only bet two dollars."[7]

Even though Waple and Omar worked well together, there was some friction between Waple and Mary. Waple described Mary's character as being in direct opposition to Omar's, revealing an interesting insight into the conflicts within the Bradleys' marriage. Waple's remarks paint Mary as a very stern, rigid, and frugal woman, yet they also reveal a deeper side to the family dynamics during this time. For example, Omar genuinely enjoyed going to parties and entertaining; however, as noted previously, Mary could not stand them. This led Waple to note that "these parties soon stopped as soon as Mrs. Bradley heard the tingling of glasses and smelled the General's breath upon arriving home."[8] Thus, she is presented as being a "stick-in-the-mud," depriving Omar of his fun and enjoyment.

Waple does not try to hide the fact that he and Mary never got along well with each other. One of the reasons for this might have been that Mary favored his friend, Pickerel, whom she lovingly nicknamed "Picky."[9] Despite this personality conflict, Waple carefully explained the differences between Mary's and Omar's convictions. He recounted that Omar played golf weekly, though he insisted on driving himself in his own car, viewing this leisure time as an unofficial trip. But it seemed his wife had an opposing perspective. Several instances are cited by Waple that reveal an inconsistency between Omar's and Mary's view of "official business."

Firstly, at this time the Bradleys had two grandchildren, Mary and Hank. When Hank stayed with his grandparents, it was Waple's job to drive him to his kindergarten class, which he did often, bringing his own twin sons with him for the ride. During these trips, Hank insisted on sitting in the front passenger seat, and one day he decided to place his feet on the dashboard. Waple discouraged this activity and asked Hank not to do this again. Young Hank was offended and decided he would pass this information on to his grandmother. The following day as Waple picked Hank up, Mary came out and scolded Waple, saying, "If Hanky boy wishes to put his feet on the dash he could do so."[10]

Another time Waple was asked to give Hank swimming lessons. Every morning at 10 a.m., Waple would accompany Hank to the officers' pool. After a few such outings, Waple began to bring his own boys along with them to enjoy the pool for themselves. Again Hank "ratted" on his driver, and Mary stepped in, reminding Waple that his sons were not allowed to swim in the officers' pool.

Waple mentioned one more recurring issue, which he claimed was well known by most other members of Bradley's private staff. It seemed that Mary was known to buy clothes, take them home, and wear them, hiding the tags. The next day, she would take them back to the store and return them for a full refund.[11] This frugality was likely due to her earlier experiences in life, but it was an unbecoming behavior for such a high-ranking officer's wife. Waple told of other times when he wasted an entire day standing around waiting for Mary's call, which never came. This frustrated him, as it wasted army resources as well as his own time.

In one final comment, Waple note that Mary did not keep up her appearances, recounting that "she never dressed up for shopping and wore roll-down stockings that were up to her knees, sometimes falling half way down her leg."[12] If this was true, then it provides a means of understanding Omar's romantic pursuits with other women. While it certainly does not justify the behavior, it does provide insight into possible motivations.

Waple thoroughly enjoyed his time working for Omar and was proud to be a part of his life, even if only for a short while. However, his tense relationship with Mary finally came to a head. At the end of 1951, Omar informed him that one of them had to leave, as Mary was persistent that something be done. Bradley said, "I can't go because I am in charge of the entire military forces, but I'll tell you what [I'm] going to do. I'll promote you to 2nd Lieutenant and send you on your way." Thus Waple was promoted and reassigned.[13]

Waple's testimony might be dismissed as merely the griping of a disgruntled employee. Nevertheless, it gives a unique and personal look into an otherwise very private family dynamic. This gives the reader a glimpse into a seemingly unbalanced and frictional relationship between Omar and Mary.

Staying True to Truman

Bradley had served as the army chief of staff for only eighteen months when he was offered the position of chairman of the Joint Chiefs of Staff. He agreed to serve one term for two years, even though he was reluctant to leave the army. On August 12, Bradley went to the White House, where President Truman announced his nomination as chairman. The Senate approved his nomination, and on August 16 he was officially sworn into office. The reaction to his appointment was largely favorable, as he still had a good reputation in the media.

Bradley's final promotion would come in 1950 during the Korean War, when President Truman promoted him to the five-star rank of General of the Army. Congress had created the grade of General of the Army in 1866 for the Civil War hero Ulysses S. Grant. Since its inception, only eight other officers had been awarded this rank. A bill authorizing his fifth star was introduced in Congress, and it was passed by both houses before reaching Truman's desk on September 18. He signed it as Vice President Alben Barkley, Speaker Sam Rayburn, and General Bradley looked on. Later that day, Truman sent the fountain pen he used to sign the bill to Omar's wife Mary "as a souvenir of such a deserved recognition."[14] In the House of Representatives, Congressman Short asked for a unanimous consent for immediate consideration of the bill to promote General Bradley. "The name of Omar N. Bradley is a household word in America and is widely known all over the world," he remarked. He added:

> I am not going to try to add to his laurels because words fade in the shadow of this man's deeds.... Anyone who had studied the life and read the record of accomplishments of this great Missourian, I think, will agree that when history is written in the future with open eyes and without prejudice the name of Omar Bradley will shine like Mars itself in the heavens in the pages of our military annals.[15]

On September 22, the official ceremony was held and Truman swore in Bradley as General of the Army. Bradley officially became the "last" and youngest of the five-star World War II Generals of the Army, and his salary was raised to $17,000 a year. Bradley had already accomplished a lifetime of achievements, yet his golden years would prove to be every bit as interesting as his earlier life. This exciting next chapter began with his chance meeting of a young, sexy writer named Esther "Kitty" Buhler. The year 1950 was not the beginning of the end for the general; it was merely the end of the beginning.

18

In Love with Kitty

    Omar's relationship with Kitty Buhler reads like a typical bestselling romance novel. A high-ranking, married general meets an intelligent, adventurous reporter through a field interview; they develop a sensual connection that they carefully pursue throughout the course of their lifetimes.

    It all began in Okinawa on February 6, 1950. Kitty had been called in at the last minute by her editor to interview the chairman of the Joint Chiefs. Apparently, the original reporter who had been assigned to this story had become ill. This didn't give Kitty much time to prepare for the meeting, which was scheduled to begin at 10:06 a.m.

    Kitty navigated her gray Jeep, with no hubcaps and a cracked windshield, over the unforgiving terrain along the war-torn roads of Okinawa on her way to the airfield in Naha. She worked as a freelance writer for United Press and such publications as *Yank* and *Tokyo Fanfare*. She also had her own column, "Rycom Kapers by Kit," which was published in the popular military magazine *Stars and Stripes*.[1]

    Kitty used her column to update soldiers and their families on the "goings-on" and social life of the military men serving on these islands. These reports included anecdotes about anything from Rycom's star hitchhiker, "the dog nobody owns," to an amusing story about a student's pocket alarm going off in the middle of a military justice class.[2] This day would prove to be different. Today she was going to meet a very important commanding officer—a general.[3] As she made her way to the base, she had no idea what would be waiting for her, and she never suspected that this interview would set off a chain of events that would forever change her life.

    As she swerved to the left in order to avoid a pothole, she passed one of the many signs on the occupied island. This one read: "Drive carefully. The man you hit might be your own replacement."[4] As she approached the airfield, she made out the sound of an aircraft flying overhead. Off to the right was the rubble of a movie house that had been leveled by Typhoon Gloria, and flapping gently in the light morning breeze was an ironic sign that read: "Now playing *Gone with the Wind*."[5]

The *Gray Goose* and the C-54 descended on the airfield at virtually the same moment. After the reporters exited their vehicles, there was a flurry of activity as the passengers disembarked, but Kitty was able to identify immediately the man she had come to meet. Tall and trim and dressed in uniform, General Omar Nelson Bradley picked his way through the crowd of officers with a slow, steady gait.

Kitty conducted the interview with her typical demeanor, asking the obvious questions that her readers expected of her. However, she was more curious about personal details, such as: Was he six-foot-one or six-foot-two? Was he interested in music? Had he read Chaucer? Did he like hot fudge sundaes? As she finished the interview, she got a funny feeling that destiny would bring them together again and that this "quiet, lanky, cragged-face man" would become an important part of her future.[6]

Omar was thirty years older than Kitty. In fact, she had been only seven years old when Omar graduated from the Command and the General Staff School in 1929 and was assigned as an instructor in tactics and weapons at the Infantry School. No matter how they had arrived at this interview, as the conference drew to an end, and the reporters began filing out, Kitty made herself busy—lingering behind on purpose.

Bradley looked her way and asked her: "Is there anything I can do for you, young lady?"

She gathered her notes, pads, and pencils together and shook her head, responding: "Not right now, sir." She placed the forefinger of her right hand in the air and said, "But hold my place, General.... I'll be back."[7] That was their first official meeting, but fate would bring them together again. Next time, things would really heat up.

A Second First Impression

Kitty and Omar's second meeting was even more coincidental than their first. It occurred three years later, in June 1953, when the two met

18. In Love with Kitty 131

randomly in an elevator at the Hollywood Turf Club (one source claimed that Omar was with Mary at their second meeting).[8] The Hollywood Turf Club was originally founded under the chairmanship of Jack L. Warner of Warner Bros., and its initial shareholders composed a notable list of movie stars, directors, and producers that included Al Jolson, Bing Crosby, Sam Goldwyn, and Walt Disney. It opened on June 10, 1938, and was the location of the 1938 Hollywood Gold Cup, at which the legendary Seabiscuit began his racing career.

In the mid–1950s, after returning to Los Angeles from Okinawa, Kitty went on some unusual assignments, one of which included covering a Hollywood nudist colony. She wrote about this experience in an article titled "Under the Skin," in which she gained entrance to the Fontana Nudist Colony during a convention called "Week for Nudists of Southern California." She made her entrance wearing only earrings and high heels. Kitty was both a successful reporter and Hollywood scriptwriter. She had been married and divorced twice and took an active involvement in thoroughbred racing. All of these events would lead her to the Hollywood Turf Club that day in the summer of 1953, when she would again bump into the famous though "homely" General Omar Bradley.[9]

Kitty had kept abreast of Bradley's career, applauding President Truman's decision to name him the fifth of the five-star generals, which had occurred on September 20, 1950. Following this, he served as the first chairman of NATO, after gracefully stepping down as Chairman of the Joint Chiefs in August 1953. These were his last years as an official in Washington, D.C., and he began to branch out into the private sector, though he continued to serve and consult on various presidential commissions.

Bradley's role as a five-star general was not just an honorary title with no specific duties. Five-star generals were expected to remain on active-duty status as long as they lived. Bradley's position as a popular general earned him a level of celebrity status. In one month's time, he claimed to have processed 1,542 pieces of official correspondence and received forty-two invitations for major speeches, evidencing his wide "fan base." He was also still considered an "active" military leader, drawing a salary of roughly $20,000 per year until it was increased in the 1970s to $30,000. His position entitled him to certain fringe benefits, including renting government office space at no cost, free travel opportunities, and the use of military aides. He was also called on for certain public appearances, including the occasional speaking engagement at the Department of Defense or D-Day anniversaries on the beaches of Normandy, as well as Veterans Day, Memorial Day, and Independence Day celebrations and engagements.[10]

It already has been noted that he was involved with the Bulova Watch Company through multiple wartime contracts and with the Bulova School while directing the VA. Bradley took a position with the Bulova Watch Company as its head of research for a salary of $25,000 per year, and in 1958, following the death of Bulova's chairman, Arde Bulova, Bradley was elected chairman, for which he earned $75,000 per year plus stock options.[11] He used his organizational and problem-solving skills to reorganize the company and its operations so that each person knew his duties and responsibilities. Furthermore he used his connections with NASA to have a Bulova Accutron clock installed in astronaut capsules, lunar orbiter vehicles, and unmanned satellites.[12]

Following his retirement as chairman, Mary and Omar decided to relocate from Washington to Southern California. In December 1953, they rented the same house that had once been owned by movie star Loretta Young on South Rodeo Drive in Beverly Hills.[13] Tragedy soon struck the Bradley family; on January 19, 1954, Omar's son-in-law, Maj. Hal Beukema, was killed at age twenty-nine when his air force F-86 jet crashed into the James River. This left Elizabeth a widow and her four children—Henry (Hank), Mary Elizabeth, Omar Bradley (Brad), and Anne—fatherless. Hal was buried at West Point.[14]

Bradley continued to indulge the passion he had developed in the postwar years in Washington: horse racing. His penchant for mathematics made him a capable handicapper, and he approached the races as he did his battles and golfing—there was a system and a challenge to it. As one biographer noted, "He rarely won, but he never gave up trying."[15] Regardless, it was this "passion" that led Omar to visit the Turf Club at Hollywood Park that one midsummer afternoon, when he was reacquainted with Kitty.

This chance encounter would lead to many more meetings, even though Omar was a married man. He and Kitty shared some of the same interests, and they were soon spending lots of time together, confiding in each other with intimate details and personal issues. One day, they realized over a bowl of shredded wheat, sliced bananas, and skim milk that they were in love. Kitty remarked that "Omar had the theory that we had lived before and had come back to find each other."[16] They believed that theirs was the original love story that played out over the course of their lifetimes.

The "incubation period," as Kitty referred to it, lasted eight months, during which time they shared afternoons at the local Turf Club, leisurely lunches at cozy restaurants near Kitty's studio, and long walks across the streets of Beverly Hills. They even enjoyed "languid nightcaps of antihistamine pills and Bourbon" together.[17] It seemed that Kitty enjoyed many of the things that Omar's wife couldn't tolerate, including social parties and drinking. It is no wonder that her personality appealed to Omar.

They spent hours together going over the personal details of their lives, discussing their emotions and the specific events that brought them together.[18] Kitty never lost sight of the fact that she was the other woman in this relationship despite her best efforts to put this out of her mind; yet she did not allow this fact to affect her relationship with Omar. Nevertheless, she remained painfully aware that Mary was "Mrs. Omar Bradley," who kept herself busy playing in bridge clubs and maintaining their new Brentwood estate.

In 1954, Elizabeth and the grandchildren went to live with the Bradleys in Beverly Hills, which significantly altered the Bradleys' lifestyle. Needing a bigger home, they bought a house on Saltair Avenue in Brentwood and were joined by two orderlies.[19] It was not easy for Omar and Kitty to keep their relationship secret, and they carried on as quietly as possible in order to avoid hurting Mary and tainting Omar's public image without "denying what we knew we could not be without."[20] They seemed to have been largely effective in carrying on this indiscretion, as even today most people do not know about this affair.

One of Kitty's producers, who was never identified, had spotted the two together a few times at the studio and at various luncheons. On the day they were married, this anonymous producer sent them a wire saying, "That had to be the best kept secret since the Atom Bomb." This certainly seems to have been the case. In all of Omar's previous biographies, the focus has been placed mainly on his wartime record, with his family mentioned only as a secondary point of interest, yet the question remains: Who was this young, beautiful reporter who had so captivated the aging U.S. general?

The Lively Life of Kitty Buhler

Esther Dora Biolo (later Kitty Buhler and Esther Kitty Bradley) was born on July 23, 1922, in New York City. On the day of her birth, the front-page headlines of the *New York Times* included one about the Ku Klux Klan, which had agreed not to wear hoods in public in exchange for the governor of Georgia not pursuing their "allegations of violence"; a pair of newlyweds who had been electrocuted in their bathtub in the Bronx; a gunfight that broke out in Brooklyn, where "Liverpool Jack" managed to kill four cops; and a recording of President Harding's honorary membership into the Flathead Indian tribe.[21]

Growing up on Manhattan's Lower East Side, she was the child of Jewish immigrant parents who owned and operated a local corner candy store. This store naturally became the local social club for the neighborhood children. Several of Kitty's earliest memories included the Mafia-style execution of her neighbor, the Orson Welles radio broadcast of the aliens from Mars, and her belief that she may have been adopted (though this does not seem to be the case).[22] In her writings, Kitty recalled the sights and sounds of her childhood during long, hot summer nights in New York with the windows open and the sounds of the popular soaps of the '30s blaring over the radio. Her penchant for writing began at the age of twelve, when she wrote her first short story on a notepad using the back of her parents' candy store as her unofficial office. It was a detective story. She attended Manhattan Business College but left to embark on what she called the "real life." Kitty underwent a sobering realization, as her first job paid a mere twelve dollars per week.[23]

One of her childhood memories included falling in love with a five-gaited mare. When her parents refused to buy it for her, she stole her brother's law library and sold it in order to come up with the down payment. Her brother later decided that if she wanted Leading Lady that much, she should have her, and *he* bought the horse for her instead.[24] This reveals the drive that Kitty possessed; she was a girl who worked hard to get what she wanted, one way or another.

Kitty dabbled in real estate management while residing in Forest Hills, New York, and she took evening courses in literature, languages, and psychology. She initially planned a career as a lawyer, and her first script was called *Legal Affair* for a Franchot Tone and Nina Foche television production.[25] One time, Kitty was even invited to take a ride to Los Angeles on the *Super Chief*, known as the "Train of the Stars" due to the high number of celebrities it transported between Chicago and L.A. Kitty secured her first studio assignment at Goldwyn Studios, where she accidentally bumped into a lion sunbathing outside Stage 2 between takes on a Harold Lloyd picture. Based on this information, it seems that the film Kitty referred to was *The Sin of Harold Diddlebock* (1947), which starred silent-film actor Harold Lloyd. By this point, she had studied at Kansas Wesleyan University, University of Southern California, and UCLA, though between assignments she spent weekends with tutors in French, Spanish, early English literature, and music.[26]

In her later years, Kitty sported a pair of horn-rimmed glasses, and from 1949 to '51 she worked for United Press, covering general news and the operation of B-29s in Okinawa during the Korean conflict. During this time, she also wrote a daily column for *Stars and Stripes* called "Kapers by Kit." In the mid–1960s, Kitty began to focus on her writing, which included the first twenty-six episodes of the popular television show *Dragnet*.[27] She also wrote for *The Ray Milland Show*, *General Electric Theater* (which Ronald Reagan hosted), *Bonanza*, *My Three Sons*, *The Untouchables*, and an episode of *Bewitched*. In all, she wrote forty-eight different television shows and even wrote the script for the major motion picture *China Doll* for John Wayne's Batjac Productions. This was the beginning of her long-term friendship with "The Duke."[28]

This friendship came full circle in 1978 when Wayne received the first General Omar N. Bradley Spirit of Independence Award in Shreveport, Louisiana. Then, in 1979, while Wayne was conducting his valiant battle against cancer, Kitty and Omar (along with many of his other friends) urged Congress to confer upon him the Congressional Gold Medal. In June 1980, Omar and Kitty traveled to Los Angeles from their home in Texas for the Army's 205th Birthday Ball, at which the Army Distinguished Civilian Service Medal was presented to Wayne posthumously.[29]

Kitty also worked on the editorial staff of an Okinawa weekly paper called the *Ryukian Review*. Furthermore, she was on the editorial staff at *Tokyo Fanfare* and wrote human interest and nonfiction articles in national and other international magazines. Some of these titles included: "Twenty-one Days of Clarity," which described her twenty-one-day water fast and "Tombs and Typhoons," which was based on her experience waiting out a typhoon in one of the tombs in Okinawa.

Additionally, many of her articles were culturally and anthropologically based, such as "Government Girl in Tokyo," which focused on the government girls and their relationship with the occupation forces in Japan, and "Buckles and Bows," which explored the psychology behind the Asian custom of bowing. She even wrote an article on religion titled "Christ and Shintoism," which examined the influence of

Japanese native religion on the occupation forces. She dabbled in different genres, writing one fictional story titled "The Ghosts of Shuri," about five Japanese artists living in an abandoned castle in Okinawa. Perhaps one of the most interesting of these writings was her own diary, which she organized into the book *Husbands I Have Known*.[30] It is unfortunate that Kitty never formally published this last work, as it surely would have been an intriguing book. At this stage, Kitty and Omar's relationship remained a secret, though it would soon be partly revealed following a very unexpected and unfortunate event.

19

From Mary to Kitty

From 1953 to the mid–1960s, Omar and Kitty carried on this love affair; however, Omar's wife soon became suspicious that something was going on. In the spring of 1957, she decided to move the family back to Washington. Omar wrote to George Marshall about the primary reason for this move: "Proximity to our daughter and our ... grandchildren is our most compelling motive." But Kitty herself admitted that this was not the whole truth—it was Mary's intent to put some distance between Omar and his ongoing mistress.[1]

Despite the truth of this statement, Kitty claimed in a later interview that "Mary and I became great friends. We had the same interests, many of the same friends, and just found we had a lot in common. Even when the Bradleys moved to Washington to be nearer their grandchildren we kept up our friendship."[2] By this time, Elizabeth had returned to Chevy Chase, Maryland, and had married an attorney named Benjamin H. Dorsey. They went on to have two children, a daughter named Melanie and a son named Benjamin Dorsey III, giving the Bradleys a total of six grandchildren. This desire to be close to the grandchildren provided a valid cover excuse to satisfy the media for the Bradleys' return to the East Coast. They settled there and purchased a six-bedroom home on Indian Lane in northwestern Washington.[3]

This forced Kitty and Omar to transition into a long-distance phase of their relationship. A need to visit Bulova's West Coast Research and Development provided a good cover story and a valid excuse for his frequent return trips to Los Angeles. As to the specifics of to how they maintained this relationship, Kitty revealed some insight:

> We always booked him a suite at the Beverly Hills Hotel. He never used it. On occasion, I managed a few days between writings assignments to

get into New York where Omar had use of Bulova's company suite at the Astor Hotel. We always were careful to book my accommodations at the far end of the hall, but the housekeepers were old hands at this. One day Omar left his red plaid robe (which we still have) in *my* suite and it was returned without comment to a hanger in *his* closet [emphasis added].[4]

They even adopted code names for each other that they employed when writing letters to one another: "Mr. George" was Omar's alias, and "Mr. Kennedy" (not intended to have any relation to John F. Kennedy) was Kitty's. Despite their best efforts to hide this relationship, their respective secretaries eventually figured it out, but their main goal was to protect Mary, which they seemingly accomplished. Though Omar had discussed divorcing Mary and marrying Kitty, this was not a realistic option given his high-profile public persona. Besides, Mary had been both a gracious and supporting lifelong partner, and it would be unfair to leave her at this later stage. In his later "autobiography," only six pages are dedicated to Bradley's postwar life, and it was merely noted that he "kept busy with Bulova matters and his other corporate directorships."[5]

In 1958, Bradley was elected chairman of the Bulova Watch Company. He was already serving on the board and executive committee of Metro-Goldwyn-Mayer as well as on a number of other corporate boards all on the East Coast. This meant that his occasions and cover stories for traveling west and meeting Kitty were rapidly dwindling.

This pushed Kitty to pour herself into her work, and at one time she reportedly spent six and a half months straight at her desk aside from the occasional nap. In 1960 she travelled, and in 1961 she purchased the contract of a successful professional fighter in Los Angeles, a 147-pound welterweight.[6] In 1962, Kitty was married; however, this wouldn't last long, and by 1963 the marriage had ended in divorce (yet again).

On the day of her final decree, Bradley came out to California and they resumed their relationship, even though things had become more complicated and frustrating for both parties. In January 1965, Kitty traveled to India to help on the set of a movie being filmed by MGM. In transit, Kitty arranged for a layover in New York, where she met with the general for a romantic getaway before her Indian adventure. Kitty's entire family showed up to send her off, including her father, mother, brother, his wife, and her sister along with her brother-in-law, her three nephews, and her two nieces. They were surprised to meet her new "friend"—the celebrated and "happily married" General Omar N. Bradley. Kitty's mother shot her a bewildered glance and asked her, "What are you doing with Omar Bradley?"

Don't Go Breaking My ... Leg?

On her return flight, Kitty stopped in New York. She and Bradley flew on to Los Angeles, where, two days after her arrival home, Kitty slipped on an oil slick in her garage and broke the femur of her left leg. This incident was more than inconvenient for the active and ambitious Kitty Buhler; it forced her to become virtually bedridden. She was stuck in an adjustable bed at her Beverly Hills apartment, forcing her to manage a host of visiting nurses, who came on a twenty-four-hour rotation, along with a steady flow of housekeepers and cooks. After surgery, the doctors debated as to whether she would ever walk again, making this a very traumatic experience for her.

Kitty was not going to allow this accident to get her down, and instead she made the best of it. She spent her days immersed in reading and reflective writing, which served as a relief from the normative deadlines to which she had become accustomed throughout her writing career. The early weeks were difficult, as she could not turn her body without help, but eventually the pain subsided, and as her body healed, she slowly felt more comfortable. One day, Bradley stopped by to visit her, and Kitty claimed:

> ... he had come to make certain I would not hurt my handicapping when I pulled myself up by the trapeze over my bed. He never had (and still hasn't) gotten over my prowess at the races. Years later, Omar was with me when I received my first Ph.D., and he advised everybody in the auditorium that I was the best handicapper in the country. The assembly was puzzled; my doctorate was in Humane letters, not horses.[7]

Omar was a frequent resident at Kitty's home during this time period, registering himself at the Beverly Hills Hotel even though they took an apartment for him just down the hall from Kitty's place.[8] It seemed something good had come out of Kitty's broken femur; it brought her closer to her "Omie," Kitty's pet nickname for the general. She told an amusing anecdote about Omar and his title: "Omar would have been known as Field Marshal Bradley except that when the five-star ranks were handed out George Catlett Marshall, the recipient of one of them, did not wish to be addressed as Field Marshal Marshall."[9] During his tenure as the Chairman of the Joint Chiefs, Omar had many opportunities to meet a great number of high-profile movie stars. He even had a cameo role in several pictures, including a scene with Rosalind Russell in "Never Wave at a WAC." He would later star in the series *This Is Your Life* with Kitty.

Omar and Hollywood

Bradley also served on the board at Metro-Goldwyn-Mayer. At the time when he joined the board, there was talk about liquidating MGM and distributing the proceeds to the stockholders. The board felt that selling these assets would be worth more than the stock price was selling for at that time. Being on the board was an important position that brought Bradley into close contact with some high-profile figures. The board approved the making of every picture filmed as well as the contracts with the various actors and actresses whom MGM employed. One of the biggest fiascos for MGM during this time was with the movie *Mutiny on the Bounty*.

The company had sent the actors and everybody else involved in the movie over to Tahiti to shoot the picture. Once they got over there, somebody didn't like the script and insisted on it being rewritten. As they waited for the script to be redone, MGM paid for the entire crew to lay around on the beaches. The picture ended up costing MGM $20 million instead of the initial budget of $10 million. This fiasco resulted in the board firing the president.[10] The cause of the problem was none other than legendary actor Marlon Brando. He started this "mutiny" by objecting to the script, forcing MGM to rewrite it. This pushed the company to adopt a new rule that they would not hire a leading man or a leading lady until that person approved the script. The board also approved the budget for the picture, the salary for actors and actresses, the location, and so on.[11] Bradley served on the board for roughly five years (and later served on the executive committee).[12]

He also consulted elsewhere in Hollywood. One rival entertainment company, RKO, offered him payment, but the general always refused it. Instead, RKO sent him a set of five-star golf clubs and a souvenir silver box, which he reluctantly accepted.[13] From 1953 to 1957, Omar and Mary lived in Brentwood and had the opportunity to meet and interact with many different movie stars, including Bob Hope and

Bing Crosby. Furthermore, Bradley had met more than his fair share of Hollywood stars and starlets through the USO during the war, including his supposedly "scandalous" relationship with Marlene Dietrich. Thus, Omar was at ease with Kitty's high-profile guests, and they were in turn comfortable around him.

Kitty's health issue was followed by months of physical therapy, which she combined with the practice of hatha yoga in order to make a fuller recovery, both physical and spiritual. Her desire was to fully heal so that she could engage in the activities that were such a part of her life, including horseback riding, tennis, and taking long, leisurely walks. She slowly recovered and resumed her writing for both film and television. Bradley continued to fly out to California and Kitty continued her trips to the Hotel Astor in New York, until something unexpected occurred in 1965.

The Death of Another Loved One

Mary was just seventy-three years old when she started getting easily tired and constantly had to rest and lie down.[14] Then she began having stomach problems and finally decided to check into the Walter Reed Hospital in Washington on a Friday. By the following Wednesday, December 1, 1965, she had passed away. The cause of her death was determined to have been leukemia. She died one year shy of her fiftieth wedding anniversary, and she was buried in Arlington National Cemetery. A private service was held at the Fort Myer chapel.[15] Kitty sent two dozen long-stemmed pink Sweetheart roses to Arlington Cemetery and noted, "To this day, whenever Omar and I are in or near Washington, D.C., we stop by the grave with pink Sweetheart Roses. Mary loved pink."[16]

Following her death, by Bradley's own account, he was a "lonely, grief-stricken man of seventy-two, completely at loose ends."[17] As one orderly noted, "he was just lost when Mrs. Bradley died," and friends recalled that during this time when they visited the general they "had never seen a man so utterly alone."[18] There is no denying that Omar loved Mary; that much is obvious to anyone who delves into Omar's life. Thankfully, he had someone to help him through it.

In a later interview, Kitty expressed her own feelings on Mary's passing: "Mary may be dead, but we are still friends. The general and I visit her grave each time we are in Washington, and always bring pink flowers—pink was her favorite color. I love her. If she were still here she'd want to do just what I'm doing—making him happy. We'll all be together in Arlington when we die, in the same plot."[19] It should be noted that Kitty went to great lengths to keep Omar's affairs private, not wishing to upset Mary or her memory. However, one must wonder about Mary's own feelings on being buried with Omar and his mistress for all eternity.

In February 1966, Kitty picked Omar up at the airport in California, and they silently drove directly to the Turf Club at Santa Anita in her Jaguar sedan. They were finally together, which was enough for now. Later that evening they made plans, mapping out the remainder of their lives. There was a lot to think about: Elizabeth, the six grandchildren, Kitty's writing career, Omar's public image, and the Washington community. During this time, Omar made many visits west, Kitty made many visits east, and the two enjoyed a premarital summer at Del Mar.

Marrying After Mary

Finally, they decided that enough was enough and made their decision to forget waiting the full "respectable" year and just make it legal. On Monday morning, September 12, 1966, following a wedding breakfast of waffles in La Jolla, the two were married in the chambers of a San Diego judge right before the Daily Double horse races at Del Mar. Judge Mahedy, a former naval officer, respected their desire for privacy and performed the ceremony in his chambers, but by the time they had arrived at the Turf Club their table was swarmed by paparazzi. It had never occurred to the newlyweds that the reporters and photographers had a direct line into the Marriage License Bureau.

Bradley settled down with his racing form and waived the inquisitive reporters aside. "Go away," he demanded, and he meant it. "It's a secret."[20] They were trying to get in touch with Elizabeth and tell her the news directly, but they were having trouble connecting with her since she was in Europe. They did not want her or the grandchildren to learn of their marriage secondhand through the media. By the next morning, the whole world knew of this celebrity wedding. The media made a lot of the fact that Kitty had been previously divorced twice, but in the end this would turn out to be her final marriage. To give the reader an idea of the level of celebrity status Bradley obtained, the following week on his Sunday night show, Ed Sullivan announced their love, closing with this line: "This has been some week. There was an earthquake north of San Francisco. The Mauna Loa volcano on the island of Hawaii erupted. And Omar Bradley got married."[21]

Sex and the Senior Citizen

Kitty and Omar continued to maintain an active sex life. Omar was seventy-three and she was forty-four when they were married, but Kitty claimed, "The general is the youngest man I know, he's got a lot more energy than I have," indirectly referring to his sex drive. Their main problem in engaging in sexual activity was finding an occasion to be alone, as their household was always filled with sergeants, aides, grandchildren, and multitudes of other visiting houseguests.

One time a visiting houseguest decided he wanted a glass of milk at 2 a.m. Omar, thinking the commotion was something more serious, leaped out of bed and raced down the stairs to see what was going on as their two poodles cheered him on, barking loudly. Kitty slipped on a robe and reached the head of the stairs just in time to witness the police and the alarm system's security at the front door; their guns were drawn and pointed at her husband, who was standing there completely naked. Though it took some convincing, Omar explained that he was in fact General Bradley, the owner of the household.[22]

It wasn't until an airplane accident in 1975 at age eighty-two that Omar's sex drive began to fail him. For Kitty and Omar, sex was more than just a physical act; "sex was the spiritual coupling of two souls."[23]

In order for this marriage to work, Kitty had to close her residence and office in Los Angeles, wrapping up her current assignment "Where Do You Hide an Elephant?" for MGM's *Please Don't Eat the Daisies*. However, Kitty claimed that she was "much happier being a full-time wife" than she ever was as a writer. Together they enjoyed swimming, playing golf, attending the races twice a week, entertaining, and being entertained. One time they played gin rummy all the way from New York to California, but Omar always won due to his math skills. Kitty's dedication to take care of Omar extended from her "privilege of working with him" to sharing what she called her "method of play" at the racetrack, where the Bradleys won enough one year "to make some tidy investments," or so he would later claim.[24] Kitty and Omar believed that their love story was the real deal, and Kitty made the general happy.

R-E-S-P-E-C-T

This marriage opened up a whole new world for Kitty that she had never imagined. Before their wedding, she didn't realize that from that day on, they would be trailed by a ceaseless entourage of army sergeants and aides. These aides helped them get through the "breathless settling-in" as Kitty and Omer traveled directly east on the morning after their wedding back to their home in Washington. Kitty found it unusual that the same "sergeants" who just a year before had taken care of Mary Bradley were now taking her in and respecting her as the new Mrs. Omar N. Bradley. It was from these soldiers that Kitty learned the power of her position. She now understood why two hundred ladies would jump to their feet whenever she walked through a reception room at West Point—she was now the senior officer's wife. Kitty jokingly explained, "I thought the ladies had to go to the powder room."[25]

It was from these sergeants that she learned what the word *aplomb* really meant. One time when their limousine developed ignition trouble while at a White House ceremony, Sergeant Bruce picked them up at the White House steps driving his old Chevrolet and dressed in his chauffeur's uniform. He smiled as he swung open his car doors for the two to enter. As the new woman in Omar's life, Kitty had to socialize with all of his friends and colleagues, including the same network of military wives that had previously befriended and accepted Mary into their inner circle. The first week that the two were married, the wife of a U.S. senator from Oklahoma telephoned her and assured Kitty that if she didn't make Omar happy, the social community would tar and feather her, running her out of Washington. In her usual joking manner, Kitty replied by promising that if that should occur, she would supply the tar herself.[26]

Kitty was both elegant and classy; she was described by one reporter as being "at home" in a turquoise silk pantsuit, decorated with silver and gold brocade. "Her short cut coiffure caps her head like a silvery helmet, and when she speaks in a soft voice, picking her words carefully, she punctuates them with a broad and fleeting smile." She always dressed with "style and distinction" and was known to wear a "circlet of five star shaped diamonds."[27] After all, as Omar became the last living five-star general, Kitty was the only woman in the country who could legitimately pull this look off.[28]

At home, the staff consisted of two sergeants and an aide, assigned by order of Congress to all five-star generals. Kitty noted, "I like having a household of men. Their job is their livelihood; therefore, they are completely reliable and take excellent care of us." Kitty did not hold Mary's view of liquor and cigarettes, and as such the couple attended numerous parties, making the most of their time in the nation's capital. They loved to entertain and throw parties.

The Bradley parties were legendary, and the couple thoroughly enjoyed their time together. Kitty later referred to herself as the "Perle Mesta" of northwest Washington.[29] Over the course of their relationship, Kitty developed a deep admiration for her husband, which was revealed in the following statement from her memoirs: "There are sects in India in which the women count their birthdays from the date of their marriages. I understand them completely."[30] Kitty and Omar had a fun-filled relationship that she compared to a spiritual rebirth in her life.

Home, Home on the Range

At any given time in the Bradley household, there were at least five cooks along with household aides, five nurses, and five administrative staff members in residence. Five-star generals do not retire in the traditional use of the term and are considered on active duty the remainder of their lifetimes. Also, they are assigned their own staffs—soldiers with special skills assigned for average tenures ranging from one to three years. One sergeant remained with the Bradleys for twenty-one years, another for eight, and another for six.

These soldiers brought with them "fresh guts of vigor" and were involved and dedicated. They became like long-lost family members to the Bradleys. These young men became particularly protective of Kitty, at times taking on the role of defensive sons looking out for their "mother." They would offer their opinion as to what they preferred her to wear, worry about her if she took on too heavy a schedule, and got nervous as to how she drove the car. Kitty alluded to this maternal relationship, writing that "in truth, each becomes our son, leaving an indelible emotional imprint. Through the years we have had quite a parade of sons, and the parade goes on."[31]

These various aides and assistants made it possible for Kitty and the general to maintain the Omar N. Bradley Library at West Point and to administer the Bradley Fellowships, Scholarships, and Awards. Their assistance also allowed them to respond to the literally thousands of letters and requests that they received on a regular basis. In short, these soldiers remained a vital part of their official lives, freeing the general and his wife to continue on with their trips and maintain their busy lifestyle.

The Bradleys were also animal lovers. They kept several dogs in residence, including their two poodles, Omaha and Utah. They even took in a police dog named Damon who was trained in a most unusual way; it seemed the trainer was an alcoholic who introduced the poor dog to Scotch and milk. Damon the dog continued his love for this particular "beverage" and refused to go to bed without it. Omar also had his own Persian cat named Texas George, but apparently the kitty acted like a movie star (Kitty compared this cat to Marlene Dietrich, of all people!) and nothing they could do would change the cat's mind.[32] Kitty joked that the dog-training manual provided her with a general structure for running a house that was full of animals, aides, and assistants—rewards for good behavior, punishment for bad. This manual was also applied to the general!

20

The Final Years

Due to his military service, Bradley had become a national hero and an international celebrity. He and Kitty toured the world, visiting various U.S. embassies. They toasted Queen Elizabeth's birthday with champagne, strawberries, and whipped cream at the embassy of Great Britain; they marked the anniversary of the Battle of the Bulge at the embassy of Belgium; and they celebrated the liberation of Luxembourg at its U.S. embassy.[1]

As noted previously, following the extraction of his teeth at age thirty-five, Bradley had allergies, which became more severe as he grew older. He was especially allergic to seafood, corn, and rice. Kitty recalled that embassy meals typically included a bisque or bouillabaisse that could be made of any number of the above ingredients, and embassy dinners often began with her racing to the far end of the table to stop Bradley from eating that first spoonful. Kitty herself developed several allergies to butter and potatoes, and later in life she became a vegetarian.[2]

Through their years in Washington, Bradley carried on many different odd jobs concurrently, but they always found time to visit the local track, including the nearby Laurel, Pimlico, and Bowie. They were frequent visitors to the White House and rubbed elbows with many different politicians. They appreciated the beauty of cherry blossoms in April and watched as people protested on the Pentagon steps.

In the foyer of their home stood a duplicate of Bradley's bust that rested on a pedestal outside the entrance to the superintendent's office at West Point. It had even become an unofficial tradition at West Point that any cadet called to the "Supe's" office for reprimand would rub Omar's nose for good luck before he entered. Kitty recollected that whenever they left for a day's races, she too would rub the nose on

Omar's bust. There were times at the track, while they were sitting out a photo finish, that she would rub the real thing. She humorously noted that "some afternoons that gleamed brightly, too."[3] Together they enjoyed afternoons of "playing the odds" at the racetrack.

The doting couple went on nationwide trips for various Veterans Day appearances. On such engagements, Bradley typically delivered a speech, flashed a smile, and gave a wave of his hand, following it up by working the crowd and shaking the hands of as many attendees as possible. On one receiving line in Birmingham, Alabama, the senior aide counted 4,103 hands that they had shook. While they carefully screened all invitations, there were so many worthwhile ones that they clocked up hundreds of thousands of miles travelling throughout the country and abroad.

Vietnam

In August 1967, Bradley made a fourteen-day visit to South Vietnam, bringing with him his blushing young bride. Kitty had sensed Omar's desire to go see the Vietnam situation for himself in order to acquire firsthand knowledge of the troops' morale there. Kitty supported the general's belief that there was no substitute for talking to the men in the field. Bradley's only hesitation was his health situation; he had recently undergone surgery to remove his kneecap, making it impossible for him to walk without a limp or pain. As a general officer on active duty, Bradley's trip to Vietnam was a business expense, and the government would foot the bill; however, Kitty's costs would not be covered. Because of this, she arranged with *Look* magazine to serve as a correspondent with the stipulation that they pay her travel expenses and that all payment and proceeds for the article be turned over to the USO, the organization that had provided Bradley and his men with entertainment throughout the war and continued to do so for troops both at home and abroad.

Omar referred to Kitty as a quiet but determined woman, invaluable, and "great for morale." He recalled his wife's incisive questions about the war at the Pentagon briefing just before their departure for Southeast Asia. After they left the briefing, one colonel turned to another, not realizing that Bradley's aide was still in the room, and asked admiringly, referring to Kitty, "How do you get one like that?" The other officer replied, "I guess you got to be a five-star general."

20. The Final Years

One reporter described Kitty as "a small, young-looking woman with a trim figure, blue eyes, and ginger-colored hair." From all of the pictures available, it seems undeniable that Kitty was an attractive individual.[4]

Kitty had promised the servicemen in Vietnam that upon their return to the States, she would correspond with the family of each soldier. This translated into a phone call or personal letter sent to 917 families. Kitty made good on her promise. There was one hang-up, though. She had to send all letters to the Pentagon first and have them checked out through the casualty department before they were sent out so as not to give the family false hope.[5] During this visit, she went everywhere with her husband, even to the hostile areas.[6]

Vietnam presented a very different military necessity from the wars that Omar had fought previously. It was like nothing he had ever experienced before. There were no wall maps on which to draw lines and say "here is the front." The front was everywhere.[7] The enemy utilized guerrilla warfare tactics that relied upon the element of surprise and hit-and-run strategies. Bradley's overall conclusion was this: "I am convinced that this is a war at the right place, at the right time and with the right enemy."[8]

In 1969, 1974, and 1979, the couple visited Normandy in France, joining with the Allies who gathered on the beaches from all parts of the world to celebrate their triumphs. In 1968, they traveled to North Africa, revisiting the battlefields at Kasserine Pass, El Guettar, and Gafsa while searching out authentic locales for their new project—they both served as senior advisers for 20th Century–Fox's film *Patton*. Fox had also bought the screen rights to Bradley's book, *A Soldier's Story*, which was used as a partial basis for the movie.[9] Tunis, Brussels, Luxemburg, Copenhagen, Frankfurt, Switzerland, Israel, Paris, London, Canada, Hawaii, the Virgin Islands—Omar and Kitty visited them all, many of them several times.

In his later travels, Bradley was confined to a wheelchair. This made their entourage look like what one observer referred to as a "band of Gypsies." They were accompanied by two officers, two enlisted aides, two nurses carrying emergency medical equipment, freezer-packed picnic baskets for special diet food, and tons of assorted luggage. This long list prompted Kitty to remark humorously:

> Our trips would require more manpower and equipment except for the local Army and Embassy assistance at every stop. Thus far this year, with Omar eighty-seven, we have logged four trips to the East Coast,

two to California, one to Louisiana. We have traveled to Paris, Normandy, and Amsterdam, and we have been to London to visit the Queen. The staff lifts Omar and his wheelchair up and over all steps and obstacles, and away we go. We are rewarded by Omar's special grin. He knows we would wheel him to hell and back. As I often tell him, he has taken all of us this far; let us help him the rest of the way.[10]

Another Aide: Frank Kindred

In 1975, due to Bradley's failing health, a clinical specialist named Frank Kindred was assigned to become the latest member of Omar's support staff. By this time, the general struggled with numerous medical issues, and it was Kindred's job to serve as his medical assistant. These duties included many different tasks such as carrying him up the stairs, picking him up, and helping him get into and out of the car. However, the job was not without its perks, because as noted throughout this section, Bradley was a celebrity in his own right, and Kindred shared in his life's adventures.

Kindred accompanied the Bradleys on their various trips across the United States. As he told one reporter, "We went everywhere together." These adventures also included many international trips, on one of which they met with the queen of England in order to dedicate a crypt in St. Paul's Cathedral for soldiers of war. Kindred recollected, "I met President Reagan; we went to Jimmy Stewart's birthday party," and they even met Karl Malden together. Bradley and Malden actually became close friends later on.

Kindred further noted that Omar loved to dine at the 21 Club, an upscale restaurant in New York City. There, together, they met actress Lauren Bacall, and on one occasion President Nixon stopped by their table "to pay his respects" to the aging war hero. While he and Bradley got along well, Kindred did make a note about Kitty's strong personality. It seemed that the general was attracted to strong-willed women. According to an article about his time with Bradley, Kindred claimed that "Kitty could be a demanding taskmaster to some members of her husband's staff, but ... he and Kitty always got along well."[11] When asked about his overall opinion of the five years that he spent as Bradley's assistant, Kindred exclaimed, "He was so laid back that you would never know he was a five-star general.... It was quite an honor, not many people got that honor."[12]

Death of a Real-Life G.I. Joe

On August 13, 1973, at 1:30 a.m., Kitty was walking around the pool at their California home when she heard an unfamiliar sound—it was Omar's emergency buzzer alerting her that he was in serious trouble. Kitty raced into the bedroom and found Bradley pale white, gasping for breath, trying to get out his final farewells to her. She responded, "You die, and I'll kill you," and she proceeded to apply mouth-to-mouth resuscitation.[13]

As soon as she got him breathing again, she rushed him to the UCLA Medical Center, where over the next three days, Bradley suffered five massive pulmonary embolisms. The doctors concluded that he could not survive another attack, and the decision was made to take him into surgery for the placement of a Mobin-Uddin umbrella to shelter the lungs from further clots. Ten days later, Bradley was taken off the critical list; he made a quick recovery. When Kitty was allowed to see him, Omar was sitting up in bed for the first time since this life-threatening operation.

During his hospital stay, Omar received numerous telegrams and pieces of mail, and he answered each one. They donated all of the flowers and plants that they had received to veterans hospitals with five-star cards stating: "From a fellow veteran, Omar N. Bradley."[14] They were finally able to return home, where Omar continued the recovery process. During this time of recuperation, the couple could not throw their typical parties or go out on the town; instead, they had to content themselves with quiet dinners with intimate friends and small poolside parties.

To keep herself occupied, Kitty decided to start learning the flamenco guitar, and as a result she had a steady stream of concert artists over the house teaching her how to play. This music served as therapy for Omar, who would sit and patiently listen while Kitty learned to play. Her teachers loved to play for Omar, and he was happy to listen; he would keep time with his fingers and his feet. One day, he surprised his wife by whipping the afghan off his lap and into the air, and like a matador yelled out, "Olé!"[15]

Their life gradually regained its normal balance of duty, family, horse races, and travelling, until March 16, 1975, when Omar suffered from a cerebral embolism. He was rushed again to UCLA where, after twenty-one seizures, he went into a coma. Previously, he had suffered a head injury, though the exact cause remains a subject of debate. Some sources claim that this trauma had been the result of an old football injury from his days at West Point sixty years earlier, while others claimed that the concussion was caused by a blow to the head while exiting an airplane.[16] Once again Omar faced surgery, this time to relieve the pressure on his brain. On March 17, 1975, Omar, at age eighty-two, underwent surgery to remove a blood clot from his brain, which had caused a non-paralytic stroke.

As he began slowly slipping away into unconsciousness, Kitty whispered repeatedly into his ear: "Where do you think you're going, soldier? You don't have a pass."[17] The doctors noted that he came through the operation "very well" and that when all was said and done, he was in "excellent" condition.[18] During this hospital stay, Kitty visited him several times daily, and the White House doctors called every morning to check on his progress. The army even sent him the best neurosurgeons they could muster to diagnose his case and to plan out the best procedures for his health. It was a critical time in Omar's life.

This particular surgery had a longer recovery period, which left Omar in a near-comatose state for many weeks, yet Kitty remained vigilant. She was given a beeper/pager that allowed her to move about and leave the hospital suite without fear of missing any critical news regarding her husband's state. Kitty occasionally left the hospital to visit the nearby famed St. Joseph's Chapel, where she offered up prayers for her husband's health and recovery. From time to time, she would find herself wandering into Schoenfeld Hall, where she sat and listened to the practicing students playing piano, waiting for her beeper to go off. Then one afternoon it finally did.

Five weeks after the surgery, Omar began to stir in his bed and gradually regained his mental capacities. The first words out of his mouth to Kitty were: "You scream. I scream. We all scream for ice cream."[19] Kitty knew then that his sense of humor remained intact, and so the two began the recovery process all over again.

The couple spent their last four years together living at Fort Bliss in Texas, where they had moved in 1977. Omar occasionally lectured on leadership and other such topics and would sparingly accept speaking engagements when the topic appealed to him. He had cheated death on several occasions from his first day on the battlefield in North Africa years before. Kitty made Omar feel young again, and this seems to be one of the reasons he lived as long as he did.

Of course, no one can elude death for very long. On April 8, 1981, Omar passed away at the age of eighty-eight.[20] He had visited New

York to attend a dinner of the local chapter of the Association of the United States Army when he was rushed to the St. Luke's-Roosevelt Hospital at 7:15 p.m. Kitty accompanied him, along with three of his military aides. By 7:35 p.m., he was pronounced dead. The cause of death was listed as cardiac arrest.

Following his demise, Bradley's flag-draped casket was displayed at the Center Chapel at Fort Bliss for three days. His remains were then transported via the presidential jet to Washington for a full military funeral. President Ronald Reagan was represented at his funeral by Vice President George Bush, who spoke admiringly of Bradley.[21] So passed the last living five-star general, and since his death, the rank has officially been retired. It seems that Omar Bradley truly was the last of his kind.

21

Reflections

Bradley's life intersected many others, and some of these individuals deserve special mention for the tremendous impact they made upon him. This included all of the U.S. presidents under whom he served, especially Harry Truman (1945–1953), Dwight Eisenhower (1953–1961), John Kennedy (1961–1963, though Omar admitted he did not know him very well), Lyndon Johnson (1963–1969), Richard Nixon (1969–1974), Gerald Ford 1974–1977), and Jimmy Carter (1977–1981). These men supported Bradley and extended to him the hospitality of the White House. There were also a number of military leaders whom Bradley had fought beside, including Prime Minister Winston Churchill, General Douglas MacArthur, General Bernard Montgomery, General George Patton, and General Matthew Ridgway.

There were key national leaders who assisted and visited with Bradley in his travels, such as Dean Acheson, Ronald Reagan, the Rockefellers, and Dean Rusk, who graced the Bradleys' home and table.[1] There were major writers whom the Bradleys had befriended, including Harold Robbins, Cornelius Ryan, Irving Stone, and Irving Wallace. Finally, there were some of the great performers of the day who developed meaningful friendships with the Bradleys, including Greer Garson, Cary Grant, Beverly Sills, Frank Sinatra, Jimmy Stewart, and Bob Hope. Hope was especially close with the general, and the two considered each other "dearest friends."[2]

On June 14, 1975, for the army's bicentennial, Bradley and Bob Hope were the guests of honor. Fifteen hundred people came together at the Beverly Hills Hotel for this celebration. According to one account, this party looked more like a movie premiere, as the ebullient Sammy Davis, Jr., played a lively show. This led one reporter to comment, "The Army had its birthday bash—Hollywood style."[3] Omar's marriage to Kitty had provided an inadvertent connection between Hollywood and Washington.

Omar and Kitty also became associated with Hollywood screenwriter Carl Foreman, though he was blacklisted as a Communist during the McCarthy era. The press was anxious to get Bradley's comments about this situation, to which he replied: "I didn't know about his blacklisting at the time and I don't care now that I do."[4] Not one to indulge in gossip, Bradley was there to discuss with Foreman the possibility of making a movie based on his autobiography, though nothing ever came out of these conversations.

On another occasion in 1975, Omar and Kitty went to see the San Francisco Ballet perform *Serenade* by Peter Tchaikovsky, when halfway through the performance a bomb threat was called in. It was believed to have been made in protest to the Russian-born Panovs, who were making their home in Israel. While all occupants were forced to leave their seats, Omar and Kitty refused to be intimidated. Kitty exclaimed, "Bombs are nothing new to the general," and while the Los Angeles bomb squad searched the Greek Theatre, Kitty entertained some of the guests with her piano playing in the Chinese Room.[5]

Bradley also participated as the guest of honor for Marina del Rey's weekend celebration for the 200th anniversary of the United States of America.[6] For this event, he was accompanied by their supposed neighbors Grace and Walter Lantz. Walter was a cartoonist who was most famous for his creation of the cartoon character Woody Woodpecker.[7] It was not unusual for the Bradleys to be invited to various "star-studded parties" that included such celebs as dancer, singer, and actress Ann Miller, composer Henri Berger, actor Walter Pidgeon, silent-film star Carmel Myers, talent agent Minna Wallis, director and screenwriter Jean Negulesco, Hollywood actor/writer Richard Carlson, vaudeville dancer June Levant, director and producer William Wyler and his wife Tally, actor Tom Drake, and MGM executive L.B. Mayer, among others.[8]

At another army ball held in 1972, Bradley was honored, and Pat O'Brien, the actor with more than a hundred stage credits, made a special appearance. So too did socialite and actress Zsa Zsa Gabor among other Hollywood celebrities, including Mickey Rooney.[9] Rooney had first been introduced to Bradley in Germany during one of his many performances for overseas troops with the USO (which won him a Bronze Star). They both enjoyed going to the track and betting on horses. They used to get together for lunch regularly at the Hollywood Park track before Bradley moved to El Paso in 1977.[10] Bradley even

True Comics #18 (1941)

This image illustrates Gen. Bradley's celebrity status, as he was depicted in *Real Life Comics* no. 21 (1945) and *True Comics* no.18 (1941).

21. Reflections

maintained a loose relationship with the famous army veteran Elvis Presley, the "King of Rock 'n' Roll" himself. However, the exact nature of this relationship remains unknown.[11]

In 1981, just before his death, Omar participated in another glamorous Hollywood event. Following the inauguration of Ronald Reagan, an all-star inaugural gala was thrown celebrating the first actor to be elected president. Bradley attended this gala along with Johnny Carson, Bob Hope, James Stewart (who announced the wheelchair-bound Omar and his wife, Kitty), Charlton Heston, Debby Boone, Dean Martin, Rich Little, Ben Vereen, Donny and Marie Osmond, Charlie Pride, Mel Tillis, and Frank Sinatra, who sent Bradley a thank-you letter for his attendance. This is not to say that Bradley was close, personal friends with each of these individuals, but his name was mentioned alongside these famed entertainers as a special guest, further evidencing his celebrity status.[12]

Originally renamed to honor "Moberly's Favorite Son," in 1943, the Moberly airport was rededicated on April 26, 1964, as General Omar N. Bradley Airport (courtesy Carlisle Military Museum, USAHEC).

General Bradley (left) with Bob Hope and professional golfer Cary Middlecoff ca. 1949 (courtesy Carlisle Military Museum, USAHEC).

These are just a few of the headlines that Omar and Kitty made together during the later "celebrity" years of his life. It is amusing to think of Bradley and his wartime "short snorter"—it seemed that Bradley himself had now become the celebrity giving out the autographs.[13] Bradley used his influence and fame for some noteworthy causes, including the Omar N. Bradley Foundation at Carlisle Barracks, Pennsylvania (this includes the General Omar Bradley Memorial Library and Museum that was opened on May 8, 1970), which gives grants to students and researchers. Also, the Omar N. Bradley Library was built at West Point. It has recently been assimilated into the larger West Point library.

Conclusion

Thus concludes the life story of one of the most high-ranking and fascinating generals the United States has ever produced. It is a shame

This G.I. Joe of Gen. Bradley comes from the Classic Collection released in 1998.

that his life has been neglected largely because most media outlets dubbed him unexciting or mundane, but as the reader is now aware, his life was anything but boring!

Omar Bradley lived life to the fullest. He took a liking to many different things, including gambling at the horse track, golf, and ice cream. He enjoyed the company of his two wives, his grandchildren, and his only daughter, Elizabeth. Omar sacrificed more than most people for his country, and he had a gentleman's disposition with an unusual deep-seated integrity that is rarely practiced any more. He did not seek out publicity as others had done; nor did he allow his celebrity status to go to his head.

Yet, for all of the positive traits that the general possessed, this biography has also uncovered some of the skeletons that he kept locked away in his closet, including his extramarital affair with Kitty and possibly with other ladies. These are no doubt the things that Bradley wished to hide from the media, and for good reason—they are embarrassing and they call into question the long-held image of him as a soft-spoken, Boy Scout figure. Perhaps *this* image of Omar Bradley will be a more palatable and realistic hero for the modern era: a man who struggled with his own desires but still loved his family, his children, and his country and sacrificed for them. What more could anybody ask from a national hero?

While other biographers have attempted to focus solely on Omar's

A half-dollar coin depicting Omar Bradley and Henry Arnold, which was part of the 5-Star Generals Commemorative Coin Act signed by President Obama on October 8, 2010.

role in World War II and his leadership skills, it seems the real value of his life achievements has been neglected. It is Bradley's legacy that remains a valuable part of American history, as it exemplifies the typical "American dream." He worked his way up through the ranks of the U.S. Army, thereby revealing that even a poor country boy from Missouri has the ability, with hard work and perseverance, to earn himself a spot as a national hero and celebrity. While it is unfortunate that in recent years Bradley has not received the same treatment as leaders such as Eisenhower, Churchill, or Patton, in his time Bradley was a highly regarded figure whose celebrity status remains unquestionable. It is only in these later years that the name Omar N. Bradley has slowly faded out of the nation's collective memory.

Bradley's leadership style further proved that one could advance and achieve this "American dream" without having to be self-serving, rude, or arrogant; rather, Bradley was the complete opposite of this personality. He genuinely cared about his men and was both polite and courteous even among his subordinates, earning himself the nickname "The GI's General." His life serves as an example to future generations that one can achieve his dreams without having to be vicious or cut-throat. Furthermore, Bradley lived life with strong, passionate love—he loved his family, he loved his God, and he loved his country. It is for these reasons that it is finally time for Omar Bradley to get the recognition he deserves. It is the author's hope that this book will contribute to a renewed interest in the life of this American patriot.

Appendix I:
General Omar Nelson Bradley
Leader or Lucky?

Omar Nelson Bradley was just an ordinary boy from Missouri who, with a lot of hard work, solid leadership qualities, and a little bit of luck, was able to climb his way up the ranks of the army ladder, eventually earning the rank of a five-star general. He became the champion for the "ordinary Joe" and the "little guy," working hard to make sure soldiers were treated with respect and that new recruits felt comfortable in their new environment. Though some have criticized Bradley's tactics and style, none could deny the effectiveness of his leadership abilities and the results they produced. After all, he did command a force of 1.3 million men, which was the largest unit ever assembled under one leader's command.

With determination and drive, Bradley worked himself into one of the highest-level leadership positions in the entire country, a role that was achieved by only a handful of other soldiers during World War II. As such, his approach to leadership remains invaluable. This article will dissect and identify some of the key traits of Bradley's leadership style and articulate them in a practical way that can then be replicated in any environment.

Even though Bradley was a strong leader and a highly effective general, several researchers and tacticians have criticized his decisions, style, and approach; thus, this article has two main purposes: (1) To explore these critical perspectives and analyze them in their context. These critiques will then be answered through a detailed examination of the people who knew him well and served directly under his leadership. (2) To systematically identify and define the core traits that made Bradley such an effective leader.

I. Leadership Critique

Given the far-reaching impact Omar Bradley made on the U.S. Army and the world at large (during World War II and after), it is not surprising that many differing opinions about his life and leadership skills have been circulated over time. It should be acknowledged at the outset of this article that regardless of what any researcher may write in modernity about Bradley, it is always easier to analyze military decisions from the safety and comfort of a desk chair than it is from the middle of a battlefield when the future lie ahead undetermined. Omar's caution in World War II remains the source of many of these accusations; thus, this time period warrants further investigation. The purpose of this section is to analyze the various academic and personal opinions of Bradley coming from both modern scholars and those who served under him.

Several researchers have claimed that Bradley's reputation as "the GI's General" was solely the result of U.S. propaganda. As Williamson Murray and Allan R. Millett noted recently in their combined work *A War to be Won* (2000):

> Bradley was not at all the soldier's general of media legend. A soldier's general saves their lives; he doesn't just dress like them. None of Bradley's frontline soldiers ever wrote of him in terms like those veterans of the Burma campaign used to describe his general, William Slim.... Only hacks among American journalists called Omar Bradley a soldier's general.[1]

This is a strong assertion, and if it is true then this entire article is not worth the paper it is printed on. However, the questions remain: Was Bradley's reputation as the soldier's general a minority opinion held only by the "hacks among American journalists" who turned it into American propaganda? Or did the majority of soldiers view Bradley in this positive light? The next section will answer these very questions by examining the differing views provided by modern history.

World War II Researchers

One of the earliest critiques to be leveled against Bradley and all World War II leaders was that there was no clear measuring stick by which to gauge them. Charles Whiting (1926–2007), the British military writer, expressed the sentiment below, from a highly optimistic perspective. Note that he did not cite any sources to back up this view:

> ... At the most the German offensive could mean a setback but never a defeat.... Thus we have no yardsticks to measure Omar Bradley as a great captain, like those great captains in the greatest war ever fought by the United States, that of 1861–1865.... But if Bradley cannot be regarded as a great captain, he will be remembered as a very able soldier, who grew appreciably in stature as the campaign went on and one who was a great advocate of the much maligned U.S. Army; a jealous guardian of its honor and its prestige.... He was very definitely a dedicated and highly professional American soldier, who did the best he could for his calling and his country....[2]

Whiting minimized the threat of Nazi Germany (and the Axis forces) and was very optimistic of the Allied forces' success. This attitude clearly affected any serious analysis he could have made of Bradley, and it was not just denigrating to the general but to all of the soldiers who risked their lives in this bloody war. Though there are a number of inaccuracies throughout this work published in 1971, his opinion of Bradley remains positive.

Charles Kirkpatrick, a historian for the Histories Division of the U.S. Army Center of Military History, implied a similar critique:

> There is no standard against which to compare Bradley as an army group commander. During the fighting in Europe, his calm and effective presence was important in times of crisis, as was his deft touch in handling subordinates. It is difficult, for example, to imagine Patton without Bradley, who exploited the talents of that volatile commander as well as any man could have done. Finally, it was his superb wartime record, combined with his reputation for fairness and honesty, that made him effective in what was probably his most difficult job, Chairman of the Joint Chiefs of Staff.[3]

Kirkpatrick's analysis was flattering of the general, confirming that he was also effective in his role as the chairman of the Joint Chiefs.

Bradley's role in closing the Falaise Pocket in Normandy has recently been criticized by the esteemed military researcher Martin Blumenson (1925–2005), who commented:

> Criticism of Bradley has been subdued ... yet whispers of bad judgment on his part have scratched the surface of his modest portrait.... Bradley attempted to play the role of the bold leader, then was troubled by doubt. He made instant decisions, then second-guessed himself and wondered whether his quick-trigger timing was little more than ill-

considered impulse. He initiated potentially brilliant maneuvers, then aborted them because he lacked confidence in his ability to see them through to completion. As a consequence, he backed and filled, and in the end mismanaged the affairs on the southern side of the pocket from Argentan to the Seine.[4]

Blumenson accuses Bradley of making instant decisions and second-guessing himself along with possessing a strong lack of confidence in the fall of 1944. Several of the more "instant" decisions that Bradley made seemed due to the influence of men such as General Patton, who were prodding him along (as Blumenson records throughout *The Patton Papers*).[5]

As Blumenson himself admitted elsewhere, "Somewhere in the middle [of Patton and Monty] was Bradley, who affected humility. He played by the book. Admired for his soundness and dependability, he preferred to take no chances. Bradley, they said, was solid and safe."[6] Bradley seemed more balanced in his decision-making process than these other two leaders; however, what in one situation could be deemed "sound" and "cautious" could in another be viewed as "indecision." Yet history has proven Bradley to be both cautious and calculative even if Blumenson personally believed that this was a negative trait in this particular period of the war.

Carlo D'Este (1936–), the former U.S. Army lieutenant colonel, is another well respected military historian and for good reason. His writings on World War II are unmatched and his research has influenced the field on many different levels. D'Este had the unique privilege to interview individuals and probe sources that are no longer accessible to the public, which makes his works all the more indispensible; however, one must be careful to compare his opinions with the facts. Such is the case with Omar Bradley, who seems to get a bad rap throughout his writings.

D'Este recaps the negative image of Omar first put forth by S. L. A. Marshall (examined more fully below) and even adds to this by saying:

> ... the public was fed the perception of a plain, soft-spoken general with whom the average civilian back home could readily identify. If truth is the first casualty of war, so it was with the image of Omar Bradley as a general of the masses, one that Bradley himself encouraged for the remainder of his life. The real Omar Bradley was rather narrow-minded and utterly intolerant of failure.[7]

These judgments appear subjective and seem to be a matter of personal opinion rather than fact and deduction. For instance, "narrow-minded" to one person might be seen as "resolute" to another. Also, it would be expected that most army officers would be "intolerant of failure." Yet D'Este did go on to speak positively of Bradley, giving him some credit for his leadership abilities, however indirectly.

In his biography of Patton, D'Este points out that "one of the war's most decorated and respected heroes," paratrooper commander James M. Gavin, admired Bradley for "his fine appreciation of the tools of his trade" and his "tactical hands-on knowledge."[8] D'Este's treatment of Omar has led another more recent researcher to conclude that "Bradley has incurred harsh censure from some critics, notably the American historian Carlo D'Este, who dismisses him as a plodder."[9] If the worst charge against Omar is that he is a cautious plodder, than it seems that his leadership abilities remain unscathed; yet if Omar was the "plodder" of World War II, then Patton could be seen as the "prodder."

Caleb Carr (1955–), the bestselling author and former editor of *MHQ: The Quarterly Journal of Military History*, spoke of Omar Bradley as "the GI General" who was "surrounded by a sea of prima donnas during World War II, never stopped quietly learning his trade, until he became, during the conquest of Germany in 1945, arguably the most progressive and important senior American commander in the European theater."[10] Again, Bradley's leadership abilities remain untarnished.

A.J. Liebling (1904–63), the journalist who in 1951 interviewed Bradley for *The New Yorker*, sang his praises, especially for his leadership abilities. He wrote about the general: "Men went as fast and as far for him as they ever went for the rhetorical Bonaparte." Elsewhere, Liebling recorded: "This reputation for sincerity even when it hurts makes General Bradley a star attraction as a witness before Congressional committees, which try to book him as often as the Copacabana books Joe E. Lewis."[11] Republican congressman Dewey Short (1898–1979) had his own opinions of his fellow "Missourian," noting that "Bradley does not boast. He looks after his men. He is selfless and only wants to win for his country. God never made a better man...."[12]

Vietnam war hero General Wesley K. Clark (1944–) also noted some of Bradley's leadership traits, observing that he was "low-key, substantive, solid, loyal and practical. Leaders in the Bradley mold repress or contain their personal insecurities and idiosyncrasies, abjure the florid personalities, overt militarism, and preening that civilians have traditionally associated with military high-command, and patiently do their part for the team effort.... They are 'organization men,' not 'Einsteins.' They aim not to 'standout' but to 'keep standing in.' They are survivors. And for its own survival and effectiveness the army and other large organizations need leaders like Omar Bradley."[13]

British reporter Max Hastings (1945–) criticized Bradley for being "prone to outbursts of savage temper. He showed himself far more ruthless than Montgomery in sacking corps and divisional commanders." Again, this critique appears subjective, comparing Omar to a British cultural value system that D'Este wittily identified: "The British tended to retain unsatisfactory commanders far too long before relieving them, while the exact opposite occurred in the U.S. Army, where senior commanders were frequently relieved for the slightest transgression, often without adequate time to grow into a job."[14] Yet Hastings's accusation goes against the core of Bradley's leadership beliefs. The fact is that Bradley prided himself in putting the right people in the right places, and it was one of the core tenets of his leadership style, as he later identified.

Bradley was also known as the polite general who rarely raised his voice. Even the fiery General George Patton in his autobiography noted there was only one time to his knowledge that Bradley ever lost his temper.[15] Therefore, Hastings's conclusion does not hold up to the historical testimony. Another of Bradley's core leadership traits was an ability to train up leaders. Bradley's contributions to improving officer training in the army are well documented, most notably through his founding of the Fort Benning OCS program.[16]

Based on the above sampling of the diverse opinions regarding Bradley and his leadership abilities, any critique of his leadership skills can largely be reduced to subjective judgments. While he was certainly cautious in his decisions, most researchers acknowledged his leadership qualities even if they questioned his motives. Alan Axelrod, in his biography of Bradley, discussed his traditional leadership style:

> In none of these profound undertakings was Omar Bradley a dramatic, mercurial, or colorful presence. The threats and issues he faced were bigger than life, but he never was. And he never wanted to be. Everything Bradley did was rooted in the values of his Missouri childhood, youth, and young manhood: values of common sense, Populist patriotism, basic decency, a commitment to hard work, a willingness to learn, a desire to teach, and a quiet, unassuming, selfless passion to serve.[17]

Because of his mild personality and this lack of aggressive self-promotion, Bradley has recently even become a target for modern researchers to scapegoat. It seems that every critique reveals some form of truth; thus, the question that must now be asked is: What did the men who served with him and under him think of his leadership abilities? The following section will attempt to piece together the type of military leader Omar Bradley was known to be among his contemporaries.

Fellow Officers

It is obvious that those who knew Bradley best and could more genuinely assess his leadership abilities were his troops and fellow officers. As such, their testimony is crucial to determining whether Bradley was in fact a strong leader as history has come to know him or if he was merely a master manipulator who was continually in the right place at the right time.

Walter Bedell Smith (1895–1961) was first acquainted with Bradley at infantry school at Fort Benning, where he asked Bradley to make use of his trapshooting range.[18] At first their personalities clashed, as Bradley categorized Smith as a "bit of a Prussian, and brutally frank," comparing him to Joseph Stilwell. Yet over time, these two personalities would become close friends. Regarding Smith, Bradley said he was "quite taken with this young captain."[19] Yet Smith also revealed some of the general's underlying defects. He believed that Bradley's decision not to take Berlin and instead push to the Elbe and Mulde may have in part been fueled by his disdain for Monty.[20]

Smith's view contradicts Bradley's own writings and rationale that the reason for this push to the Elbe and Mulde was in order to cut the Germans off from any possible retreat into the Austrian Alps. A rumor had been circulating among the Nazis that somewhere in the Alps lay a secret hideout where weapons, stores, and aircraft were stored for a "last-ditch, all-out defense."[21] This turned out to be nothing more than a fanatical Nazi myth; it seems unlikely that the cautious Bradley would risk his men's lives and seek the prestige of taking Berlin all for the sake of damaging another officer's reputation.

Ernie Pyle (1900–45) was a front-line news reporter who wrote articles about World War II for the folks back in the States. While it is certain that Pyle was concerned with boosting the morale of U.S. citizens, nevertheless, his views cannot be wholly discounted. Pyle was the one who actually nicknamed Bradley "the GI General." Pyle painted the general in a very positive light, candidly admitting, "I make no bones about the fact that I am a tremendous admirer of General Bradley. I don't believe I have ever known a person to be so unanimously loved and respected by the men around and under him."[22]

Pyle's account of Bradley has been disputed by Hastings and D'Este as being more a matter of myth than fact. To defend this belief, they have cited the unpublished interview with the World War II leader and military historian S. L. A. Marshall (1900–77), which will be critiqued below. Marshall's opinions have been cited by researchers to prove that Pyle's report was American propaganda and therefore does not factually resemble the true Omar Bradley. But is it true?

It seems that if any leader would have negative remarks about Bradley it would have been the British general with whom he clashed—Field Marshall Bernard Montgomery. Yet Montgomery's memoirs are suspiciously absent of any blatant anti–Bradley remark, and they seem to have been censored to such a degree that most researchers do not take them at face value; these too must be read critically.

Throughout *The Memoirs of Field-Marshal the Viscount Montgomery of Alamein, K. G.*, any denigration of Bradley is by implication. One such "obvious" implication is recorded in the section "The Battle of the Ardennes," where Monty declares that Bradley's 12th Army Group "was split in two. His headquarters were at Luxembourg, whence he could not control the northern half of his Army Group…. I found the northern flank of the bulge was very disorganized. Ninth Army had two corps and three divisions; First Army had three corps and fifteen divisions. Neither Army Commander had seen Bradley or any senior member of his staff since the battle began, and they had no directive on which to work."[23]

Yet elsewhere Monty regarded Bradley highly, with such remarks as "I would willingly serve under Bradley" or "if public opinion in America was involved, he should let Bradley control the battle and I would gladly serve under him."[24] He also wrote, "If Ike had adopted Bradley's plan he … [wouldn't have] failed to get any of his objectives…." The British general publicly praised Bradley for his ability to firmly hold onto Bastogne.[25] Monty's entire representation remains consistent with history, and taken at face value it defends the historical personality of "the GI General."

Dwight Eisenhower, who became the supreme commander of the Allied Forces in Europe, spoke very highly of Bradley. This was especially evident in his writings to Marshall, as exemplified on September 6, 1943, when he compared Bradley to Patton: "Bradley … is, in my opinion, the best combat leader I have yet met in our service. While he possibly lacks some of the extraordinary and ruthless driving power that Patton can exert at critical moments, he still has such a force and determination that even in this characteristic he is among our best."[26] Ike even went so far as to call Bradley "a jewel to have around" and spoke highly of him throughout his communications and writings.[27]

Bradley entered the war as the "understudy" of the famous General George Patton. However, Patton had his own changing opinions on Bradley and his approach to leadership. For example, in his diary on July 14, 1944, he wrote that Bradley didn't have "any backbone."[28] Yet he spoke very highly of Cobra, an operation for which Bradley is often criticized for being too rash. Patton noted, "Cobra ... is the best operation which has been planned so far"—if it worked, of course. Writing to Eisenhower on July 28 of that same year, Patton said, "Bradley certainly has done a wonderful job. My only kick is that he will win the war before I get in. However, nothing can be done about that."[29] A few weeks later on August 17, Patton noted to H. H. Arnold that it was "a great pleasure and privilege to work with General Bradley...."[30]

While Patton's alternating opinion of Bradley seems generally positive, he would also write privately to his wife, Beatrice, that Omar the "tent maker" liked to have "large discussions and took no chances" and that he was "too conservative," wishing Bradley were a little more daring.[31] On November 11, 1944, Patton wrote to Eisenhower concerning the 83rd Division in reserve for the First Army. Patton noted, "I suppose that Hodges and Middleton have been working on Brad for a week and this, added to his natural timidity, caused him to make this decision. I hope history records his moral cowardice."[32]

By December 27, Patton again changed his opinion, recording in his diary, "Bradley left at 1000 to see Ike, Montgomery, and Smith. If Ike will put Bradley back in command of the First and Ninth Armies, we can bag the whole German army. I wish Ike were more of a gambler, but he is certainly a lion compared to Montgomery, and Bradley is better than Ike as far as nerve is concerned."[33]

Then on January 12, Patton again wrote approvingly in his diary of Bradley, stating that if Bradley were assigned control of the First Army, it "will be very advantageous, as Bradley is much less timid than Montgomery."[34] Still later on January 23, Patton wrote that Bradley's plan to attack "is good and I think it will succeed."[35] One of Patton's final reflections on the general was recorded in his diary on January 26, 1945, where he wrote, "Bradley leaves for his new command post at Namur today.... I called on him ... to say goodbye. He is a good officer but utterly lacks 'it.' Too bad."[36] Elsewhere, Patton claimed Bradley was "a swell fellow," observing that after he left II Corps he wrote to him, saying, "I want to repeat that I never enjoyed service with anyone as much as you and trust that someday we can complete our warlike operations."[37]

It seems from Patton's inconsistent writings that Bradley's caution was personally frustrating to him at times (as Blumenson critiqued); however, what Patton deemed slow and cautious must be seen in light of Patton's own aggressive leadership style. This style is laid out in Patton's personal and emotional definition of leadership, which he explained in a letter to his son George on January 16, 1945:

> Leadership ... is the thing that wins battles. I have it—but I'll be damned if I can define it. Probably it consists in knowing what you want to do and then doing it and getting mad if anyone stepps [sic] in the way. Self-confidence and leadership are twin brothers...."[38]

Patton's leadership style, which involved emotion, passion, and confidence, can be juxtaposed to Bradley's steady and calculative process. These different approaches to leadership were based on two very different personalities; however, when combined with each other, both styles were highly effective in battle. Still, there is nothing in Patton's writings that would discredit Bradley's ability as a leader.

Historian and British soldier Constantine FitzGibbon, who knew Bradley only marginally during World War II, noted that General Omar Bradley was "a soldier and a man for whom I had, have, and shall always retain, a feeling of total and quite unabashed hero-worship, an emotion to which I may say I was no more susceptible then than I am now [1971]."[39]

George H. Waple, III, who served as Omar's personal aide from 1948 to '49, called him a "great man." He noted his kindness to strangers and that he helped people whenever he could.[40] He told an anecdote that again evidenced Bradley's warm nature:

> Even though rank has its privileges many officers took great pride in introducing themselves with their rank preceding their name. I had lived with this policy all my service years, however, there was one man who really impressed me once or twice, and once in particular. I was chauffeuring Five Star General Omar N. Bradley back to the Pentagon and as we got to the Memorial Bridge circle there were several cars that seemed lost. The General stated, "Waple, pull up beside that car," with this he put his window down and stated, "I am Omar Bradley, can I help

you?" Usually the folks in the car were very surprised to see the General, in fact, so surprised that they could not answer.[41]

S. L. A. Marshall's infamous testimony is commonly used to question Bradley's leadership ability, but when taken in context, it actually tells quite a different story. Marshall spoke highly of Bradley, stating that his "relations with General Bradley were always of the finest." Though Marshall did note, "I have to say, I don't rate him as highly as General Eisenhower did or some others of his contemporaries do. As a commander, I think, he had some high qualities. He was steadfast."[42] This quote proves that even one of the most historically negative remarks against Bradley was not really as harsh as it may first seem when considered in its entirety. Marshall also claimed that he did not consider Bradley to be "an inspired thinker" and he believed that Montgomery's staff were more "competent" as planners than Bradley's. "Most of the inspired ideas," Marshall wrote, "came out of the 21st Army Group rather than out of Bradley's headquarters."[43]

There is also the infamous quote that D'Este (who seems to have held something against Bradley) cited to question Bradley's leadership abilities and role as the GI's General:

> He was played up by Ernie Pyle.... The GIs were not impressed with him. They scarcely knew him. He's not a flamboyant figure and he didn't get out much to troops. And the idea that he was idolized by the average soldier is just rot....

Yet this reference was part of a larger context in which Marshall was actually complimenting Bradley. Note the rest of Marshall's full statement:

> He didn't make that much of an imprint. For instance, the imprinting couldn't compare with Patton's on the minds of troops. I say my relations with him were extraordinary. He did me countless favors. Whenever I asked him to do anything, he was more than gracious and willing and he figured prominently in several of my key moves.... It was his steering of this through his staff and their prompt return to us that made us feel at least that we had freeway and that we could operate."[44]

Marshall claimed that Patton's imprint on the troops was greater than Bradley's had been. This squares with what is known about the historical personalities of each officer and makes more sense in this context. D'Este's referencing of this snippet seems strange as it seemingly puts a harsher tone into Marshall's "oral history" and omits the appreciative words from the end of it. Regardless of this context, the overwhelming proof of history validates the leadership skills of Bradley based on the men who knew him and served under him. One such proof can be found in the remarks of Russian General Marshal Ivan S. Konev (1897–1973) when Konev awarded Bradley the Order of Suvorov, first class.

Konev recorded his own impressions of Bradley and his leadership style. He noted that Bradley was a man of his word and apparently a very genuine individual. He also respected his penchant for history, as Bradley eagerly listened while Konev told him tales of the legendary Russian military leader Alexander Suvorov (1729–1800) and his Italian and Swiss campaigns. After all, Bradley was assigned the same level of rank (honorary) as Suvorov, and it was only fitting that he would understand the prestige that such an award afforded.[45] It was the highest award the Russians had for commanders of large formations, and Konev had been personally instructed by Stalin to present this award to Bradley directly.

Though they spoke through interpreters, Konev later wrote in his memoirs the following favorable impression:

> A professional soldier, he was strong, calm, and reserved. Judging from our exchange on military subjects, his analysis of events was accurate and interesting, and he realized the importance that powerful artillery, tanks, and aviation had acquired during the war. He understood the nature of modern warfare well and accurately differentiated the primary from the secondary. I felt he also had a profound understanding of artillery matters and appraised our tanks, their armament, armor, engines, etc. with a knowledgeable eye. In sum, I both felt and could see that the man beside me was well oriented in the use of all arms of the services, and this, in my opinion, is the primary mark of a highly qualified commander. I had the impression that here was a military man in the full sense of the word, an army leader worthy of representing American troops in Europe.[46]

While there are certainly differing views of Bradley's leadership, it seems that very few of his fellow soldiers disputed his leadership prowess. The very fact that he earned the highest rank available in the army proves that this was not the case of blind chance or dumb luck. Bradley was for all intents and purposes an extremely capable leader.

Conclusion

As the director of *This Is Your Life* noted in a personal letter to General Bradley, "From the fields of Missouri to the five star general of the U.S. is a difficult journey to make." The overall picture conveys that while Bradley had shortcomings as a leader, his life served as an authentic picture of what true leadership looks like across a number of fields, including both military and business. As one reporter for *Life* reflected in an article on June 5, 1944: "Since he has none of the theatrical qualities of a Patton or a Montgomery, his place in history will depend entirely on his performance. But if he does prove to be a great general, the kindness and simplicity which now make him a good man will make him a very great man."[47] History has shown Bradley to be that "very great man," and his life serves as an inspiration to leaders of all sorts. As such, this next section will examine the key tenets of Omar's leadership style.

II. Key Leadership Traits

Some of Bradley's major military characteristics were systematically identified by Alan Axelrod in his book *Bradley*. These included:

1. Understanding terrain and its importance in battle
2. Looking at the battle from the perspective of the enemy
3. Figuring out the logistics of every battle
4. Remembering the importance of each individual soldier

While these principles have become typical practices in modern warfare, Bradley kept them at the forefront of his leadership style. His focus on the individual soldier was evident in his nickname "the GI General" and "the Soldier's General." Bradley's abilities speak for themselves, and his concentration on the individuality of each soldier is still reflected in the military today, most notably through slogans such as "Be All You Can Be" and "Army of One." One can question Bradley's conservative nature and criticize his "thinking before acting approach," but few can deny he was both a capable and effective leader. This section will attempt to identify some of the key traits that made Omar Bradley such an effective leader.[48]

Leadership Development

Omar identified several key "laws of leadership," one of which was a core trait: leadership development. He adamantly believed that leaders should always be training up other leaders beneath them. Bradley had his own process for identifying new leaders among his people and began by first looking for men and women who knew their business well and were equipped to handle the task at hand. He developed a certain criteria for picking new leaders and officers, which he explained. First, "you look for a man who has leadership and many other qualities. He must have mental and physical energy and a strong work ethic." As Bradley noted, "you never hear of a lazy man getting very far." Above all else, he must have character and the "courage of his convictions. He must have human understanding and consideration for others." The general remarked, "Usually, leaders have all of these qualities, but an exceptional military leader has one or more of these qualities to an outstanding degree." Thus, leadership development is based on character, energy, and an ability to identify and train up new leaders.

Bradley was adamant about this skill and explained, "I don't want to overemphasize leadership of senior men. My interest extends to leaders of all ranks. I would caution [anyone] to remember that an essential qualification of any good leader is the ability to recognize, select, and train junior leaders."

Bradley even had a generic system for testing out new leaders. He noted, "There is no better way to develop leadership than to give the youngster or other individual a job involving responsibility and let him work it out. Try to avoid telling him how to do it. That, for example, is the basis of our whole system of combat orders. We tell the subordinate unit commander what we want him to do and leave the details to him. I think this system is largely responsible for the many fine leaders in our services today. We are constantly training and developing younger officers and teaching them to accept responsibility." This quote indirectly reveals another universal leadership trait that cannot be overlooked—problem-solving skills. A good leader is able to solve issues and deal with any complications that may arise. Bradley's leadership style avoided micromanaging and provided a healthy span of accountability and freedom.

Good Leaders Lead

Bradley claimed that "while it takes a good staff officer to initiate an effective plan, it requires a leader to ensure that the plan is properly executed." This is the very reason that he taught that the work of collecting information, studying it, drawing a plan, and making a decision are 10 percent of the job while seeing that plan through is the remaining 90 percent.

The general told a story on this point concerning World War I hero General Pershing. While inspecting a certain area, Pershing found a project that was not going very well, even though the second lieutenant in charge seemed to have a pretty good plan. General Pershing asked the lieutenant how much pay he received, and when the lieutenant replied: "$141.67 per month, sir," General Pershing said: "Just remember that you get $1.67 for making your plan and issuing the order, and $140.00 for seeing that it is carried out." Bradley noted his own interpretation of this story: "I am not sure that I would go to that extreme. Certainly in these days, problems are complex and good staff work plays a large part in resolving them. I have known commanders who were not too smart, but they were very knowledgeable about personnel and knew enough to select the very best for their staffs." Thus, a good leader is one who causes or inspires others, staff or subordinate commanders, to do the job at hand. Effective leadership goes past the theoretical and becomes both practical and applicable.

Furthermore, Bradley insisted, no leader knows it all. A strong leader should encourage the members of his staff to speak up if they think the commander is wrong in his decision or on a particular course of action. "A confident leader should invite constructive criticism and it is a grave error for any leader to surround himself with a 'Yes' staff. All leaders should inform the members of their staffs that anyone who does not disagree once in a while with what is about to be done is of limited value and perhaps should be shifted to some other place where he might occasionally have an idea."

In the following quote, Bradley refers specifically to the decision-making process: "After a decision is made, everyone must be behind it 100 percent. I thought the British were admirable in this respect during World War II. No matter how much discussion there had been on a subject, as soon as a decision was made you never heard any doubts expressed. You had to believe that everyone involved in making the decision had never entertained any ideas except those expressed in the decision." And so Bradley identifies solidarity as another key trait of dynamic leaders—they must be able to agree to disagree but then get past their own disagreements for the sake of the greater cause.

Another main requirement for the successful leadership of any organization is having the proper organization and structure. Bradley noted, "The military has to have organization. I am a very strong believer in the proper organizational structure because it keeps too much power from getting into the wrong hands. Everybody knows what they are supposed to do, what their colleague is supposed to do, and they know their responsibilities."[49] A good army is an organized army, and having the proper infrastructures in places is absolutely crucial to success.

Putting the Right People in the Right Places

Once, Bradley was asked in an interview how he responded when a particular soldier's performance had disappointed him. He replied: "Sometimes a man doesn't turn out quite as well as you had hoped, but it usually doesn't take too long to discover that before he can do any great damage. A man might make an error once in a while which you could overlook and let him profit by that error, but when a man proves without question that he is not capable of handling a certain job, then he should be removed at once."[50]

There were many instances when Bradley had to reassign subordinate officers. Though several researchers have viewed this as proof that he was too demanding, he nevertheless had high expectations for his officers, and rightfully so, as they were responsible for implementing key battle decisions/directives. One example of this could be seen in his dealings with the 8th Division. Following D-Day, Bradley inspected the 8th Division, having heard of its training. It was not moving the way he expected it to move.

Bradley decided to meet with the commanding officer, who immediately asked to be replaced. Bradley was confused at this situation, as he had received word that this was a "beautifully-trained division," and believed that its major flaw was that they looked to their commander for every decision. In today's jargon, this leader would be labeled as a "micromanager"; he did not delegate his authority very well. This commander's main downfall was that he had failed to train up his younger regimental, battalion, and company commanders to think and act for themselves. This broke what Omar considered a main tenet of good leadership.

This unit would move ahead ten or fifteen miles on the front, getting outside the range of the division commander, and then they would have to stop and wait. Bradley told the commander that he would be back in 48 hours and in the meantime he should get his troops moving forward. When he returned a couple days later, Bradley found that the commander had failed to obey this order. The commander greeted him and said, "Brad, I guess you'll have to relieve me," to which Omar responded, "Bill, I don't think I have any choice. You are just not getting anywhere, and we've got to get this division going."[51]

In the end this commander was replaced, along with sixteen other officers, but within two weeks this group became one of the army's most effective divisions.[52] This goes to show how important it is to put the right people in the right places. It is a matter of record that Omar relieved several other commanding officers over the course of the war, including the commanders of the 90th and 79th divisions. He noted, "You couldn't take the risk, you couldn't delay it, you replace them."[53]

Lead by Example

There were numerous reasons why Bradley would replace various officers in the field under his command. Sometimes the officer just did not possess the necessary leadership skills in battle, but it could sometimes be more complicated. There was one trait that Bradley firmly believed was essential for leadership: An officer should lead by example.

He commonly dismissed officers if he found out that they were hiding out behind the front lines and making their men take risks while they commanded from the comforts of a basement. Bradley believed that a commander could not inspire his men by sitting in a basement far away from the front line of action.

Bradley further noted that as an effective officer, "you got to get out and show them you are interested and you are willing to take chances with them."[54] When Bradley reassigned these officers, it usually marked the end of their advancement and careers; this included a reduction (i.e., demotion) that could mean they would become permanent colonels with no opportunity to climb the ranks. They were also taken out of the field of battle and sent back stateside.

Reassigning men was never an easy task, especially for Bradley, who knew many of these officers personally. Once Bradley even had to relieve one of his closest friends, a commander named Pinky Ward. Ward had been a cadet in his company at West Point and they had served together a number of times, yet he was just not the right man for the position. Being able to reassign leaders, as difficult as it may be, remains an essential element in being an effective leader, especially when fighting in war.[55]

Bradley acquired the reputation of moving too close to the action on the front lines of battle, contrary to what S. L. A. Marshall and Monty implied. Bradley's own commanding officer, General George C. Marshall, spoke to him about this very issue, to which Bradley responded,

"General, the men take their chances getting shot at up at the front line, and I have to take my chances going around to visit them."[56]

The general also believed that a great leader must be willing to come alongside his troops and read his men. One day, General Bradley called in an aide and ordered nighttime forced marches for the green troops. They would be in stages. Five miles, then ten, and finally twenty-five. Bradley issued instructions that he would take part in the twenty-five-mile march.

Sometime later, in the dark of night, Bradley fell in with his troops. He eased his way into the ranks. There was much grousing and complaining. A GI bellowed, "I'd like to get my hands on the SOB who thought this one up." A soft Missouri voice came out of the darkness. "Yup. He ought to be hanged." It was a long time before the marchers learned that voice belonged to Bradley.

Self-Confidence

Another key leadership trait that the general identified was self-confidence. Bradley noted, "The men won't have confidence in a leader who doesn't have confidence in himself."[57] He also observed, "You must have confidence in yourself, your unit and your subordinate commanders—and in your plan."

Bradley related an incident in which he had to relieve a senior commander because his men had lost confidence in him. This meant, of course, that he could not expect maximum performance from that particular division. After being relieved, the officer came to Bradley at his headquarters and showed him a file of references given to him at his request by the governors of all the towns his division had passed through. Bradley remarked, "If he had confidence in himself, he would not have felt the need for those letters. After seeing the letters, I told the officer that if I had ever had any doubts as to whether I had to relieve him, those doubts were now removed. His letters proved beyond question that he had lost confidence in himself, so it was no wonder the men had lost confidence in him."

Know Your Business

When asked about the DNA of leadership, Bradley responded:

> ... there are many essential characteristics that a good employee must possess, but a few come to mind as perhaps the most important.... He

must know his job, without necessarily being a specialist in every phase of it.

Specialties dominate almost every problem faced today by the military leader or the business manager [or religious facilitator]. This individual must get deeply enough into his problem that he can understand it and intelligently manage it, without going so far as to become a specialist himself in every phase of the problem.

Thomas J. Watson of IBM once said that genius in an executive is the ability to deal successfully with matters he does not understand. This leads to another principle of leadership which I have often found neglected, both in the military and in business [and church]. While you need not be a specialist in all phases of your job, you should have a proportionate degree of interest in every aspect of it—and those concerned, your subordinates, should be aware of your interest. A leader should be well-rounded whenever possible, with adequate experience in the field.

Energy/Ability

Bradley believed that both mental and physical energy were essential to successful leadership. He asked the rhetorical question, "How many really good leaders have you known who were lazy, or weak, or who couldn't stand the strain?" General Sherman was a good example of a leader with outstanding mental and physical energy. During the advance from Chattanooga to Atlanta, he would go for days at a time with only two or three hours of sleep per night, yet he was constantly in the saddle reconnoitering, and he often knew the dispositions and terrain so well that he could maneuver the enemy without a serious fight and with minimum losses.

Conversely, a sick commander is of a limited value. It is not fair to the troops under him to have a leader who is not functioning at 100 percent capability. Bradley noted that he had to relieve several senior commanders during World War II because of illnesses, and he pointed out that Napoleon didn't lose a major battle until Waterloo, where he was a sick man.

Recognition and Consideration

Omar also maintained that recognition was a key trait of effective leadership:

> You must get around and show interest in what your subordinates are doing, even if you don't know much about the technique of their work.

And, when you are making these visits, try to pass out praise when due, as well as corrections or criticism.

We tend to speak up only when things go wrong. This is such a well-recognized fact that a "Complaint Department" is an essential part of many business firms. To my knowledge, no comparable facility exists anywhere to expedite the handling of praise for the job well done—it need not be extravagant.

Bradley claimed that "a leader should possess human understanding and consideration for others. A good leader must remember that men are not robots and should not be treated as though they were machines." Bradley was not suggesting coddling subordinates, but understanding that men "are highly intelligent, complicated beings who will respond favorably to human understanding and consideration. By this means their leader will get maximum effort from each of his employees/subordinates. He will also win their loyalty—and in this connection, it is well to remember that loyalty goes down as well as up. The sincere leader will go to bat for his subordinates when such action is needed."

Resolve

Bradley also firmly believed that a good leader must at times be stubborn and resolute. He made reference to the opening stanza of the West Point cadet prayer, which begins:

> O God, our Father, Thou Searcher of human hearts, help us to draw near to Thee in sincerity and truth. May our religion be filled with gladness and may our worship of Thee be natural.
> Strengthen and increase our admiration for honest dealing and clean thinking, and suffer not our hatred of hypocrisy and pretense ever to diminish. Encourage us in our endeavor to live above the common level of life. *Make us to choose the harder right instead of the easier wrong*, and never to be content with a half truth when the whole can be won.[58]

Bradley believed that when a leader has come to a decision after thorough analysis, and when he is sure he is right, he must stick to it even to the point of stubbornness. Ulysses S. Grant furnished a good illustration of this particular trait. He never knew when he was supposed to be defeated. A less stubborn man might have lost at Shiloh.

Bradley was of the opinion that there is usually one best solution, but that any good plan, boldly executed, is better than indecision. He noted, "There is usually more than one way to obtain results."

The general revealed his own decision-making process, which began with first weighing out the problem and then asking himself two questions: (1) What solutions are there? (2) What are the pros and cons of each solution? He would then decide upon the best course of action. Omar noted, "We have a lot of that, of course, in the military. Every decision we make has to go through that process, particularly in combat."[59]

A great leader will also possess some degree of imagination. He must be able to visualize and think through his decision ahead of time. Whether it be an administrative decision, or one made in combat, the possible results of that decision must be plain to the one making it.

Character

While there are other qualities that can contribute to effective leadership, one of the key traits that the general promoted through his life and constant example was character. While this word can have many different meanings, Bradley applied it in a broad sense to describe a person who has high ideals, who stands by them, and who can be trusted absolutely. "Such a person will be respected by all those with whom he is associated. And, such a person will readily be recognized by his associates for what he is."

"It has been said that a man's character is the reality of himself," Bradley remarked. "I don't think a man's strength of character ever changes. I remember a long time ago when someone told me that a mountain might be reported to have moved, I could believe or disbelieve it, as I wished, but if anyone told me that a man had changed his character, I should not believe it." An effective leader must have a strong sense of character and integrity.

Luck/Opportunity

Bradley believed that a good leader must have both luck and opportunity. He must be able to recognize when opportunity is knocking and be able to rise and open the door when it does.

Experience

Bradley never discounted the value of experience, as it forged good judgment. He noted:

Someone may remind you that Napoleon led armies before he was 30; and that Alexander the Great died at the age of 33. Napoleon, as he grew older, commanded larger armies. Alexander might have been even greater had he lived longer and had more experience. In this respect, I especially like General Bolivar Buckner's theory that "Judgment comes from experience and experience comes from bad judgment."

Patience/Perseverance

Patience was another attribute that Bradley believed was one of the unsung keys to great leadership. This is curious since some have faulted his decisions as a general by claiming that he was not aggressive enough in battle (i.e., too patient); however, there was a deep-seated reason behind Bradley's belief in this particular attribute. After the war was over, Omar told a story concerning a childhood memory:

> Before my father died, when I was very young, he used to say, "Be patient, son." I guess every father has said that to every son many times. It took me many years to understand it. I first learned what he meant when I tried to fish in a hurry. I found that it doesn't work. For a boy to catch a fish with an angleworm, he has to carefully seek out and find worms. Then he has to bait the hook and patiently wait for a fish to take the lure. He has to be calm and quiet. Most of all, to fish successfully, he has to keep trying.

Bradley carefully explained that his father didn't mean the "sittin'" type of patience," but rather the "workin'" type. In other words, whatever one's goal may be, don't sit and wait, but keep on working at it. Bradley believed that patience is a commodity equally as important as power. His belief in this trait was rooted in his interpretation of the Bible, referencing Habakkuk, the minor prophet, who cried to God: "O, Lord, how long shall I cry, and thou wilt not hear? Even cry out into thee of violence and thou wilt not save!" The general believed that America had been founded on "the Christian ideal for every man" and that "Christianity itself, with the help of faithful men, has lasted almost 2,000 years." He concluded that there is no chance of failure unless it be through haste.

Bravery

This article has assembled all of the general's various self-proclaimed laws of leadership, compiling them from a number of his writings. However, the final key to Bradley's view of leadership can best be summarized in one word: bravery. Bravery is the steering wheel that directs each leader. One must be willing to take some risks in his role. Bradley defined bravery thus:

> ... courage in action. It is that quality which enables a man to face up to a challenge with decision and purpose—whether that challenge be imminent physical danger, or the defense of a moral principle, or a pioneering effort in new fields of progress.
>
> In each case, the brave man stakes everything, with conviction and fortitude, whether risking his life in open combat, or barricaded behind a desk to meet the attacks of his critics. Fully aware of the dangers, he coolly carries out a plan of action without regard for the cost to himself. He follows through when lesser men are turned aside by doubt or fear for personal safety [or comfort].
>
> Foolhardy heroics are not bravery. The truly brave man is quiet, calm and self-possessed. He makes no display of audacity. His emotions are held in check while he calculates the outcome of the most drastic move. Bravery is courage in action. It produces the deed which sets the hero above the coward.[60]

Bradley exemplified each of these traits, especially bravery. He rode to the front lines with his men and had several close calls with death, yet he adamantly believed that a good leader leads through example.

Conclusion

Bradley listed the key attributes of leadership: leadership development, delegation (thereby avoiding micro-management), organization, putting the right people in the right places, self-confidence, leading by example, recognition and consideration, energy and ability, patience and perseverance, resolve, character, luck, experience, and—perhaps most importantly of all—bravery. Despite his strong opinions concerning leadership, Bradley was quick to point out that he believed leadership could be taught and learned to some degree through experience and dedication.

While Bradley's leadership abilities have been called into question by certain military researchers and personalities, this article has shown that none of these disputes really hold up to careful scrutiny and appear to be more the personal reflections and opinions of the minority. Bradley was both kind and compassionate. He strove to be fair, and he maintained that competent soldiers should advance even if they aren't the most capable leaders at that time. This is not to say that Bradley did not have his fair share of faults and shortcomings, because he certainly did. He was known to countermand Patton's orders, and he occasionally ignored direct orders from Eisenhower. He was cautious and, like most people today, he preferred the company of those who were most like him and his personality. He was also not a very faithful husband to his first wife, Mary. Yet despite these faults, he was able to orchestrate one of the largest military forces in history and thereby secure a victory for the Allied forces. Regardless of these issues, there were few generals in history finer than Omar Nelson Bradley.

Appendix II:
The Screen Credits
of Kitty Buhler Bradley
Connecting Washington, D.C., to Hollywood

Esther Kitty [Buhler] Bradley was a prominent Hollywood writer. Given her strong work ethic, her natural beauty, and her penchant for writing, Kitty's success in Hollywood is not surprising. As a result of her writing, she came into contact with many famous personalities. This list of her screen credits presents the reader with an understanding of Kitty's indirect connections to various Hollywood stars. Her relationship to these individuals also serves to bridge the gap between Washington, D.C., and Hollywood, as America turned to both during World War II.

World War II overlapped a period in American history known as the "Golden Age of Television." During the 1940s, FM radio became the standard that was used to relay news about the Second World War, and television was rapidly becoming a common form of news and entertainment. Also, many famous stars served in the army and participated in World War II, as did many starlets who toured the front lines with the USO. Washington and Hollywood teamed up to inspire the men and women serving overseas and reminded them what they were fighting for.

Kitty herself was extremely successful in her writing endeavors, yet when she married Bradley she traded in this fame to become "Mrs. Omar Nelson Bradley." She never regretted this decision, as she openly claimed that she preferred to be remembered for her fifteen years as Bradley's wife rather than for her own career as a Hollywood writer. It seems that history has granted her this wish and validated her dedication to the general.[1] Despite her own choice to focus on her role as "Mrs. Omar Bradley," it should be clarified that Kitty's life was fascinating in its own right and she had many accomplishments.

Her earliest experiences in the entertainment industry began with a childhood enchantment with radio programs that she listened to daily. She described a picture of her childhood during the long, hot summers spent in New York City. The windows of her parents' small apartment would be propped open and the popular soaps of the '30s would blare through her radio and her neighbors.' She recalled the significance of one program in particular that could be seen as foreshadowing her own later relationship with "Omie":

> "Our Gal Sunday" asked the same question five times a week at 12:45 p.m.
> "Can this girl from a mining town in the West find happiness as the wife of a wealthy and titled Englishman?" To paraphrase that: "Can this girl from Manhattan's lower Eastside find happiness as the wife of an attractive and legendary American hero?"
> You bet your ass she can—in America.[2]

Kitty did find happiness in the end, both in her relationship with Omar Bradley and through her career as a writer.

On February 3, 2004, twenty-three years after Omar's death, Kitty joined her husband on the other side of existence. At eighty-one years of age, Kitty died of pneumonia while residing in Rancho Mirage, California. Her body was laid to rest just as she predicted, in Arlington National Cemetery alongside Omar and his first wife, Mary. Upon her death, most of her materials and papers were donated to the University of Texas in El Paso.

* * * * *

Television

The Untouchables
　"Come and Kill Me" (November 27, 1962)
　Starring: Robert Stack (1919–2003), the future co-star in the comedy *Airplane* (1980) and eventual host of the hit television series *Unsolved Mysteries* (1987); and Dan Dailey, who happened to be the first actor to receive the Golden Globe Award.

My Three Sons for Don Fedderson Productions
  1. "The Second Time Around" (January 25, 1962)
  Starring: Fred MacMurray (1908–1991), the later star of *The Shaggy Dog* (1959) and *The Absent Minded Professor* (1961); William Frawley (1887–1966), who played the famed landlord "Fred Metz" on the long-running sitcom *I Love Lucy*; Patricia Barry (1922–), the television actress known for her over 130 television and movie appearances, most notably *The Donna Reed Show, The Twilight Zone, Alfred Hitchcock Presents*, and *Perry Mason*.

  2. "Cherry Blossoms in Bryant Park" (March 12, 1964)
  Starring: Fred MacMurray and William Frawley.

  3. "Charley and the Kid" (January 21, 1965) (appears to be listed as "Bub's Other Family" in Kitty's personal resume)
  Starring: Fred MacMurray and William Frawley.

The 20th Century–Fox Hour
  1. "Threat to a Happy Ending" for Twentieth Century–Fox (May 29, 1957)
  Starring: William Bendix (1906–1964), the star of *The Babe Ruth Story* (1948); and Lori Nelson (1933–), a co-star in the *Creature from the Black Lagoon* (1954) who was also briefly engaged to Burt Reynolds.

  2. "Men in Her Life" (April 17, 1957)
  Starring: Phyllis Kirk (1927–2006), who appeared with Vincent Price in *House of Wax* (1953); Kendall Scott, the actor known for *The Young Lions* (1958) and *The 20th Century–Fox Hour* (1955); and Malcolm Broderick (1944–) who starred in *Man on Fire* (1957).

  3. "City in Flames" (March 6, 1957)
  Starring: Ann Jeffreys (1923–), who is best known for her work in *The Delphi Bureau* (1972) and for playing David Hasselhoff's mother in the television show *Baywatch*; Jeff Morrow (1907–1993), the actor who served in the army during World War II and starred in such series as *Bonanza* and *Perry Mason*; Kevin McCarthy (1914–2010), who appeared in over two hundred television and movie roles and whose part in *Death of a Salesman* (1951) got him nominated for an Academy Award for Best Supporting Actor; and the multi-talented actress Lurene Tuttle (1907–1986), who was known as the "First Lady of Radio," appearing in everything from *I Dream of Jeannie* to *The Munsters* to *Little House on the Prairie* and others. She later pursued a career as an

acting coach and was known for re-training radio actors returned from fighting in World War II.

Legal Affair for NBC (live)
   Starring: Franchot Tone (1905–1968), the star of *Mutiny on the Bounty* (1935), and Nina Foch (1924–2008), the Dutch-born actress who is remembered for her portrayal of "cool, calculating female roles" such as in *An American in Paris* (1951), which won the Best Picture Oscar.

The Ray Milland Show
   1. "Tryout" for Revue Productions (March 10, 1955)
   Starring: Ray Milland (1907–1986), one of Paramount's most "durable" actors who was under contract with them from 1934 to 1948 and is best known for his Academy Award-winning portrayal of an alcoholic writer in *The Lost Weekend* (1945); Phyllis Avery (1922–2011), who played Peggy McNutley in the CBS comedy show titled *Meet Mr. McNutley* (which was renamed *The Ray Milland Show* during its second season); and Hans Conried (1917–1982), famous especially for his voice-over roles including Captain Hook and Mr. Darling in Disney's *Peter Pan* (1953), Snidely Whiplash in *The Rocky and Bullwinkle Show* (in the segment "Dudley-Do-Right"), and the Grinch/narrator from *Dr. Seuss's Halloween is Grinch Night*, among others. He was also a film and television actor who appeared in *I Love Lucy, The Beverly Hillbillies, The Love Boat, Hogan's Heroes*, and many more.

   2. "Faculty Wife" (May 26, 1955)
   Starring: Ray Milland and Phyllis Avery.

Dragnet for Mark VII Productions [1952]
   1. "The Human Bomb"
   2. "The Big Actor"
   3. "The Big Death"
   4. "The Big Mother"
   5. "The Big Cast"
   6. "The Big Speech"
   7. "The Big Parrot"
   8. "The Big Moody"

The Screen Credits of Kitty Buhler Bradley 191

9. "The Big Blast"
10. "The Big Trial"
11. "The Big September Man"
12. "The Big Phone Call"
13. "The Big Casing"
14. "The Big Lamp"
15. "The Big Jump"
16. "The Big Sorrow"
17. "The Big Elevator"
18. "The Big Seventeen"
19. "The Big Trio"

Starring: Jack Webb (1920–1982), most commonly known for his starring role in this television series, though he was also the founder of the production company called Mark VII Limited, which produced another popular police show, *Adam-12* (1968–1975); Barton Yarborough (1900–1951), the actor who tragically, after filming the second episode of this series, suffered a heart attack and died four days later at the age of 51; and Barney Phillips (1913–1982), another actor who served in World War II and played his role as Sgt. Ed Jacobs in this series. He is also known for his minor roles in various television series as *I Love Lucy*, *Perry Mason*, and *The Andy Griffith Show* and for starring in the iconic *Twilight Zone* episode titled "Will the Real Martian Please Stand up?"

Dateline Tokyo for Mickey Rooney Productions
Starring: Dane Clark (1912–1988), known for his ability to play an "average Joe" character and voted the sixteenth most popular star in 1945.

The Cara Williams Show for CBS
Starring: Cara Williams (1925–), actress best known for her role as the mother in *The Defiant Ones* (1958) and for her Emmy nomination in the category of Best Lead Actress in a Comedy.

Valentine's Day for Twentieth Century–Fox
"Cherry Blossoms in New York" (1964)

Starring: Tony Franciosa (1928–2006), well-known for his portrayals of "moody, troubled characters" as exemplified in his appearance as a morphine addict in *A Hatful of Raid* (for which he was nominated for a Tony award).

Tightrope for Greene-Rouse Productions, Screen Gems
   "Gangster's Daughter" (1960)
   Starring: Mike Connors (1925–), the actor and producer best remembered for playing the role of Detective Joe Mannix in the CBS series *Mannix*; and Barton MacLane (1902–1969), the actor, playwright and screenwriter who played General Martin Peterson on the hit 1960s NBC television show *I Dream of Jeannie*.

Petticoat Junction for Filmways
   "Billie Jo's First Job" (1965)
   Starring: Bea Benaderet (1906–1968), the radio and television personality who starred in *Petticoat Junction* and in *Green Acres*, played the Shady Rest Hotel owner Kate Bradley. She was also the original voice of Betty Rubble during the first four seasons of *The Flintstones*, played the role of Jed's cousin, Pearl Bodine, in *The Beverly Hillbillies*, and was the voice of "Granny" in the original Sylvester the Cat and Tweety segments on the cartoon *Looney Tunes*.

The Beachcomber for Filmasters, Inc.
   Starring: Cameron Mitchell (1918–1994), the actor and television star who also served as a bombardier in the U.S. Army during World War II. He was a founding member of the Actor's Studio in New York City.

Bewitched for Screen Gems
   Starring: Elizabeth Montgomery (1933–1995), the famous actress who played "Samantha" in the series *Bewitched*. This ultimately earned her five Emmy Awards and four Golden Globe nominations.

The Jan Clayton Show for Sam Marx, Metro-Goldwyn-Mayer
   Starring: Jan Clayton (1917–1983), the film, television, and musical theater actress probably best known today for playing Jeff Miller's mother on the television series *Lassie* (1954) (which was syndicated under the title *Jeff's Collie*).

Tessa for Sam Marx

The Screen Credits of Kitty Buhler Bradley 193

You Can't Take It with You for Screen Gems
    Starring: Cecil Kellaway (1890–1973), the South African actor remembered for his work on *The Luck of the Irish* (1948) and *Guess Who's Coming to Dinner* (1967); and Barbara Britton (1919–1980) who was known for her Western film roles and especially for her role of Pam North on the mystery television series *Mr. and Mrs. North* (1952).

Irene (based on the Broadway play) for Producing Artists Corporation

Those Whiting Girls (1957)
    "The Feminine Touch" for Metro-Goldwyn-Mayer

Mother Carey's Chickens for Walt Disney Productions (adapted from the novel by Kate Douglas; however, it was never released in these one-hour segments).

Daniel Boone for Mickey Rooney Productions
    Starring: Mike Connors

A Scene with a Star for H-L Productions
    Starring: Barbara Jo Allen (aka Vera Vague) (1906–1974), best remembered for her catch phrase "You dear boy," her appearance in at least 60 movies and television series, and for her introduction in 1939 on the NBC Matinee where she became a regular along with Bob Hope. Most modern readers would know her primarily from her voice-over work for several Disney pictures, including the fairy Fauna in *Sleeping Beauty* (1959) and the Scullery Maid in *The Sword in the Stone* (1963).

Lady with a Badge for Robert Lord, Screen Televideo Productions

Crossroads for Ted Lloyd

J. D. (Juvenile Delinquency) for Goodson-Todman Productions

Roommates for Freed TV Productions

Chaos for Ted Kneeland Productions

Soldier of Fortune, 13 teleplays for half-hour series for Volcano Productions

The Hal Roach Rascals for Seven Arts Productions
Produced by: Hal Roach, Jr.

* * * * *

Films

China Doll for Batjac Productions
  Starring: Victor Mature (1913–1999), the Italian-American actor who tried to enlist in the navy but was rejected because he was color-blind. The same day he was rejected, he also signed up for the coast guard, where he was accepted. He is known primarily for this film as well as *One Million B. C.* (1940) and *Lady in the Dark* (1944); Li LiHua (1924–), the Chinese-born actress nicknamed "The Evergreen Tree" of Chinese cinema, most famously remembered for this film and several Chinese movies; Sue Whitman (1946–), the English actress best known for her roles in *A Nice Girl Like Me* (1969), *Smashing Time* (1967) and *Crossroads* (1964); Ward Bond (1903–1960), who played Bert in the Christmas movie *It's a Wonderful Life* (1946) as well as Captain Clayton in *The Searchers* (1956). Bond is well-known for starring in various Western films and worked on 23 films with the legendary actor (and personal friend of Kitty) John Wayne.

A Dram of Love for Frank Borzage and Charles M. Tanner Productions

Private Custody for Joseph Turner Productions

Two on a Tour for Ted Kneeland Productions

Tokyo Police for Mickey Rooney Productions

Green Okinawa documentaries made for the U.S. State Department

The Other Love
  Starring: Barbara Stanwyck (1907–1990), the American actress who made 85 films in 38 years before she began working in television. While she worked in many different movies, some of the most notable include *Stella Dallas* (1937) (which led to two Academy Award nominations for Best Actress, Leading and Supporting), *The Thorn Birds*

(1983) (which won her a Golden Globe award), and for her own television series *The Barbara Stanwyck Show* (1961), for which she also won three Emmy awards; David Niven (1910–1983), the English actor and renowned novelist who had several iconic roles including Phileas Fogg in *Around the World in 80 Days* (1956) and Sir Charles Lytton (aka the Phantom) in *The Pink Panther* (1963). Niven also served in World War II, where he was re-commissioned as a lieutenant; and Richard Conte (1910–1975), the Italian-American actor who worked in many movies, most notably in the heist film *Ocean's 11* (1960) (which was remade in 2001) and *The Godfather* (1972). His career picked up during World War II, when most of the time he played a soldier, most notably in *The Purple Heart* (1944) and *A Walk in the Sun* (1945).

Eugene Aram, based on the novel by Bulwar-Lytton

Variety, based on E. A. Dupont's film

Cairo Incident
　　　Starring: John Garfield (1913–1952), the American actor known for his portrayal of rebellious and working-class characters. Curiously enough, Garfield's career ended early when his name became unfairly associated with the Communist paranoia of the 1950s. He was actually called to testify before the U.S. House Committee on Un-American Activities (HUAC), but the mere accusation alone was enough to have him blacklisted in Hollywood. He died from a heart attack on May 9, 1952.

＊ ＊ ＊ ＊ ＊

Newspapers

United Press
　　　Kitty traveled through the Orient from 1949–1951, covering general news stories during the Korean conflict.

Stars and Stripes
　　　Kitty was in charge of writing her daily column titled "Kapers by Kit."

Ryukian Review
　　　She was on the editorial staff of the Okinawa weekly.

＊ ＊ ＊ ＊ ＊

Magazines

Tokyo Fanfare
 Kitty was also on the editorial staff of this Tokyo magazine.

Additionally, she wrote several human interest pieces and non-fiction articles, which were published in various national and international magazines. Some of these titles included the following: "Twenty-one Days of Clarity" for which she subjected herself to a 21-day complete water fast; "Under the Skin," a curious article that Kitty wrote during her stay at the Fontana Nudist Colony, where she made her entrance wearing only earrings and high heels; "Government Girl in Tokyo," which was based on Kitty's contact with the government girls during the occupation in Japan; "Tombs and Typhoons" was based on her experience while hiding out during a typhoon in Okinawa; "The Ghosts of Shuri" was a story that followed five Japanese artists who lived in an abandoned castle in Okinawa; "Rice Cakes and Wine" surveyed the influence that the Eastern culture made on the French Impressionists; "Buckles and Bows" focused on the psychology behind the custom of bowing in the Orient: "Pen with a Feather" was based on Eastern literature; "Christ and Shintoism" explored the influence that the occupation forces had on the indigenous Japanese ancestral religion known as Shintoism; and finally, "Husbands I Have Known," which was based on her own diary and the men that Kitty loved and left throughout her lifetime. It is a shame that this manuscript has been lost, as it surely would have revealed some of the intimate details of Kitty's private yet glamorous life.

* * * * *

Other Projects

 Lectures before cultural, professional groups, and various Universities
 Guest panelist on radio and television programs
 Dialogue director, with Mervyn LeRoy (1900–1987), the noted film director and producer at 20th Century–Fox
 Story editor, Beeman Productions, Sam Goldwyn Studios

* * * * *

Associations
Writers Guild of America West, Inc.
Greater Los Angeles Press Club
The National League of American Pen Women, Inc.
El Paso Arts Alliance

Chapter Notes

Preface

1. Throughout his work, Blumenson appears overtly critical of Bradley and even puts motivation and emotions into his personality that are speculative at best. These opinions are exemplified in the following statement; no sources are cited to indicate how he arrived at such a deep-seated, personal opinion of Bradley:
> But secretly [Bradley] chafed under the idea and often wished that he could be a star performer too. During the campaign he would enjoy a flush of success beyond his wildest dreams. That moment would induce in him a self-exhilaration close to dizziness.... Bradley, to a certain extent, would lose sight of the established objectives and pursue unrealistic goals.

Martin Blumenson, *The Battle of the Generals: The Untold Story of the Falaise Pocket—The Campaign That Should Have Won World War II* (New York: William Morrow, 1993), 31, 80.

2. Carlo D'Este, *Patton: A Genius for War* (New York: HarperCollins, 1996), 2.

3. D'Este in his biography of Patton insisted that Bradley despised Patton even though there is ample evidence to the contrary. D'Este, *Patton*, 5. Bradley also wrote, "The fact of the matter is that not in Tunisia, nor ever, did I feel a 'professional rivalry' with George Patton, or any sort of jealousy...." Omar N. Bradley and Clay Blair, *A General's Life* (New York: Simon & Schuster, 1983), 139.

4. My theory of why Bradley's papers were destroyed could also possibly begin to explain why his fellow officer, Walter Bedel Smith, seemingly destroyed his own personal correspondence with his wife, Nory. D. K. R. Crosswell, *Beetle: The Life of General Walter Bedell Smith* (Lexington: University Press of Kentucky, 2010), 1045.

5. Blumenson, *Battle of the Generals*, 27.

Introduction

1. Kitty Buhler, "Horses Make Strange Bedfellows or My Life with Omar Bradley: Outline for an Autobiography" (ca. 1981), 12.

2. Adrian Lewis, *Omaha Beach: A Flawed Victory* (University of North Carolina, 2001), 162.

3. Jim DeFelice, *Omar Bradley: General at War* (Washington, D.C.: Regnery History, 2011), 357.

4. "World Battlefronts, WESTERN FRONT: Destroy the Enemy," *Time*, December 4, 1944. Accessed January 28, 2013. http://content.time.com/time/magazine/article/0,9171,796955,00.html#ixzz2pxZ5qCRX.

5. DeFelice, *Omar Bradley*, 22.

6. Ibid., 109.

7. Alan Axelrod, *Bradley: A Biography* (London: Palgrave Macmillan, 2008), 186.

8. Charles Whiting, *Bradley* (New York: Ballantine Books, 1971), 159.

Chapter 1

1. Omar N. Bradley, "What We Owe Our Country," *Reader's Digest*, August 1949.
2. A. J. Liebling, "Profiles: Five Star Schoolmaster II," *The New Yorker* (March 10, 1951): 50.
3. Omar N. Bradley, "General Bradley's Handwritten Memoir of his Army Career before World War II," West Point Library Archives, n.p.
4. Bradley, "General Bradley's Handwritten Memoir," 17.
5. Ibid., n.p.
6. Kitty Buhler, "Research for the Breakout Between 1955 and 1970," Special Collections Department, University of Texas at El Paso, 36.
7. Bradley, "General Bradley's Handwritten Memoir," 1.
8. Buhler, "Research for the Breakout," 38.
9. Blair, *A General's Life*, 24.
10. Bradley, "General Bradley's Handwritten Memoir," n.p.
11. Blair, *A General's Life*, 26.
12. Liebling, "Profiles: Five Star Schoolmaster II," 54.
13. Ibid.

Chapter 2

1. Alan Axelrod, *Bradley: A Biography* (London: Palgrave Macmillan, 2008), 16.
2. Bradley, "General Bradley's Handwritten Memoir," 1–2.
3. Ibid.
4. Liebling, "Profiles: Five Star Schoolmaster II," 56.
5. Ibid., 58.
6. Ibid.
7. Colonel Red Reeder, *Omar Nelson Bradley: The Soldiers' General* (2011), Kindle edition.
8. Blair, *A General's Life*, 33.
9. Bradley, "General Bradley's Handwritten Memoir," 19.

Chapter 3

1. Bradley, "General Bradley's Handwritten Memoir," 16–18.
2. Blair, *A General's Life*, 36.
3. Bradley, "General Bradley's Handwritten Memoir," 446.
4. Ibid.
5. Blair, *A General's Life*, 37.
6. Ibid., 40.
7. Mary had seemingly contracted it from her next-door neighbor in Columbus, Missouri. Bradley, "General Bradley's Handwritten Memoir," 52.
8. Blair, *A General's Life*, 42.
9. Ibid.
10. DeFelice, *Omar Bradley*, 27.
11. Bradley, "General Bradley's Handwritten Memoir," 52.
12. Blair, *A General's Life*, 43.
13. Kitty Buhler, "Research for the Breakout," 133.
14. Blair, *A General's Life*, 43.
15. "We find that 32.17% of veterans report extramarital sexual relationships, which is twice the rate among nonveterans in this sample ... [and] conclude that veteran status is strongly associated with extramarital sex and divorce ... the higher rates of infidelity among veterans may be related to selection factors; military experiences, such as deployment; or postmilitary factors." Andrew S. London, Elizabeth Allen, Janet M. Wilmoth, "Veteran Status, Extramarital Sex, and Divorce: Findings from the 1992 National Health and Social Life Survey," *Journal of Family Studies* 34:11 (September 23, 2013).
16. Mary Quayle Bradley, "To the Ladies Who Come Up in June," *The Pointer* (April 18, 1952): 132–133.

Chapter 4

1. Blair, *A General's Life*, 46.
2. Bradley, "General Bradley's Handwritten Memoir," 11.
3. Blair, *A General's Life*, 48.
4. DeFelice, *Omar Bradley*, 34.

Chapter 5

1. Blair, *A General's Life*, 50.
2. Steve Harrison, "Brad" *The Missouri Freemason* (Spring 2008): 47.
3. He had several works in his library on betting; one such title was marked up and written in. This book was titled *Betting Horses to Win* by Les

Conklin (fifth printing, 1958) and in its pages was a loose cut-out called "Pointers for Serious Players" by J. D. Smith.

4. Bradley, "General Bradley's Handwritten Memoir," 31.

5. Blair, *A General's Life*, 55.

Chapter 6

1. Bradley, "General Bradley's Handwritten Memoir," 54–55.

2. "Profiles: Five-Star Schoolmaster I," 39; Liebling, "Profiles: Five Star Schoolmaster I," 69–70.

3. Omar N. Bradley, "Golf is my Antidote," *The Golfer* (November 1949).

4. Blair, *A General's Life*, 58.

5. Jim DeFelice noted that at his next post his interests would change, as he cared for a friend's horse and rode it for about an hour per day. DeFelice, *Omar Bradley*, 38.

6. Bradley, "General Bradley's Handwritten Memoir," 44.

7. Ibid., 45.

8. Ibid., 60.

Chapter 7

1. Liebling, "Profiles: Five Star Schoolmaster I," 74.

2. Ibid., 66.

3. Omar N. Bradley, "Golf is my Antidote," *The Golfer* (November 1949).

4. Frank E. Grizzard, "False Teeth" in *George Washington: A Biographical Companion* (Santa Barbara, Calif.: ABC-CLIO, 2002), 103–105.

5. Blair, *A General's Life*, 61.

6. Ibid.

7. Blair, *A General's Life*, 63.

8. Liebling, "Profiles: Five Star Schoolmaster I," 38.

9. Buhler, "Research for the Breakout," 30.

10. Blair, *A General's Life*, 74.

11. Though it remains uncertain how Hitler would have dealt with the U.S. in a post–World War II context, Gerhard L. Weinberg noted: "The trajectory of Hitler's view of the future was as terrible as it was consistent. He began with an aspiration for world domination by the racially superior Germans and ended, in his last testament, with an admonition to the German people to adhere to his racial concepts. And he wanted them to do so under the leadership of a successor whose vision reached across the oceans to the wider world that might yet, someday, fall under German domination." Gerhard L. Weinberg, *Visions of Victory: The Hopes of Eight World War II Leaders* (Cambridge University Press, 2005), 37.

12. Blair, *A General's Life*, 76.

13. Bradley, "General Bradley's Handwritten Memoir," 81.

Chapter 8

1. Blair, *A General's Life*, 81.

2. Ibid., 83.

3. Ed Cray, *General of the Army: George C. Marshall, Soldier and Statesman* (Lanham, Md.: Rowman & Littlefield, 2000), 150.

4. Blair, *A General's Life*, 86.

5. Ibid., 89.

6. Blair, *A General's Life*, 89.

7. Ibid., 92.

8. Ibid., 93.

9. "Leadership: General of the Army Omar N. Bradley," *The New Age*, February 1975.

10. Blair, *A General's Life*, 102.

11. Bradley, "General Bradley's Handwritten Memoir," 108.

Chapter 9

1. Blair, *A General's Life*, 107.

2. Ibid., 104.

3. Ibid., 105.

4. Ibid.

5. Ibid., 106.

6. Ibid., 107.

7. Liebling, "Profiles: Five Star Schoolmaster II," 57.

8. Blair, *A General's Life*, 111.

Chapter 10

1. Bradley, "Handwritten Memoirs," 148–149; Blair, *A General's Life*, 142.

2. Blair, *A Soldier's Story*, 29.

3. Bruce Watson, *Exit Rommel: The Tunisian Campaign, 1942–43* (Mechanicsburg, Pa.: Stackpole Books, 2007), 93.

4. Steven Zaloga, *Kasserine Pass*

1943: Rommel's Last Victory (Oxford, England: Osprey Publishing, 2005), 90.
5. Buhler, "Research for the Breakout," 158.
6. Blair, *A General's Life*, 138.
7. Ibid., 139.
8. Blair, *A General's Life*, 159.
9. Ibid.
10. Benjamin F. Schemmer, "A Visit with the Soldier's General: General of the Army, Omar N. Bradley," *Armed Forces Journal* (June 1972).

Chapter 11

1. Blair, *A General's Life*, 170.
2. Ibid.
3. Ibid., 178.
4. Ibid., 179.
5. Ibid., 181.
6. Ernie Pyle, *Brave Men* (Lincoln, NE: Bison Books, 2001), 326–327. Patton biographer Carlo D'Este disagreed with Pyle's sentiments, disputing Bradley's popularity. He quoted Marshall, observing: "The GI's were not impressed with him. They scarcely knew him. He's not a flamboyant figure and he didn't get out much to troops. And the idea that he was idolized by the average soldier is just rot." D'Este, *Patton*, 467. Despite D'Este's highjacked claims, it seems based on the overwhelming reports of soldiers who had served with Bradley (Pyle included) that he was mistaken in his critique. One such "soldier" was none other than General Dwight Eisenhower, who noted his own opinion of Bradley:

> Bradley was the master tactician of our forces and in my opinion will eventually come to be recognized as America's foremost battle leader.... My high opinion of Bradley, dating from our days at West Point, had increased daily during our months together in the Mediterranean.... He was a keen judge of men and their capabilities and was absolutely fair and just in his dealing with them. Added to this, he was emotionally stable and possessed a grasp of larger issues that clearly marked him for high office.

The Papers of Dwight David Eisenhower: The Chief of Staff, vol. 6–9 (Baltimore: Johns Hopkins Press, 1970), 2234.
7. Buhler, "Research for the Breakout," 130.

Chapter 12

1. Blair, *A General's Life*, 204.
2. Ibid., 207.
3. Ibid., 211.
4. Buhler, "Research for the Breakout," 27.
5. Blair, *A General's Life*, 213.
6. Ibid., 214.
7. Ibid., 230.
8. Bradley, "General Bradley's Handwritten Memoir," 328.
9. Buhler, "Research for the Breakout," 139.
10. Buhler, "Research for the Breakout," 130–140.
11. Blair, *A General's Life*, 244.

Chapter 13

1. Paraphrased slightly from *The Collected Writings of General Omar N. Bradley: Articles, Broadcasts and Statements, 1945–1967*, III, 4–7 (4–5).
2. There have been many wonderful and accessible books written on the events surrounding the Normandy D-Day invasion. One such intriguing account was written by historian Stephen E. Ambrose, *D-Day: June 6, 1944: The Climactic Battle of World War II* (New York: Simon & Schuster, 2013).
3. Blair, *A General's Life*, 251.
4. Charles Whiting naively expressed this opinion, though he provided no source or documentation to back up his view:

> ... with rare exceptions they were unable to prove themselves or their true qualities, for they were never faced with those adverse conditions which show a general for what he really is. Even the surprise German counterattack in the Ardennes does not allow us to see General Bradley under these circumstances, for in spite of the seriousness of the situation after 16th December 1944 ... no one ever thought that it could lead to a defeat.... At the

most the German offensive could mean a setback but never a defeat. Whiting, *Bradley*, 159.
  5. Buhler, "Research for the Breakout," 27.
  6. Bradley, "General Bradley's Handwritten Memoir," 353.
  7. Ibid., 352–353.
  8. Buhler, "Research for the Breakout," 171.
  9. Ibid., 191.
  10. Ibid., 195.
  11. Ibid., 192.
  12. Pyle, *Brave Men*, 329.
  13. Bradley, "General Bradley's Handwritten Memoir," 396–397.
  14. Ibid., 397–398.
  15. Buhler, "Research for the Breakout," 29.
  16. Chet Hansen's diary, May 1, 1945.

Chapter 14

  1. Blair, *A Soldier's Story*, 308–309.
  2. Chet Hansen's diary, June 25, 1944.
  3. Chet Hansen's diary, June 27, 1944.
  4. Blair, *A Soldier's Story*, 313.
  5. Bradley, "General Bradley's Handwritten Memoir," 357.
  6. Buhler, "Research for the Breakout," 177.
  7. Blair, *A Soldier's Story*, 314.
  8. Buhler, "Research for the Breakout," 143.
  9. A. J. Liebling, "Profiles: Five Star Schoolmaster I," *The New Yorker* (March 3, 1951): 70. As Clay Blair noted in a letter to Carlo D'Este on March 11, 1986, through his research on Bradley, he discovered that no heavy drinkers "ever got anywhere with Bradley" with the sole exception of Col. B. A. "Monk" Dickson, the II Corps G-2, "whom he greatly admired but who was the only principal staff officer on Bradley's First Army staff who failed to be promoted to brigadier general." D'Este, *Patton*, 892.
  10. Russel F. Weigley, *Eisenhower's Lieutenants: The Campaign of France and Germany, 1944–1945* (Indiana University Press, 1990), 152.
  11. Blumenson, *The Battle of the Generals*, 138.
  12. Kenneth W. Hechler, "VII Corps in Operation 'Cobra,'" *CMH*, 64.
  13. Blair, *A General's Life*, 280–281.
  14. *The Patton Papers, 1940–1945*, ed. Martin Blumenson (Boston: Houghton Mifflin, 1974), 489.

Chapter 15

  1. Buhler, "Research for the Breakout," 169.
  2. Ibid., 96.
  3. Blair, *A General's Life*, 352.
  4. Ibid., 354.
  5. Ibid., 356.
  6. For more information on Smith, see D. K. R. Crosswell, *Beetle: The Life of General Walter Bedell Smith* (Lexington: University Press of Kentucky, 2010).
  7. Blair, *A General's Life*, 357.
  8. Ibid., 380–381.
  9. DeFelice, *Omar Bradley*, 301.
  10. Blair, *A General's Life*, 382–383.
  11. Ibid., 401.
  12. Ibid., 404.
  13. Bradley, "General Bradley's Handwritten Memoir," 415.
  14. Blair, *A General's Life*, 418.
  15. Ibid., 428.
  16. Bradley, *A Soldier's Story*, 540. This story has recently been adapted into a best-selling book (and movie starring George Clooney) written by Robert M. Edsel and titled *The Monuments Men: Allied Heroes, Nazi Thieves and the Greatest Treasure Hunt in History* (New York: Center Street Publishing, 2010).
  17. Blair, *A General's Life*, 436.
  18. Buhler, "Research for the Breakout," 33.
  19. Jim DeFelice, "Bradley & Marlene." Accessed January 29, 2014. http://www.jimdefelice.com.
  20. Buhler, "Horses Make Strange Bedfellows," 27.

Chapter 16

  1. Kitty Buhler, "The Omar Bradley Story," 83.
  2. Ibid., 84.
  3. Ibid., 83–84.
  4. This incident is briefly alluded to in Merle Miller, "Bradley H.[sic] Bradley: People on the Home Front," *Yank* 4:21 (November 9, 1945): 6. In his memoirs, Bradley noted, "I was invited to lunch by

Marshall Konev who commanded the Russian Army Group opposite mine. It was an interesting day and I invited him and his staff to lunch at my headquarters a couple of weeks later." Bradley, "General Bradley's Handwritten Memoirs," 417.
    5. Blair, *A General's Life*, 551.
    6. Though this same meeting was attributed to Colonel Courtney Hicks Hodges, it seems possible that he went with Bradley and Allen to this luncheon meeting. G. Patrick Murray, "Courtney Hodges: Modest Star of WWII," *American History Illustrated*, January 1973, 24.
    7. Buhler, "Research for the Breakout," 103.
    8. Seweryn Bialer, ed., *Stalin and His Generals: Soviet Military Memoirs of World War II* (New York: Pegasus, 1969), 553.
    9. Buhler, "Research for the Breakout," 104–105.
    10. Bradley, "General Bradley's Handwritten Memoir," 417.
    11. Buhler, "Research for the Breakout," 106–111.
    12. Bialer, *Stalin and His Generals*, 556.
    13. Blair, *A General's Life*, 440.
    14. Bradley, "General Bradley's Handwritten Memoir," 419.
    15. Blair, *A General's Life*, 442.
    16. Ibid., 442.

Chapter 17

    1. Liebling, "Profiles: Five Star Schoolmaster II," 40–42.
    2. Blair, *A General's Life*, 446.
    3. Ibid., 462.
    4. Ibid., 449.
    5. Omar N. Bradley, "It's Ability That Counts," *County Government* (May 1961).
    6. Liebling, "Profiles: Five Star Schoolmaster I," 70.
    7. George H. Waple III, *Country Boy Gone Soldiering* (Bloomington, Indiana: X-Libris [self-published], 1998), 120.
    8. Ibid., 121.
    9. George H. Waple, III, *Country Boy Gone Soldiering* (Bloomington, Ind.: X-Libris [self-published], 1998), 124–125.
    10. Ibid., 123.
    11. Ibid., 123–124.
    12. Ibid., 119.
    13. Ibid., 125.
    14. Blair, *A General's Life*, 553.
    15. Liebling, "Profiles: Five Star Schoolmaster I," 64.

Chapter 18

    1. The acronym RYCOM was the U.S. Army's Ryukyus Command, which would later be named the (USCAR) United States Civil Administration of the Ryukyus (USCAR). This was the occupation of the Ryukyu Islands, which included the island of Okinawa.
    2. Buhler, "Rykom Kapers," *Pacific Stars and Stripes* (June 16, 1950): 2.
    3. Buhler, "Horses Make Strange Bedfellows," 1.
    4. Ibid., 2.
    5. Ibid.
    6. Buhler, "Horses Make Strange Bedfellows," 3.
    7. Ibid., 4.
    8. Carole Kass, "Mrs. Omar Bradley Lives With History," *Times Dispatch*, February 10, 1969.
    9. Charles Whiting called Bradley "the general with the homely features." Whiting, *Bradley*, 8.
    10. Blair, *A General's Life*, 665.
    11. Ibid.
    12. They hadn't mass-produced this product yet, but as Bradley noted, "... to meet our government's need we accelerated our program and turned out a timer—a two and one-half inch cube—that weighed only eight ounces and satisfactorily accomplished what had previously been done by 32 pounds of radio equipment in satellites. Without the Accutron timer our satellites would send out signals indefinitely, and in time every broadcasting wavelength in space would be occupied." "Lessons of Leadership: Organizing With Confidence," *Nation's Business* (April 1969): 114, 117.
    13. Blair, *A General's Life*, 665.
    14. Ibid.
    15. Ibid., 666.
    16. Buhler, "Horses Make Strange Bedfellows," 12.
    17. Ibid., 10.
    18. Ibid., 11.
    19. Blair, *A General's Life*, 666.

20. Buhler, "Horses Make Strange Bedfellows," 12.
21. A brief description of Kitty's estate can be found online at "Mrs. Bradley's Stuff—Not a Pretty Story." Accessed on February 26, 2014. http://writeoutloud.typepad.com/writeoutloud/2005/04/mrs_bradleys_st.html
22. Buhler, "Horses Make Strange Bedfellows," 6.
23. Ibid., 10–11.
24. Ibid., 11.
25. Kass, "Mrs. Omar Bradley Lives With History."
26. This was taken from the brief biography of Kitty's life based on a finding aid created by Julie Graham, "Finding Aid for the Kitty Buhler Scripts, ca. 1950s–ca. 1960s," Online Archive of California. Accessed February 5, 2014. http://pdf.oac.cdlib.org/pdf/ucla/pasc/buhle228.pdf
27. Anon., "Rooney, Tokyo," *The Billboard* (July 24, 1954): 2, 31.
28. Buhler, "Horses Make Strange Bedfellows," 15.
29. Ibid.
30. "Screen Credits of Kitty Buhler Bradley," University of Texas at El Paso, Special Collections Department.

Chapter 19

1. Blair, *A General's Life*, 666.
2. Kass, "Mrs. Omar Bradley Lives With History."
3. Blair, *A General's Life*, 666.
4. Buhler, "Horses Make Strange Bedfellows," 14.
5. Blair, *A General's Life*, 666.
6. Buhler, "Horses Make Strange Bedfellows," 16.
7. Ibid., 20.
8. Buhler, "Horses Make Strange Bedfellows," 21.
9. Ibid., 20–21.
10. "Tape Four of Interview Three with General of the Army Omar N. Bradley" (October 1975), 29.
11. Ibid., 29–30.
12. Ibid., 30.
13. Buhler, "Horses Make Strange Bedfellows," 21.
14. Blair, *A General's Life*, 666.
15. Ibid.
16. Buhler, "Horses Make Strange Bedfellows," 22.
17. Blair, *A General's Life*, 666.
18. Ibid.
19. Kass, "Mrs. Omar Bradley Lives With History."
20. Buhler, "Horses Make Strange Bedfellows," 24.
21. Ibid., 25.
22. Ibid., 26–27.
23. Ibid., 27.
24. Kass, "Mrs. Omar Bradley Lives With History."
25. Buhler, "Horses Make Strange Bedfellows," 29.
26. Ibid.
27. Kass, "Mrs. Omar Bradley Lives With History."
28. Ibid.
29. By her own admission in Buhler, "Horses Make Strange Bedfellows," 29.
30. Ibid., 30.
31. Ibid., 31–32.
32. Ibid., 32.

Chapter 20

1. Buhler, "Horses Make Strange Bedfellows," 33.
2. Ibid.
3. Ibid., 34.
4. Liebling, "Profiles: Five Star Schoolmaster I," 72.
5. "Organizing with Confidence," *Nation's Business* (April 1969): 115.
6. Schemmer, "A Visit with the Soldier's General: General of the Army, Omar N. Bradley."
7. "General Omar Bradley: My Visit to Vietnam, The GI's General of World War II Reports on his 14 Days with Troops," *LOOK* 31:23 (November 14, 1967): 29–35.
8. "General Omar Bradley: My Visit to Vietnam," 31.
9. "Bradley to Help on Film," *New York Times*, August 14, 1968, 31.
10. Buhler, "Horses Make Strange Bedfellows," 37.
11. Not everyone got along as well with Kitty as Kindred did. In fact, Bradley's Pentagon secretary actually resigned within three months of Kitty's and Bradley's marriage, writing him a letter that compared the two "Mrs.

Bradleys" to each other: "I don't know of any other officer's wife who expects that her husband's secretary in the Pentagon will do all her personal work. They would be aghast at the idea, Mrs. Bradley knew better. I can't recall that the second Mrs. Bradley ever *asked* for my help. She simply gave me the work as though I had no choice." "Letter from Alma Hickey to Omar Bradley," *The Bradley Papers*, USMA (December 19, 1966).

12. Dave Bakke, "Gen. Omar Bradley's Personal Assistant Looks Back," *State Journal-Register* (May 2014) http://www.sj-r.com/article/20140501/News/140509895#140509895/?Start=1&_suid=1409689442365002745789638999241> [accessed on September 2, 2014].

13. Buhler, "Horses Make Strange Bedfellows," 38.

14. Ibid., 39.

15. Ibid., 40.

16. John Dreyfuss, "Gen. Bradley Has Successful Brain Surgery," *Los Angeles Times*, March 27, 1975; "Gen. Bradley Suffers Stroke," *Los Angeles Times*, March 22, 1975.

17. Buhler, "Horses Make Strange Bedfellows," 40.

18. "Gen. Bradley Has Surgery," *Richmond Times Dispatch*, March 27, 1975.

19. Buhler, "Horses Make Strange Bedfellows," 41.

20. Alden Whitman, "Gen. Omar N. Bradley Dead at 88; Last of Army's Five-Star Generals," *New York Times*, April 9, 1981, A1.

21. "Bradley's Body Is Flown to Capital," *New York Times*, April 14, 1981, B18.

Chapter 21

1. Bradley received a "medal of honor" from the Lotos Club, an organization that included many prestigious individuals such as the Rockefellers.

2. Liebling, "Profiles: Five Star Schoolmaster I"; Army Archerd, "Just For Variety," *Variety* (May 28, 1975).

3. Larry J. Myers, "Army Birthday Bash by CPT," *Soldiers* (November 1975): 30.

4. Carol Soucek, "Screenwriter Carl Foreman Returns to L.A.," *Los Angeles Herald-Examiner*, August 28, 1975.

5. Fran Erwin, "Applause Drowns Threat of Uninvited Bomb," *The News* (Van Nuys, California), July 22, 1975.

6. Joyce Haber, "Mayer, Thalberg from Inside Out," *Los Angeles Times*, July 4, 1975.

7. Archerd, "Just For Variety."

8. Joyce Haber, "Mayer, Thalberg from Inside Out," *Los Angeles Times*, July 17, 1975.

9. "General Bradley, Viet POW's honored at Army Ball," *Association of the United States Army Newsletter* 7:1 (Summer 1972).

10. Laurie Johnston, "Notes on People: When the Private Enjoyed Dining With the General," *New York Times*, May 26, 1980, B21.

11. Presley sent Bradley an autographed picture at some point calling him General "Baby" Bradley. Also, upon seeing the movie *Patton* and Bradley's role in that movie, Presley—a gun enthusiast—sent Bradley a factory-engraved, presentation-grade Colt .45 M1911A1 (serial number 306707-C) as a Christmas present. It was delivered on December 4, 1970, along with a handwritten note on a holiday gift card that read, "To Gen. Bradley, With Love and Respect, Elvis Presley." It is currently housed in the U.S. Army Heritage Museum in Carlisle Barracks.

12. Bob Thomas, "For Inauguration Festivities," *The Victoria Advocate* (January 14, 1981): 10c.; Harold C. Schonberg, "Inaugural Spotlight Shifts to Sinatra and Show Biz," *New York Times*, January 20, 1981. The Omar Bradley exhibit at the U.S. Army Heritage Museum holds a thank-you letter written and signed by Frank Sinatra.

13. A verified autograph of General Omar Bradley in 2014 can fetch anywhere between $200 to $12,000 depending on the historical nature of the signed item/document.

Appendix I

1. Williamson Murray and Allan R. Millett, *A War to Be Won: Fighting The Second World War* (Belknap Press of Harvard University Press, 2000), 418.

2. Whiting, *Bradley*, 159.

3. Charles Edward Kirkpatrick, *Omar Nelson Bradley: The Centennial* (Washington: Department of Defense [?], 1992), n.p.

4. Blumenson, *The Battle of the Generals*, 268.

5. *The Patton Papers*, 481, 486, 608, 630, 648. Blair, *A General's Life*, 183, 208, 411–412.

6. Blumenson, *The Battle of the Generals*, 27.

7. Carlo D'Este, *Eisenhower: A Soldier's Life* (New York: Henry Holt, 2002), 404.

8. Carlo D. Este, *Patton: A Genius for War* (New York: HarperCollins, 1995), 469.

9. Max Hastings, *Armageddon: The Battle for Germany, 1944–45* (New York: Random House, 2004).

10. Caleb Carr, "Introduction to the Modern Library War Series," *A Soldier's Story* (New York: Random House, 1999), xii.

11. A. J. Liebling, "Profiles: Five Star Schoolmaster I," *The New Yorker* (March 3, 1951): 62.

12. Liebling, "Introduction," *A Soldier's Story* (New York: Random House, 1999), xviii.

13. Wesley Clark, "Foreword," *Bradley: A Biography* (New York: Palgrave Macmillan, 2008), viii.

14. D'Este, *Patton*, 468.

15. George S. Patton, *War As I Knew It* (New York: Houghton Mifflin, 1995), 225.

16. Blair, *A General's Life*, 97. Russell F. Weighley in his book *Eisenhower's Lieutenants* (1990), described Bradley as a "cool, quiet, and dominant commander," which seems to be a solid description of his leadership. Russell F. Weighley, *Eisenhower's Lieutenants* (Bloomington: Indiana University Press, 1990), 84, 195.

17. Axelrod, *Bradley*, 190.

18. D. K. R. Croswell, *Beetle: The Life of General Walter Bedell Smith* (Lexington: University Press of Kentucky, 2010), 172.

19. General J. Lawton Collins also seemingly thought highly of Bradley, as H. Paul Jeffers noted in his biographical account. H. Paul Jeffers, *Taking Command: General J. Lawton Collins From Guadalcanal to Utah Beach* (New York: Penguin Books, 2009), 276.

20. D. K. R. Crosswell, "The Chief of Staff: The Military Career of General Walter Bedell Smith," *Contributions in Military Studies* 110 (New York: Greenwood Press, 1991), 315.

21. Bradley, *A Soldier's Story*, 536.

22. Pyle, *Brave Men*, 326.

23. *The Memoirs of Field-Marshal the Viscount Montgomery of Alamein, K. G.*, (London: Collins, 1958), 276.

24. Ibid., 241, 272.

25. Ibid., 256, 277.

26. *The Papers of Dwight David Eisenhower, The War Years: II* (Baltimore: Johns Hopkins University Press, 1979), 1388.

27. Ibid.

28. *The Patton Papers, 1940–1945*, 481.

29. Ibid., 489.

30. Ibid., 517.

31. Ibid., 566.

32. Ibid., 573.

33. Ibid., 608.

34. Ibid., 622.

35. Ibid., 628.

36. Ibid., 630.

37. D'Este, *Patton*, 466.

38. *The Patton Papers, 1940–1945*, 625.

39. Constantine FitzGibbon, "The GI's General," *Bradley* (New York: Ballantine Books, 1971), 159.

40. Waple, *Country Boy Gone Soldiering*, 119, 126.

41. Ibid., 126.

42. SLA Marshall Papers, "Oral History Volume I," Section 5: Bound Copies, USAMHI, Box 14: 6.

43. Ibid.

44. SLA Marshall Papers, "Oral History Volume I": 6.

45. *Stalin and His Generals: Soviet Military Memoirs of World War II*, ed. Seweryn Bialer (New York: Pegasus Books, 1969), 555.

46. *Stalin and His Generals*, 556.

47. Charles Christian Wertenbaker, "Omar Nelson Bradley: History and 'The Plan' Place Greatness within the Grasp of a Quiet Man from Missouri," *Life* 16:23 (June 5, 1944): 112.

48. This section is derived largely

from two separate articles: Gen. Omar Bradley, "Lessons of Leadership, Part XLVII: Organizing With Confidence," *Nation's Business* (April 1969) and Omar Bradley, "Leadership: General of the Army Omar N. Bradley," *The New Age* (February 1973).

49. Gen. Omar Bradley, "Lessons of Leadership, Part XLVII: Organizing with Confidence," *Nation's Business* (April 1969), 114.

50. Bradley, "Lessons of Leadership," 116.

51. Ibid., 155.
52. Ibid., 155.
53. Ibid., 153.
54. Ibid., 154.
55. Ibid., 156.
56. Ibid., 115.
57. Ibid., 116.

58. The West Point cadet prayer is still commonly prayed by cadets today:

O God, our Father, Thou Searcher of human hearts, help us to draw near to Thee in sincerity and truth. May our religion be filled with gladness and may our worship of Thee be natural.

Strengthen and increase our admiration for honest dealing and clean thinking, and suffer not our hatred of hypocrisy and pretence ever to diminish. Encourage us in our endeavor to live above the common level of life. *Make us to choose the harder right instead of the easier wrong*, and never to be content with a half truth when the whole can be won. Endow us with courage that is born of loyalty to all that is noble and worthy, that scorns to compromise with vice and injustice and knows no fear when truth and right are in jeopardy. Guard us against flippancy and irreverence in the sacred things of life. Grant us new ties of friendship and new opportunities of service. Kindle our hearts in fellowship with those of a cheerful countenance, and soften our hearts with sympathy for those who sorrow and suffer. Help us to maintain the honor of the Corps untarnished and unsullied and to show forth in our lives the ideals of West Point in doing our duty to Thee and to our Country. All of which we ask in the name of the Great Friend and Master of all. Amen [emphasis added].

59. Bradley, "Lessons of Leadership," 115.

60. General Omar N. Bradley, "What is Bravery?" *This Week Magazine* (May 15, 1955) taken from *Magazine Articles by General of the Army, Omar N. Bradley, 1947–1969*, vol. 1. (n.d., n.p.), 86.

Appendix II

1. "Today's Newsmakers Heard Around the World," *The Lewiston Journal*, September 3, 1981, 18.

2. Buhler, "Horses Make Strange Bedfellows," 10–11.

Bibliography

Books

Ambrose, Stephen E. *D-Day: June 6, 1944: The Climactic Battle of World War II*. New York: Simon & Schuster, 2013.
_____. *The Supreme Commander: The War Years of General Dwight D. Eisenhower*. Garden City, NY: Doubleday, 1969.
Atkinson, Rick. *The Day of Battle*. New York: Henry Holt, 2009.
Axelrod, Alan. *Bradley: A Biography*. London: Palgrave Macmillan, 2008.
Bialer, Seweryn, ed. *Stalin and His Generals: Soviet Military Memoirs of World War II*. New York: Pegasus, 1969.
Bland, Larry I., ed. *The Papers of George Catlett Marshall*, 5 vols. Baltimore: Johns Hopkins University Press, 1981–2003.
Blumenson, Martin. *The Battle of the Generals: The Untold Story of the Falaise Pocket—The Campaign That Should Have Won World War II*. New York: William Morrow, 1993.
Bradley, Omar N. *The Collected Writings of General Omar N. Bradley: Articles, Broadcasts and Statements*, 5 vols. [1945–1967] (typescript).
_____. *Magazine Articles by General of the Army Omar N. Bradley*, 5 vols. [1947–1975].
_____. *A Soldier's Story*. New York: Random House, 1999.
_____, and Clay Blair. *A General's Life*. New York: Simon & Schuster, 1983.
Cray, Ed. *General of the Army: George C. Marshall, Soldier and Statesman*. Lanham, MD: Rowman & Littlefield, 2000.
Crosswell, D. K. R. *Beetle: The Life of General Walter Bedell Smith*. Lexington: University Press of Kentucky, 2010.
DeFelice, Jim. *Omar Bradley: General at War*. Washington, D.C.: Regnery History, 2011.
D'Este, Carlo. *Eisenhower: A Soldier's Life*. New York: Henry Holt, 2002.
_____. *Patton: A Genius for War*. New York: HarperCollins, 1996.
Edsel, Robert M. *The Monuments Men: Allied Heroes, Nazi Thieves and the Greatest Treasure Hunt in History*. New York: Center Street Publishing, 2010.
Grizzard, Frank E. "False Teeth" in *George Washington: A Biographical Companion*. Santa Barbara, CA: ABC-CLIO, 2002.
Hastings, Max. *Armageddon: The Battle for Germany, 1944–45*. New York: Random House, 2004.

Jeffers, H. Paul. *Taking Command: General J. Lawton Collins from Guadalcanal to Utah Beach*. New York: Penguin, 2009.
Kirkpatrick, Charles Edward. *Omar Nelson Bradley: The Centennial*. Washington, D.C.: Department of Defense [?], 1992.
Lewis, Adrian. *Omaha Beach: A Flawed Victory*. Chapel Hill: University of North Carolina Press, 2001.
The Memoirs of Field-Marshal the Viscount Montgomery of Alamein, K. G. London: Collins, 1958.
Murray, Williamson, and Allan R. Millett. *A War to Be Won: Fighting the Second World War*. Cambridge: Belknap Press of Harvard University Press, 2000.
The Papers of Dwight David Eisenhower: The Chief of Staff, vol. 6–9. Baltimore: Johns Hopkins University Press, 1970.
Patton, George S. *War as I Knew It*. New York: Houghton Mifflin, 1995.
The Patton Papers, 1940–1945, ed. Martin Blumenson. Boston: Houghton Mifflin, 1974.
Pyle, Ernie. *Brave Men*. Lincoln, NE: Bison Books, 2001.
Reeder, Colonel Red. *Omar Nelson Bradley: The Soldiers' General.* Kindle edition, 2011.
Smith, Walter Bedell. *Eisenhower's Six Great Decisions, 1944–1945*. New York: Longmans, Green, 1956.
Waple, George H., III. *Country Boy Gone Soldiering*. Bloomington, IN: X-Libris [self-published], 1998.
Watson, Bruce. *Exit Rommel: The Tunisian Campaign, 1942–43*. Mechanicsburg, PA: Stackpole Books, 2007.
Weigley, Russell F. *Eisenhower's Lieutenants: The Campaign of France and Germany, 1944–1945*. Bloomington: Indiana University Press, 1990.
Weinberg, Gerhard L. *Visions of Victory: The Hopes of Eight World War II Leaders.* New York: Cambridge University Press, 2005.
Whiting, Charles. *Bradley*. New York: Ballantine, 1971.
Zaloga, Steven. *Kasserine Pass 1943: Rommel's Last Victory*. Oxford, England: Osprey Publishing, 2005.

Periodicals

American History Illustrated
Armed Forces Journal
Association of the United States Army Newsletter
The Billboard
Contributions in Military Studies
The Golfer
Journal of Family Studies
The Lewiston Journal
Life Magazine
LOOK Magazine
Los Angeles Herald-Examiner
Los Angeles Times
The Missouri Freemason
Nation's Business
The New Age
New York Times

New Yorker
The News
Pacific Stars and Stripes
The Pointer
Reader's Digest
Richmond Times Dispatch
Soldiers
State Journal-Register
Time Magazine
Times Dispatch
This Week Magazine
The Victoria Advocate

Unpublished Sources

Bradley, Kitty [Buhler]. "Horses Make Strange Bedfellows or My Life with Omar Bradley: Outline for an Autobiography," ca. 1981. Author's personal collection.

_____. "Research for the Breakout Between 1955 and 1970," Special Collections Department, University of Texas at El Paso.

_____. "Screen Credits," Special Collections Department, University of Texas at El Paso.

Bradley, Omar N. "General Bradley's Handwritten Memoir of his Army Career before World War II." USMA, West Point Library Archives.

_____. "Interview with General of the Army Omar. N. Bradley." October 1975, USMA: West Point Library Archives. [typescript].

Hansen, Chet. *Chester B. Hansen Collection*, "Omar N. Bradley's War Diary," 7 vols., USMA: West Point Library Archives.

Marshall, S.L.A. *The Papers of Samuel Lyman Atwood Marshall, 1900–1977*, USAMHI: Carlisle Barracks, Pennsylvania.

Index

Numbers in ***bold italics*** refer to pages with photographs.

alcohol 90–91, 109, 111, 145
alcoholism 38, 146, 190
Allen, Leven C. 60, 110
Arnold, Henry H. 75, 160, 171
atomic bomb 7, 120
USS *Augusta* 78–80, 82

Ball, Lucille 85
Bastogne 97, 99, 170
Battle of the Bulge (Ardennes) 1, 5, 10, 11, 12, 85, 93, 95, 97, 98, 106, 147, 170, 202 *ch*13*n*4
Benny, Jack 85
Benson Force 68
Bergen, Edgar 43
Beukema, Hal 64, 76, 82, ***83***, 115, 116, 132
Beverly Hills 132–133, 137, 139, 154
Bewitched 135, 192
Bogart, Humphrey 85
Bolling, Alexander R. 65
Bonanza 135, 189
Boone, Debby 157
Bradley, Elizabeth 39, 40, 45, 50, 53–54, 55, 57–58, 64, 75, 76, 82–***83***, 87, 104, 115, 116, 117, 123, 132, 133, 137, 142, 147, 160
Bradley, John Smith 18–20
Bradley, Kitty (Buhler) 106–107, 128, 129–153, 155, 157–158, 160, 187–197
Bradley, Mary 3, 12, 20–22, 27–36, 38–41, 44–45, 49–50, 53, 57–60, 62, 64–65, 75, ***83***, 87–88, 104, 114–120, 122–128, 131–133, 137,–138, 140–141, 144–145, 174, 186, 188, 200*ch*2*n*7
Brando, Marlon 140

Bridge, Lewis D. 62, 64, 69, 71, 76
Bulova, Arde 121
Bulova School 121–122
Bulova Watch Company 132, 137, 138
Bush, George 153

Carson, Johnny 157
Carter, Jimmy 154
Cherbourg 89–90
China Doll 135, 194
Churchill, Winston 75–77, 98, 154, 161
concentration camps 101–102, 106
Copass, Charles B. 47
Crosby, Bing 43, 85, 131, 141

D-Day (Normandy) 3, 5, 11, 32, 67, 72, 76–79, 80–87, 115, 132, 178
Davis, Bette 85
Davis, Sammy, Jr. 154
Dean, Dizzy 43
Dempsey, Jack 43
dentures 48–49
Dick, Beatrice 28–31
Dickson, Benjamin A. "Monk" 80, 203*ch*14*n*9
Dietrich, Marlene 85, 103–107, ***105***
Disney, Walt 131, 193
dogs 32, 37, 47, 59, 62, 65, 146
Dragnet 135, 190

Eichelberger, Robert L. 58
VIII Corps 95
8th Panzer Division 67
Eisenhower, Dwight "Ike" D. 3, 6, 13, 23, 42, 65, 67–69, 71, 75, 76, 79, 86, 91, 93, 95–102, 106, 114, 122–124,

213

154, 161, 170–171, 173, 186, 202*ch*11*n*6
Elbe River 101–102, 125, 169

1st Canadian Army 99
1st US Army 75
V Corps 77
Ford, Gerald 154
Forrestal, James 125

Gabor, Zsa Zsa 155
Garland, Judith 85
Gasser, Lorenzo D. 55–56
General Electric Theater 135
Germany 94, 95, 98, 99, 100, 101, 106, 123, 155, 165, 167
Godfrey, Arthur 43
Goldwyn, Sam 131; Studios 134, 138, 140, 192, 193, 196
Grant, Cary 154
Grant, Ulysses S. 128, 182
Grove, Lefty 43

Hagen, Walter 43
Hansen, Chester "Chet" 9, 62, 64, 65, 69, 71–73, 76, 78–79, 104–106, 123
Heifetz, Jascha 108
Heston, Charlton 157
Hiroshima 120
Hitler, Adolf 53–58, 69, 72, 75–77, 82–83, 91–95, 97, 101–102, 104, 201*ch*7*n*11
Hodges, Courtney Hicks 59, 77, 95, 96, 100, 171, 204*ch*16*n*6
Hollywood Turf Club 131–134, 142
Hope, Bob 43, 85, 140, 154, 157, **158**, 193
horse 45, 48, 111–**112**, 125–126, 132, 134, 139, 141–142, 151, 155, 160
Hubbell, Carl 43
hunting 47, 62, 123

ice cream 50, 71, 79, 152, 160
Italy 54, 55, 57–58, 73, 119, 123

Japan 42–43, 54, 58, 60, 62, 120, 135–136, 196
Jews 67
Johnson, Lyndon 154
Joint Chiefs of Staff 3, 12, 124, 127, 165
Jones, Bobby 43

Kennedy, John F. 154
King George VI 77
Konev, Marshal Ivan Stepanovich 108–113, **110**, **112**, 174, 204*ch*16*n*4

Korean War 4, 12, 128
Ku Klux Klan **116**, 134

Lantz, Walter 155
Leahy, Frank 43
Lincoln, Abraham 18, 26
Little, Rich 157

MacArthur, Douglas 60, 114, 122, 154
Marina del Rey 155
Marshall, George C. 3, 49, 50, 51, 52, 56–60, 63, 67, 68, 75, 76, 114, 115, 116, 118, 120, 122, 137, 139, 140, 179
Marshall, S.L.A. 8, 10, 166, 170, 173, 179, 202*ch*11*n*6
Martin, Dean 157
Mesta, Perle 123, 145
MGM (Metro-Goldwyn-Mayer) 11, 138, 140, 143, 155, 192, 193
Middleton, Troy 95, 171
Miller, Glenn 108
Moberly, MO 15, 20–23, 26–27, 29–31, 34–35, 41, 48, 51, 57, 64, 116–117, 120, **157**
Montgomery, Bernard "Monty" 78, 90, 97–101, 104, 154, 166, 168–171, 173, 175, 179
My Three Sons 135, 189

Nagasaki 120
Nazi 36, 46, 56–58, 75, 84, 90, 91, 93, 95, 98–102, 109, 124, 165, 169
XIX Corps 77
9th Army Group 99
Nixon, Richard 150, 154

O'Brien, Pat 155
old-fashioned (drink) 90–91
Omaha Beach 11, 79, 80–82, 125
Operation Cobra 10, 91–93, 171
Operation Grenade 99
Operation Husky 67, 71
Operation Lumberjack 99–100
Operation Veritable 99
Osmond, Donny 157
Osmond, Marie 157
Overlord 72, 75–79, 84

Panzer tank 67, 93, 95–97
Patton (movie) 8, 149, 206*ch*21*n*11
Patton, George S. 3, 6, 8–9, 45, 60, 64, 68–69, 71–73, 77–78, 93, 95–97, 100, 102, 154, 161, 165–168, 170–173, 175, 186, 199*ch*Intro*n*3, 202*ch*11*n*6
Pearl Harbor 43, 60, 62, 104
Presley, Elvis 157, 206*ch*21*n*11

Index

Pride, Charlie 157
prima facie 9
Pyle, Ernest "Ernie" T. 2, 9, 69, 73, 169–170, 173, 202*ch*11*n*6

Quayle, Eudora (Goodfellow) 20

racetrack 125, 132, 139, 142, 143, 147–148, 151
Ray Milland Show 135, 190
Reagan, Ronald 135, 150, 153, 154, 157
Ridgway, Matthew B. 64, 154
RKO 140
Rommel, Erwin 67, 69, 91
Rooney, Mickey 108, 155, 191, 193, 194
Roosevelt, Franklin D. 53, 55–56, 75–76

St. Elizabeth's Hospital 29
Samuel Goldwyn Studios 34, 138, 140, 192, 193, 196
Sarazen, Gene 43
scotch 90–91, 146
VII Corps 99, 77
SHAEF 96, 98
Shore, Dinah 103–104
"short snorter" 77, 79, 105, **114**, 158
Sicily 63, 68, 70, 71–74, 78, 80, 85, 123
The Sin of Harold Diddlebock 135
Sinatra, Frank 85, 154, 157
Slim, William 119, 164
Smith, Gen. Bedel 51–52, 96, 169, 171, 199*ch*Intro*n*4, 203*ch*15*n*6
snake 26–27, 47
Snead, Sammy 43
Speaker, Tris 43
Stars and Stripes 129, 135, 195
Stewart, James "Jimmy" 150, 154, 157
Stilwell, Joe 52, 169
Sullivan, Ed 143
Summersby, Kay 100, 106
Super Chief (train) 134

X Corps 65
Third Reich 53–54, 58, 102
3rd US Army 97, 106
13th Armored Regiment 67
Thomson, Jimmy 43
Tillis, Mel 157
toilet 78
Truman, Harry S. 116, 118, 120–124, 127–128, 131, 154
Tunisia 65, 67–70, 71, 85, 199*Intro.n*3
12th Army Group 36, 98, 108, 170
21st Army Group 173
II Corps 68–70, 71, 75, 172, 203*ch*14*n*9

United Press 129, 135, 195
United Service Organizations (USO) 84, 103, 141, 148, 155, 187
Untouchables 135, 188
Utah Beach 11, 79, 80–81, 146

Vereen, Ben 157
Veteran's Administration (VA) 3–4, 111, 114–116, 118–119, 120–123, 132
Vietnam War 148–149, 167
vodka 108, 110–112
von Rundstedt, Gerd 1, 95–96
von Schlieben, Karl Wilhelm 90

Waple, George H., III 9, 125–127, 172
Warner, Jack 131
Washington, George 3, 48
Wayne, John 135, 194
West Point Academy 22–23, 25–27, 29, 31–33, 36–37, 38–40, 49, 53–54, 58, 64–65, 76, 82–83, 115, 132, 144–145, 147, 152, 158, 179, 182, 202*ch*11*n*6, 208*app.*1*n*58
Worsham, Lew 43

York, Alvin C. 62–63

www.ingramcontent.com/pod-product-compliance
Ingram Content Group UK Ltd.
Pitfield, Milton Keynes, MK11 3LW, UK
UKHW041957140426
5217IPUK00015B/850